BIG IDEAS
MATH.
ALGEBRA 1

Record and Practice Journal

- Activity Recording Journal

- Activity Manipulatives

- Extra Practice Worksheets

- Fair Game Review Worksheets

- Glossary

BIG IDEAS LEARNING.

Erie, Pennsylvania

Photo Credits

ISBN 13: 978-1-60840-311-0
ISBN 10: 1-60840-311-4

23456789-VLP-16 15 14 13 12

Contents

Contents

Contents

Contents

Contents

Contents

Contents

Contents

Name_____ Date _____

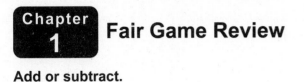

Add or subtract.

1. $-1 + (-3)$

2. $0 + (-12)$

3. $-5 + (-3)$

4. $-4 + (-4)$

5. $5 - (-2)$

6. $-5 - 2$

7. $0 - (-6)$

8. $-9 - 3$

9. In a city, the record monthly high temperature for July is $88°F$. The record monthly low temperature is $30°F$. What is the range of temperatures for July?

10. An elevator ascends five floors from the ground floor and then descends three floors. How many floors above the ground floor is the elevator?

Name _____ Date _____

Multiply or divide.

11. $-2(5)$

12. $-3(5)$

13. $-5 \cdot (-6)$

14. $-4 \cdot (-4)$

15. $-18 \div (-3)$

16. $-64 \div (-8)$

17. $-15 \div 5$

18. $-48 \div 6$

19. In a class of 30 students, each student pays $2 to go on a field trip. How much money is collected for the field trip?

20. A class of 28 students breaks up into groups of four to work on an activity. How many groups are there?

1.1 Solving Simple Equations
For use with Activity 1.1

Essential Question How can you use inductive reasoning to discover rules in mathematics? How can you test a rule?

---

1 **ACTIVITY:** Sum of the Angles of a Triangle

Work with a partner. Use a protractor to measure the angles of each triangle. Complete the table to organize your results.

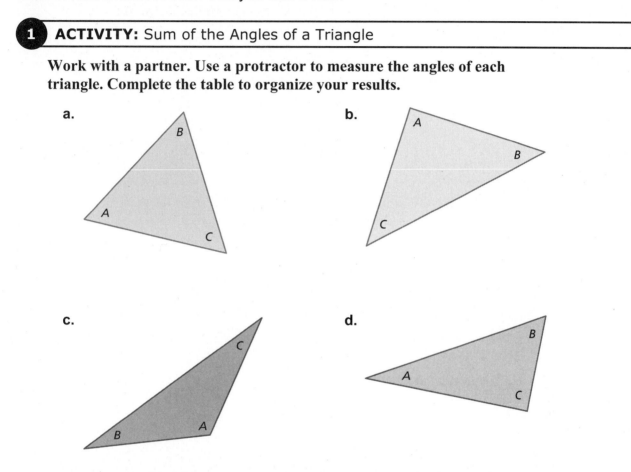

a.

b.

c.

d.

Triangle	Angle *A* (degrees)	Angle *B* (degrees)	Angle *C* (degrees)	*A* + *B* + *C*
a.				
b.				
c.				
d.				

1.1 Solving Simple Equations (continued)

2 ACTIVITY: Writing a Rule

Work with a partner. Use inductive reasoning to write and test a rule.

   a. Use the completed table in Activity 1 to write a rule about the sum of the angle measures of a triangle.

   b. TEST YOUR RULE Draw four triangles that are different from those in Activity 1. Measure the angles of each triangle. Organize your results in a table. Find the sum of the angle measures of each triangle.

Name_____ Date_____

3 **ACTIVITY:** Applying Your Rule

Work with a partner. Use the rule you wrote in Activity 2 to write an
equation for each triangle. Then, solve the equation to find the value of *x*.
Use a protractor to check the reasonableness of your answer.

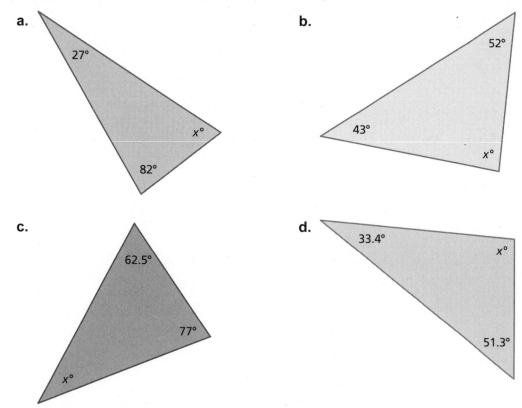

a.

27°

82°

x°

b.

52°

43°

x°

c.

62.5°

77°

x°

d.

33.4°

x°

51.3°

What Is Your Answer?

4. **IN YOUR OWN WORDS** How can you use inductive reasoning to discover
rules in mathematics? How can you test a rule? How can you use a rule to
solve problems in mathematics?

Name _____ Date _____

Solve the equation. Check your solution.

1. $x + 5 = 16$

2. $11 = w - 12$

3. $\dfrac{3}{4} + z = \dfrac{5}{6}$

4. $3y = 18$

5. $\dfrac{k}{7} = 10$

6. $\dfrac{4}{5}n = \dfrac{9}{10}$

7. $x - 12 \div 6 = 9$

8. $h + |-8| = 15$

9. $1.3(2) + p = 7.9$

10. A coupon subtracts $5.16 from the price p of a shirt. You pay $15.48 for the shirt after using the coupon. Write and solve an equation to find the original price of the shirt.

11. After a party, you have $\dfrac{1}{6}$ of the cookies you made left over. There are a dozen cookies left. How many cookies did you make for the party?

1.2 Solving Multi-Step Equations
For use with Activity 1.2

Essential Question   How can you solve a multi-step equation? How can you check the reasonableness of your solution?

1   **ACTIVITY:** Solving for the Angles of a Triangle

Work with a partner. Write an equation for each triangle. Solve the equation to find the value of the variable. Then find the angle measures of each triangle. Use a protractor to check the reasonableness of your answer.

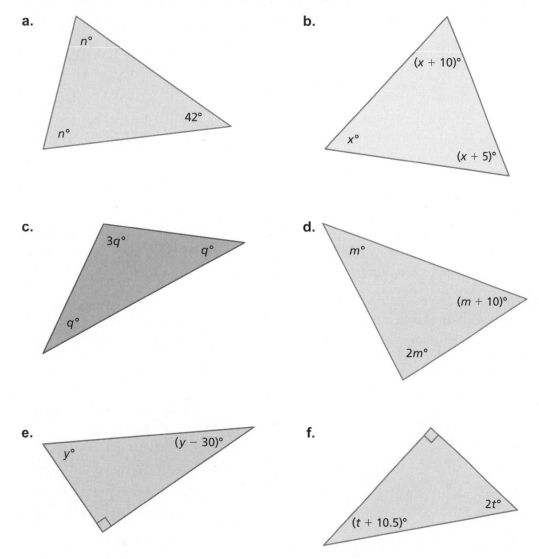

a.

b.

c.

d.

e.

f.

1.2 Solving Multi-Step Equations (continued)

2 ACTIVITY: Problem Solving Strategy

Work with a partner.

The six triangles form a rectangle.

Find the angle measures of each triangle. Use a protractor to check the reasonableness of your answers.

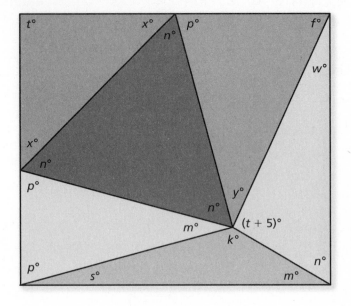

3 ACTIVITY: Puzzle

Work with a partner. A survey asked 200 people to name their favorite weekday. The results are shown in the circle graph.

a. How many degrees are in each part of the circle graph?

b. What percent of the people chose each day?

c. How many people chose each day?

Favorite Weekday

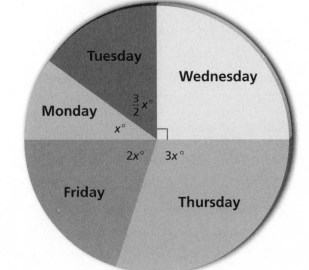

1.2 Solving Multi-Step Equations (continued)

d. Organize your results in a table.

What Is Your Answer?

4. **IN YOUR OWN WORDS** How can you solve a multi-step equation? How can you check the reasonableness of your solution?

Name _____ Date _____

Practice
For use after Lesson 1.2

Solve the equation. Check your solution.

1. $3x - 11 = 22$

2. $24 - 10b = 9$

3. $2.4z + 1.2z - 6.5 = 0.7$

4. $\dfrac{3}{4}w - \dfrac{1}{2}w - 4 = 12$

5. $2(a + 7) - 7 = 9$

6. $20 + 8(q - 11) = -12$

7. Find the width of the rectangular prism when the surface area is 208 square centimeters.

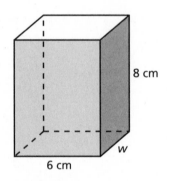

8 cm

w

6 cm

8. The amount of money in your savings account after m months is represented by $A = 135m + 225$. After how many months do you have \$765 in your savings account?

Name_____ Date_____

Essential Question How can you solve an equation that has variables on both sides?

1 ACTIVITY: Perimeter and Area

Work with a partner. Each figure has the unusual property that the value of its perimeter (in feet) is equal to the value of its area (in square feet).

- **Write an equation (value of perimeter = value of area) for each figure.**

- **Solve each equation for x.**

- **Use the value of x to find the perimeter and area of each figure.**

- **Check your solution by comparing the value of the perimeter and the value of the area of each figure.**

a.
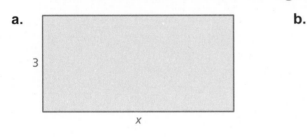

b.
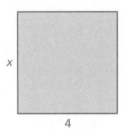

c.
d.

1.3 Solving Equations with Variables on Both Sides (continued)

e.

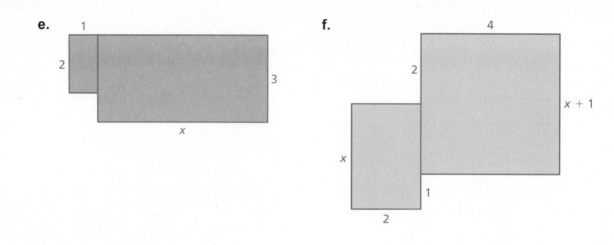

f.

g.

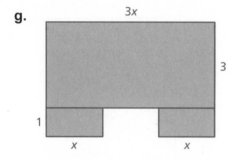

---

2 ACTIVITY: Surface Area and Volume

Work with a partner. Each solid on the next page has the unusual property that the value of its surface area (in square inches) is equal to the value of its volume (in cubic inches).

- **Write an equation (value of surface area = value of volume) for each solid.**

- **Solve each equation for** *x*.

- **Use the value of** *x* **to find the surface area and volume of each solid.**

- **Check your solution by comparing the value of the surface area and the value of the volume of each solid.**

Name_____ Date _____

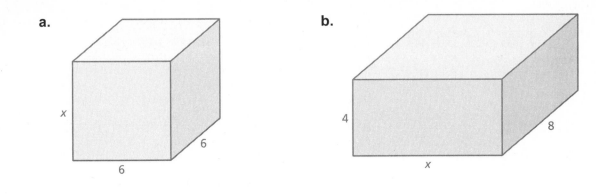

a. (cube with sides x, 6, 6)

b. (rectangular box with sides 4, 8, x)

---

3 **ACTIVITY:** Puzzle

Work with a partner. The two triangles are similar. The perimeter of the larger triangle is 150% of the perimeter of the smaller triangle. Find the dimensions of each triangle.

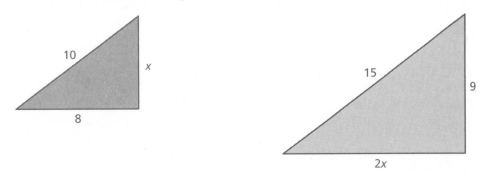

What Is Your Answer?

4. **IN YOUR OWN WORDS** How can you solve an equation that has variables on both sides? Write an equation that has variables on both sides. Solve the equation.

1.3 Practice
For use after Lesson 1.3

Solve the equation. Check your solution.

1. $x + 16 = 9x$

2. $4y - 70 = 12y + 2$

3. $5(p + 6) = 8p$

4. $3(g - 7) = 2(10 + g)$

5. $1.8 + 7n = 9.5 - 4n$

6. $\dfrac{3}{7}w - 11 = -\dfrac{4}{7}w$

7. One movie club charges a \$100 membership fee and \$10 for each movie. Another club charges no membership fee but movies cost \$15 each. Write and solve an equation to find the number of movies you need to buy for the cost of each movie club to be the same.

8. Thirty percent of all the students in a school are in a play. All students except for 140 are in the play. How many students are in the school?

1.3b Practice
For use after Lesson 1.3b

Solve the equation. Graph the solutions, if possible.

1. $|x| = 3$

2. $|x - 4| = 1$

3. $|x| = 0$

4. $|2x + 1| = 7$

5. $|3x - 2| = 10$

6. $|5x - 2| = -10$

Name _____ Date _____

7. $|2x + 5| - 5 = -2$ **8.** $3|4x + 6| = 24$

9. $-|2x - 8| - 6 = -12$ **10.** $-5|x + 3| + 3 = -17$

11. In a songwriting competition, the minimum length of a song is 2.5 minutes. The maximum length of a song is 5.5 minutes. Write an absolute value equation that has these minimum and maximum lengths as its solutions.

Name_____ Date _____

Essential Question   How can you use a formula for one measurement to write a formula for a different measurement?

1 **ACTIVITY:** Using Perimeter and Area Formulas

Work with a partner.

a. • Write a formula for the perimeter P of a rectangle.

• Solve the formula for w.

• Use the new formula to find the width of the rectangle.

w $P = 19$ in.

$\ell = 5.5$ in.

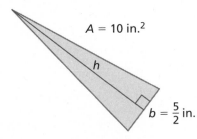

$A = 10$ in.^{2}

h

$b = \dfrac{5}{2}$ in.

b. • Write a formula for the area A of a triangle.

• Solve the formula for h.

• Use the new formula to find the height of the triangle.

c. • Write a formula for the circumference C of a circle.

• Solve the formula for r.

• Use the new formula to find the radius of the circle.

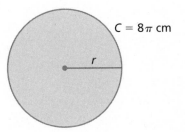

$C = 8\pi$ cm

r

1.4 **Rewriting Equations and Formulas** (continued)

- Write a formula for the area *A*.
- Solve the formula for *h*.
- Use the new formula to find the height.

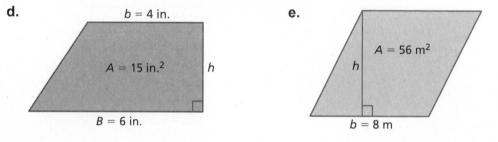

d. $b = 4$ in.
$A = 15$ in.^{2}
h
$B = 6$ in.

e. $A = 56$ m^2
h
$b = 8$ m

2 **ACTIVITY:** Using Volume Formulas

Work with a partner.

a. • Write a formula for the volume *V* of a prism.

- Solve the formula for *h*.

- Use the new formula to find the height of the prism.

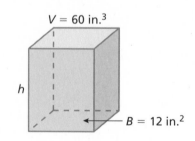

$V = 60$ in.^{3}
h
$B = 12$ in.^{2}

1.4   **Rewriting Equations and Formulas** (continued)

- Write a formula for the volume *V*.
- Solve the formula for *B*.
- Use the new formula to find the area of the base.

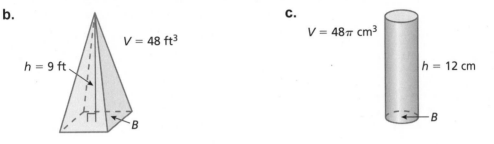

b.

$V = 48$ ft^3

$h = 9$ ft

B

c.

$V = 48\pi$ cm^3

$h = 12$ cm

B

d. • Write a formula for the volume *V* of a cone.

- Solve the formula for *h*.

- Use the new formula to find the height of the cone.

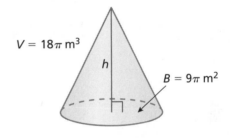

$V = 18\pi$ m^3

h

$B = 9\pi$ m^2

What Is Your Answer?

3. **IN YOUR OWN WORDS** How can you use a formula for one measurement to write a formula for a different measurement? Give an example that is different from the examples on these three pages.

Name _____ Date _____

Solve the equation for *y*.

1. $2x + y = -9$

2. $4x - 10y = 12$

3. $13 = \frac{1}{6}y + 2x$

Solve the equation for the bold variable.

4. $V = \ell \mathbf{w} h$

5. $f = \frac{1}{2}(\mathbf{r} + 6.5)$

6. $S = 2\pi r^2 + 2\pi r \mathbf{h}$

7. The formula for the area of a triangle is $A = \frac{1}{2}bh$.

   a. Solve the formula for *h*.

   b. Use the new formula to find the value of *h*.

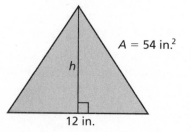

$A = 54$ in.^{2}

h

12 in.

Name_____ Date_____

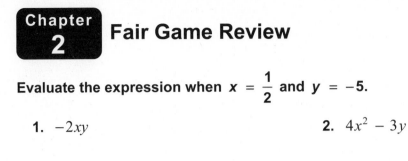

Chapter 2 Fair Game Review

Evaluate the expression when $x = \dfrac{1}{2}$ **and** $y = -5$.

1. $-2xy$

2. $4x^2 - 3y$

3. $\dfrac{10y}{12x + 4}$

4. $11x - 8(x - y)$

Evaluate the expression when $a = -9$ **and** $b = -4$.

5. $3ab$

6. $a^2 - 2(b + 12)$

7. $\dfrac{4b^2}{3b - 7}$

8. $7b^2 + 5(ab - 6)$

9. You go to the movies with five friends. Two of you buy a ticket and a bag of popcorn. The rest of your friends buy just one ticket each. The expression $4x + 2(x + y)$ represents the situation. Evaluate the expression when tickets cost \$7.25 and a bag of popcorn costs \$3.25.

Chapter 2 Fair Game Review (continued)

Use the graph to answer the question.

10. Write the ordered pair that corresponds to Point D.

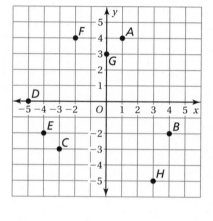

11. Write the ordered pair that corresponds to Point H.

12. Which point is located at $(-2, 4)$?

13. Which point is located at $(0, 3)$?

14. Which point(s) are located in Quadrant IV?

15. Which point(s) are located in Quadrant III?

Plot the point.

16. $(3, -1)$

17. $(0, 2)$

18. $(-5, -4)$

19. $(-1, 0)$

20. $(-2, 3)$

Name_____ Date_____

2.1 Graphing Linear Equations
For use with Activity 2.1

Essential Question How can you recognize a linear equation? How can you draw its graph?

---

1   ACTIVITY: Graphing a Linear Equation

Work with a partner.

a. Use the equation $y = \frac{1}{2}x + 1$

   to complete the table. (Choose any two x-values and find the y-values).

	Solution Points	
x		
$y = \frac{1}{2}x + 1$		

b. Write the two ordered pairs given by the table. These are called **solution points** of the equation.

c. **PRECISION** Plot the two solution points. Draw a line *exactly* through the two points.

d. Find a different point on the line. Check that this point is a solution point of the equation $y = \frac{1}{2}x + 1$.

e. **LOGIC** Do you think it is true that *any* point on the line is a solution point of the equation $y = \frac{1}{2}x + 1$? Explain.

2.1 **Graphing Linear Equations** (continued)

f. Choose five additional *x*-values for the table. (Choose positive and negative *x*-values.) Plot the five corresponding solution points on the previous page. Does each point lie on the line?

	Solution Points				
x					
$y = \dfrac{1}{2}x + 1$					

g. **LOGIC** Do you think it is true that *any* solution point of the equation $y = \dfrac{1}{2}x + 1$ is a point on the line? Explain.

h. **THE MEANING OF A WORD** Why is $y = ax + b$ called a *linear equation*?

 2 **ACTIVITY:** Using a Graphing Calculator

Use a graphing calculator to graph $y = 2x + 5.$

a. Enter the equation $y = 2x + 5$ into your calculator.

b. Check the settings of the *viewing window*. The boundaries of the graph are set by the minimum and maximum *x*- and *y*-values. The number of units between the tick marks are set by the *x*- and *y*-scales.

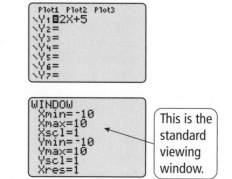

This is the standard viewing window.

2.1   **Graphing Linear Equations** (continued)

    c. Graph $y = 2x + 5$ on your calculator.

    d. Change the settings of the viewing window to match those shown. Compare the two graphs.

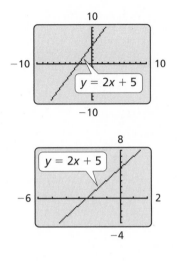

What Is Your Answer?

3. IN YOUR OWN WORDS How can you recognize a linear equation? How can you draw its graph? Write an equation that is linear. Write an equation that is *not* linear.

4. Use a graphing calculator to graph $y = 5x - 12$ in the standard viewing window.

    a. Can you tell where the line crosses the *x*-axis? Can you tell where the line crosses the *y*-axis?

    b. How can you adjust the viewing window so that you can determine where the line crosses the *x*- and *y*-axes?

5. CHOOSE TOOLS You want to graph $y = 2.5x - 3.8$. Would you graph it by hand or using a graphing calculator? Why?

Name _____ Date _____

Graph the linear equation.

1. $y = 4$

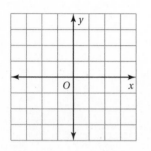

2. $y = -\dfrac{1}{3}x$

Solve for y. Then graph the equation.

3. $y + 2x = 3$

4. $2y - 3x = 1$

5. The equation $y = 2x + 4$ represents the cost y (in dollars) of renting a movie after x days of late charges.

    a. Graph the equation.

    b. Use the graph to determine how much it costs after 3 days of late charges.

2.2 Slope of a Line
For use with Activity 2.2

Essential Question How can the slope of a line be used to describe the line?

Slope is the rate of change between any two points on a line. It is the measure of the *steepness* of the line.

To find the slope of a line, find the ratio of the change in y (vertical change) to the change in x (horizontal change).

$$\text{slope} = \frac{\text{change in } y}{\text{change in } x}$$

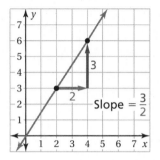

1 **ACTIVITY:** Finding the Slope of a Line

Work with a partner. Find the slope of each line using two methods.

>   **Method 1: Use the two black points.**

>   **Method 2: Use the two gray points.**

Do you get the same slope using each method? Why do you think this happens?

a.
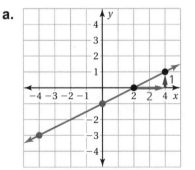

b.
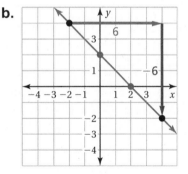

c.
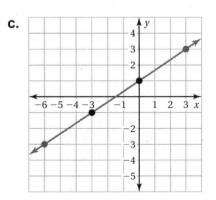

d.
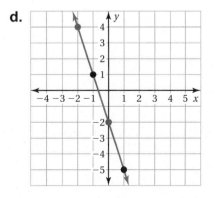

2.2 **Slope of a Line** (continued)

2 **ACTIVITY:** Drawing Lines with Given Slopes

Work with a partner.

- **Draw a line through the black point using the given slope.**
- **Draw a line through the gray point using the given slope.**
- **What do you notice about the two lines?**

a. Slope $= \dfrac{3}{4}$

b. Slope $= -\dfrac{4}{3}$

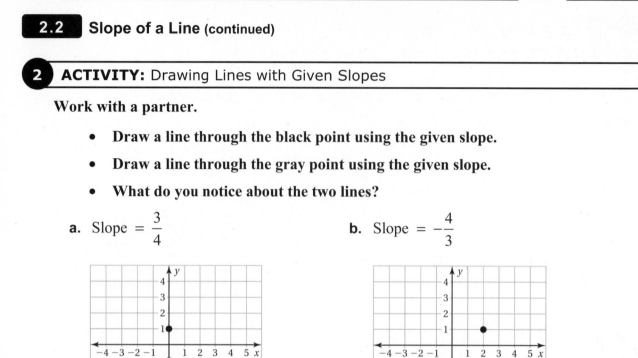

3 **ACTIVITY:** Drawing Lines with Given Slopes

Work with a partner.

- **Examine the lines drawn through the black points in parts (a) and (b) of Activity 2. Draw these two lines in the same coordinate plane.**

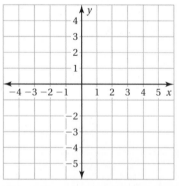

- **Describe the angle formed by the two lines. What do you notice about the product of the slopes of the two lines?**

2.2   **Slope of a Line** (continued)

What Is Your Answer?

4. **IN YOUR OWN WORDS** How can the slope of a line be used to describe the line?

5. Based on your results in Activity 2, make a conjecture about two different nonvertical lines in the same plane that have the same slope.

6. **REPEATED REASONING** Repeat Activity 3 for lines drawn through the gray points in Activity 2. Based on your results, make a conjecture about two lines in the same plane whose slopes have a product of −1.

2.2 Practice
For use after Lesson 2.2

Find the slope of the line.

1.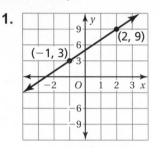

2.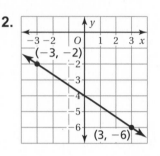

3.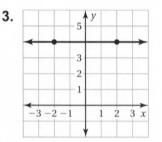

4.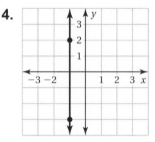

5. The back of a moving truck is 4 feet above the ground. A ramp extending from the back of the truck meets the ground 10 feet from the truck. What is the slope of the ramp?

6. Which set of stairs is more difficult to walk up? Explain.

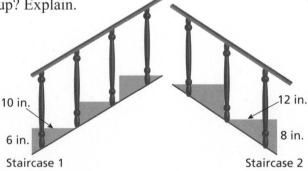

Name_____ Date_____

Which lines are parallel? How do you know?

1.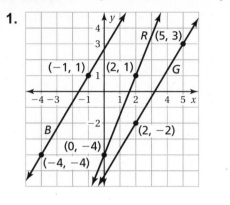

2.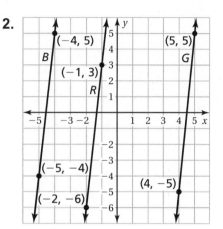

Are the given lines parallel? Explain your reasoning.

3. $y = 2, y = -4$

4. $x = 3, y = -3$

5. Is the quadrilateral a parallelogram?
Justify your answer.

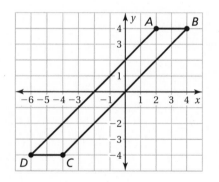

2.2b **Practice** (continued)

Which lines are perpendicular? How do you know?

6.

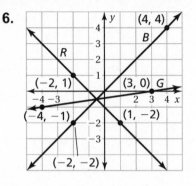

7.

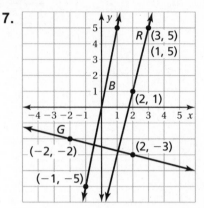

Are the given lines perpendicular? Explain your reasoning.

8. $x = 0, y = 3$

9. $y = 2, y = -\dfrac{1}{2}$

10. Is the parallelogram a rectangle?
Justify your answer.

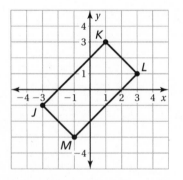

Name_____ Date_____

2.3 Graphing Linear Equations in Slope-Intercept Form
For use with Activity 2.3

Essential Question How can you describe the graph of the equation $y = mx + b$?

1 ACTIVITY: Finding Slopes and *y*-Intercepts

Work with a partner.

- **Graph the equation.**
- **Find the slope of the line.**
- **Find the point where the line crosses the *y*-axis.**

a. $y = -\dfrac{1}{2}x + 1$

b. $y = -x + 2$

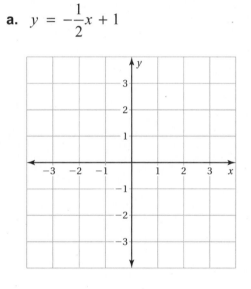

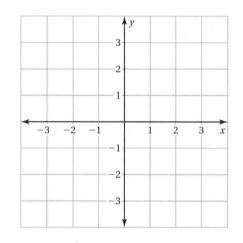

c. $y = -x - 2$

d. $y = \dfrac{1}{2}x + 1$

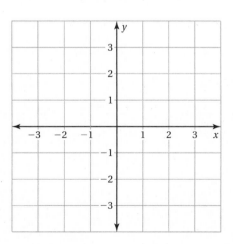

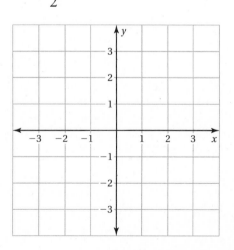

2.3 Graphing Linear Equations in Slope-Intercept Form (continued)

Inductive Reasoning

Work with a partner. Graph each equation. Then complete the table.

	Equation	Description of Graph	Slope of Graph	Point of Intersection with *y*-axis
1a	2. $y = -\dfrac{1}{2}x + 1$			
1b	3. $y = -x + 2$			
1c	4. $y = -x - 2$			
1d	5. $y = \dfrac{1}{2}x + 1$			
	6. $y = x + 2$			
	7. $y = x - 2$			
	8. $y = \dfrac{1}{2}x - 1$			
	9. $y = -\dfrac{1}{2}x - 1$			
	10. $y = 3x + 2$			
	11. $y = 3x - 2$			
	12. $y = -2x + 3$			

2.3 **Graphing Linear Equations in Slope-Intercept Form** (continued)

What Is Your Answer?

13. **IN YOUR OWN WORDS** How can you describe the graph of the equation $y = mx + b$?

    a. How does the value of m affect the graph of the equation?

    b. How does the value of b affect the graph of the equation?

    c. Check your answers to parts (a) and (b) with three equations that are not in the table.

14. Why do you think $y = mx + b$ is called the "slope-intercept" form of the equation of a line? Use drawings or diagrams to support your answer.

Name _____ Date _____

2.3 | **Practice**
For use after Lesson 2.3

Find the slope and *y*-intercept of the graph of the linear equation.

1. $y = -3x + 9$

2. $y = 4 - \dfrac{2}{5}x$

3. $6 + y = 8x$

Graph the linear equation. Identify the *x*-intercept. Use a graphing calculator to check your answer.

4. $y = \dfrac{2}{3}x + 6$

5. $y - 10 = -5x$

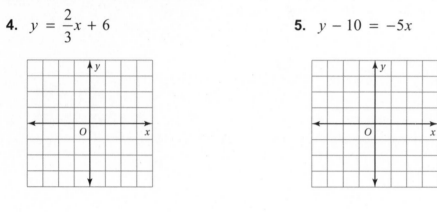

6. The equation $y = -90x + 1440$ represents the time (in minutes) left after x games of a tournament.

   a. Graph the equation.

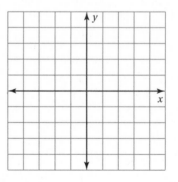

   b. Interpret the *x*-intercept and slope.

Name_____ Date_____

Essential Question How can you describe the graph of the equation
$ax + by = c$?

---

1 **ACTIVITY:** Using a Table to Plot Points

Work with a partner. You sold a total of
$16 worth of tickets to a school concert.
You lost track of how many of each type
of ticket you sold.

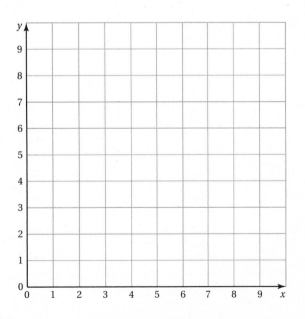

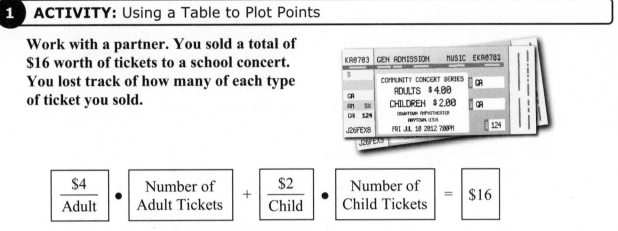

$$\boxed{\frac{\$4}{\text{Adult}}} \bullet \boxed{\begin{array}{c}\text{Number of}\\\text{Adult Tickets}\end{array}} + \boxed{\frac{\$2}{\text{Child}}} \bullet \boxed{\begin{array}{c}\text{Number of}\\\text{Child Tickets}\end{array}} = \boxed{\$16}$$

a. Let x represent the number of adult tickets.
Let y represent the number of child tickets.
Write an equation that relates x and y.

b. Complete the table showing the different combinations of tickets you might
have sold.

Number of Adult Tickets, x					
Number of Child Tickets, y					

c. Plot the points from the
table. Describe the pattern
formed by the points.

d. If you remember how many adult
tickets you sold, can you determine
how many child tickets you sold?
Explain your reasoning.

2.4 **Graphing Linear Equations in Standard Form** (continued)

2 **ACTIVITY:** Rewriting an Equation

Work with a partner. You sold a total of $16 worth of cheese. You forgot how many pounds of each type of cheese you sold.

CHEESE FOR SALE
Swiss: $4/lb   Cheddar: $2/lb

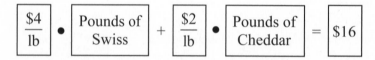

$$\boxed{\frac{\$4}{\text{lb}}} \bullet \boxed{\substack{\text{Pounds of} \\ \text{Swiss}}} + \boxed{\frac{\$2}{\text{lb}}} \bullet \boxed{\substack{\text{Pounds of} \\ \text{Cheddar}}} = \boxed{\$16}$$

a. Let x represent the number of pounds of Swiss cheese. Let y represent the number of pounds of Cheddar cheese. Write an equation that relates x and y.

b. Rewrite the equation in slope-intercept form. Then graph the equation.

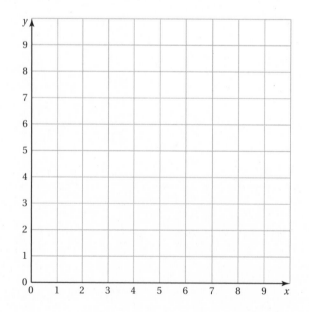

2.4 **Graphing Linear Equations in Standard Form** (continued)

What Is Your Answer?

3. IN YOUR OWN WORDS How can you describe the graph of the equation $ax + by = c$?

4. Activities 1 and 2 show two different methods for graphing $ax + by = c$. Describe the two methods. Which method do you prefer? Explain.

5. Write a real-life problem that is similar to those shown in Activities 1 and 2.

6. Why do you think it might be easier to graph $x + y = 10$ using standard form instead of rewriting it in slope-intercept form and then graphing?

Name_____ Date _____

Practice
For use after Lesson 2.4

Write the linear equation in slope-intercept form.

1. $2x - y = 7$
2. $\dfrac{1}{4}x + y = -\dfrac{2}{7}$
3. $3x - 5y = -20$

Graph the linear equation using intercepts. Use a graphing calculator to check your graph.

4. $2x - 3y = 12$

5. $x + 9y = -27$

6. You go shopping and buy x shirts for \$12 and y jeans for \$28. The total spent is \$84.

   a. Write an equation in standard form that models how much money you spent.

   b. Graph the equation and interpret the intercepts.

2.5 Writing Equations in Slope-Intercept Form
For use with Activity 2.5

Essential Question How can you write an equation of a line when you are given the slope and *y*-intercept of the line?

 ACTIVITY: Writing Equations of Lines

Work with a partner.

- Find the slope of each line.

- Find the *y*-intercept of each line.

- Write an equation for each line.

- What do the three lines have in common?

a.
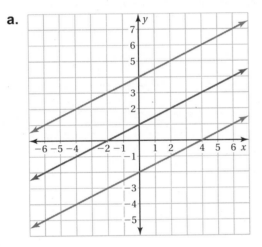

b.
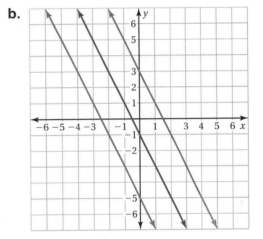

c.
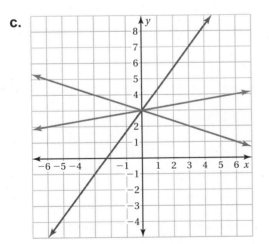

d.
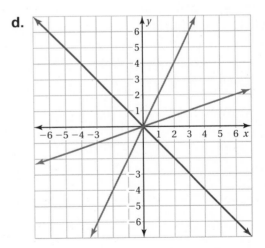

2.5 **Writing Equations in Slope-Intercept Form** (continued)

2 **ACTIVITY:** Describing a Parallelogram

Work with a partner.

- Find the area of each parallelogram.

- Write an equation for each side of each parallelogram.

- What do you notice about the slopes of the opposite sides of each parallelogram?

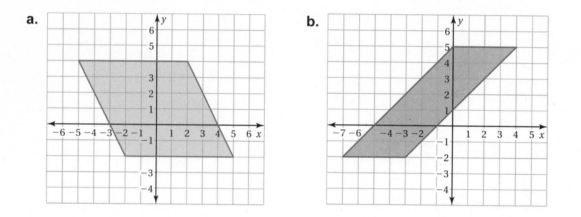

a.

b.

3 **ACTIVITY:** Interpreting the Slope and y-Intercept

Work with a partner. The graph shows a trip taken by a car where t is the time (in hours) and y is the distance (in miles) from Phoenix.

a. How far from Phoenix was the car at the beginning of the trip?

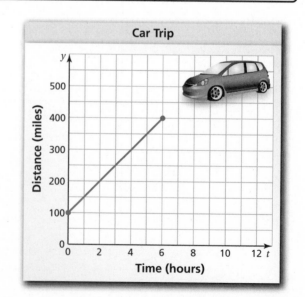

Car Trip

2.5   **Writing Equations in Slope-Intercept Form** (continued)

    b. What was the car's speed?

    c. How long did the trip last?

    d. How far from Phoenix was the car at the end of the trip?

What Is Your Answer?

    4. **IN YOUR OWN WORDS** How can you write an equation of a line when you are given the slope and y-intercept of the line? Give an example that is different from those in Activities 1, 2, and 3.

Name_____ Date _____

Write an equation of the line in slope-intercept form.

1.

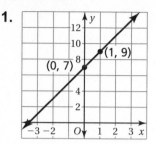

2.

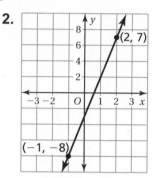

3.

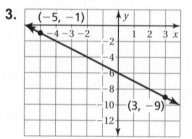

4.

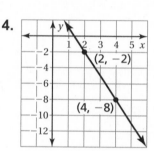

Write an equation of the line that passes through the points.

5. $(3, 8), (-2, 8)$　　　**6.** $(4, 3), (6, -3)$　　　**7.** $(-1, 0), (-5, 0)$

8. You organize a garage sale. You have $30 at the beginning of the sale. You earn an average of $20 per hour. Write an equation that represents the amount of money y you have after x hours.

Name_____ Date_____

Essential Question How can you write an equation of a line when you are given the slope and a point on the line?

 ACTIVITY: Writing Equations of Lines

Work with a partner.

- Sketch the line that has the given slope and passes through the given point.

- Find the *y*-intercept of the line.

- Write an equation of the line.

a. $m = -2$

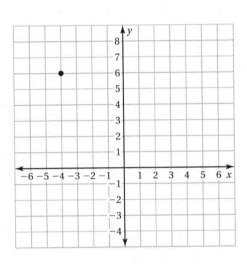

b. $m = \dfrac{1}{3}$

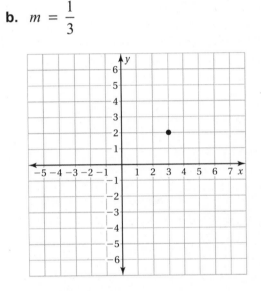

c. $m = -\dfrac{2}{3}$

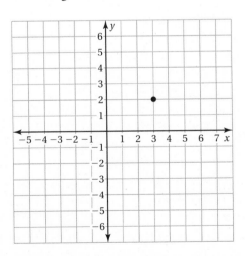

d. $m = \dfrac{5}{2}$

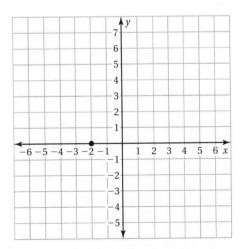

2.6 Writing Equations in Point-Slope Form (continued)

2 ACTIVITY: Developing a Formula

Work with a partner.

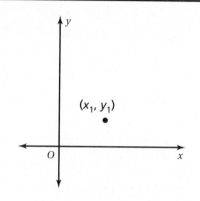

a. Draw a nonvertical line that passes through the point (x_1, y_1).

b. Plot another point on your line. Label this point as (x, y). This point represents any other point on the line.

c. Label the rise and run of the line through the points (x_1, y_1). and (x, y).

d. The rise can be written as $y - y_1$. The run can be written as $x - x_1$. Explain why this is true.

e. Write an equation for the slope m of the line using the expressions from part (d).

f. Multiply each side of the equation by the expression in the denominator. Write your result. What does this result represent?

2.6 **Writing Equations in Point-Slope Form** (continued)

---

3 **ACTIVITY:** Writing an Equation

Work with a partner.

For 4 months, you have saved $25 a month. You now have $175 in your savings account.

- Draw a graph that shows the balance in your account after t months.

- Use your result from Activity 2 to write an equation that represents the balance A after t months.

What Is Your Answer?

4. Redo Activity 1 using the formula you found in Activity 2. Compare the results. What do you notice?

5. The formula you found in Activity 2, $y - y_1 = m(x - x_1)$, is called the *point-slope form* of the equation of a line. Why is $y - y_1 = m(x - x_1)$, called the "point-slope" form? Why do you think this is important?

6. IN YOUR OWN WORDS How can you write an equation of a line when you are given the slope and a point on the line? Give an example that is different from those in Activity 1.

Name _____ Date _____

2.6 Practice
For use after Lesson 2.6

Write in point-slope form an equation of the line that passes through the given point that has the given slope.

1. $m = -3; (-4, 6)$

2. $m = -\dfrac{4}{3}; (3, -1)$

Write in slope-intercept form an equation of the line that passes through the given points.

3. $(-3, 0), (-2, 3)$

4. $(-6, 10), (6, -10)$

5. The total cost for bowling includes the fee for shoe rental plus a fee per game. The cost of each game increases the price by $4. After 3 games, the total cost with shoe rental is $14.

   a. Write an equation to represent the total cost y to rent shoes and bowl x games.

   b. How much is shoe rental? How is this represented in the equation?

Name_____ Date _____

Write an equation of the line that passes through the given point and is parallel to the given line. Use a graphing calculator to check your answer.

1. $(1, 3); y = 2x + 6$

2. $(-2, -2); y = -3x + 7$

3. $(5, 7); y = \dfrac{3}{5}x + 6$

4. $(2, -5); y = -\dfrac{7}{2}x - 2$

Write an equation of the line that passes through the given point and is parallel to the line shown in the graph.

5. $(1, 2)$

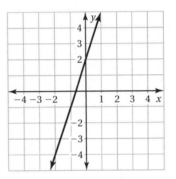

6. $(4, 7)$

7. $(0, -9)$

8. $(-6, -15)$

2.6b **Practice** (continued)

Write an equation of the line that passes through the given point and is perpendicular to the given line.

9. $(1, 1); y = \dfrac{1}{2}x + 4$

10. $(-3, 7); y = 3x - 4$

11. $(-2, -8); y = -2x - 7$

12. $(-8, 10); y = -\dfrac{4}{7}x + 2$

Write an equation of the line that passes through the given point and is perpendicular to the line shown in the graph.

13. $(4, -4)$

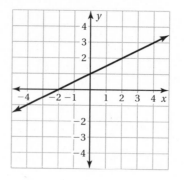

14. $(-5, 2)$

15. $(0, 0)$

16. $(0, 6)$

Name_____ Date _____

2.7 Solving Real-Life Problems
For use with Activity 2.7

Essential Question How can you use a linear equation in two variables to model and solve a real-life problem?

1 EXAMPLE: Writing a Story

Write a story that uses the graph at the right.

- **In your story, interpret the slope of the line, the *y*-intercept, and the *x*-intercept.**

- **Make a table that shows data from the graph.**

- **Label the axes of the graph with units.**

- **Draw pictures for your story.**

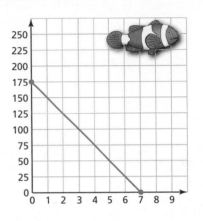

There are many possible stories. Here is one about a reef tank.

Tom works at an aquarium shop on Saturdays. One Saturday, when Tom gets to work, he is asked to clean a 175-gallon reef tank.

His first job is to drain the tank. He puts a hose into the tank and starts a siphon. Tom wonders if the tank will finish draining before he leaves work.

He measures the amount of water that is draining out and finds that 12.5 gallons drain out in 30 minutes. So, he figures that the rate is 25 gallons per hour. To see when the tank will be empty, Tom makes a table and draws a graph.

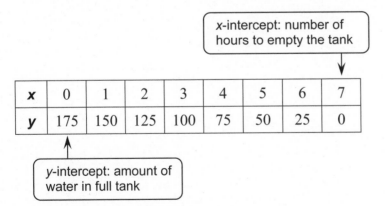

x-intercept: number of hours to empty the tank

x	0	1	2	3	4	5	6	7
y	175	150	125	100	75	50	25	0

y-intercept: amount of water in full tank

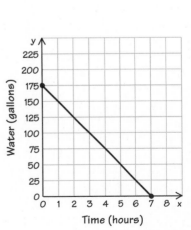

From the table and also from the graph, Tom sees that the tank will be empty after 7 hours. This will give him 1 hour to wash the tank before going home.

2.7 **Solving Real-Life Problems** (continued)

2 **ACTIVITY:** Writing a Story

Work with a partner. Write a story that uses the graph of a line.

- **In your story, interpret the slope of the line, the _y_-intercept, and the _x_-intercept.**

- **Make a table that shows data from the graph.**

- **Label the axes of the graph with units.**

- **Draw pictures for your story.**

Name_____ Date _____

3 ACTIVITY: Drawing Graphs

Work with a partner. Describe a real-life problem that has the given rate and intercepts. Draw a line that represents the problem.

a. Rate: −30 feet per second
   y-intercept: 150 feet
   x-intercept: 5 seconds

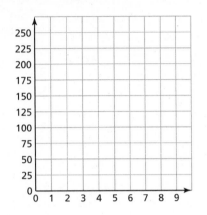

b. Rate: −25 dollars per month
   y-intercept: $200
   x-intercept: 8 months

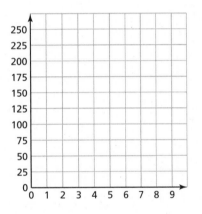

What Is Your Answer?

4. **IN YOUR OWN WORDS** How can you use a linear equation in two variables to model and solve a real-life problem? List three different rates that can be represented by slopes in real-life problems.

Name _____ Date _____

2.7 **Practice**
For use after Lesson 2.7

Describe a real-life problem that has the given rate and intercepts. Draw a line that represents the problem.

1. Rate: −6 feet per year
   y-intercept: 24 feet
   x-intercept: 4 years

2. Rate: −2 pages per minute
   y-intercept: 280 pages
   x-intercept:140 minutes

3. You are buying shirts for an organization. You have $120 to spend. The number of short-sleeved shirts y you buy after buying x long-sleeved shirts is $y = -1.2x + 24$.

   a. Graph the equation.

   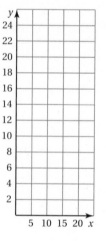

   b. Interpret the x- and y-intercepts.

4. The graph relates the percent of battery life y left in an MP3 player to the amount of playing time it has left. Write an equation of the line.

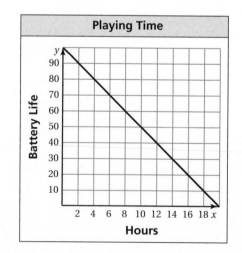

Name____ Date__________

Chapter 3 Fair Game Review

Complete the number sentence with <, >, or =.

1. $\frac{3}{4}$ _____ 0.2

2. $\frac{7}{10}$ _____ 0.7

3. 0.6 _____ $\frac{2}{3}$

4. $\sqrt{3}$ _____ 1.75

5. 6 _____ $\sqrt{12}$

6. 1.8 _____ $\frac{31}{16}$

7. Your height is 5 feet and $1\frac{5}{8}$ inches. Your friend's height is 5.6 feet. Who is taller? Explain.

Name _____ Date _____

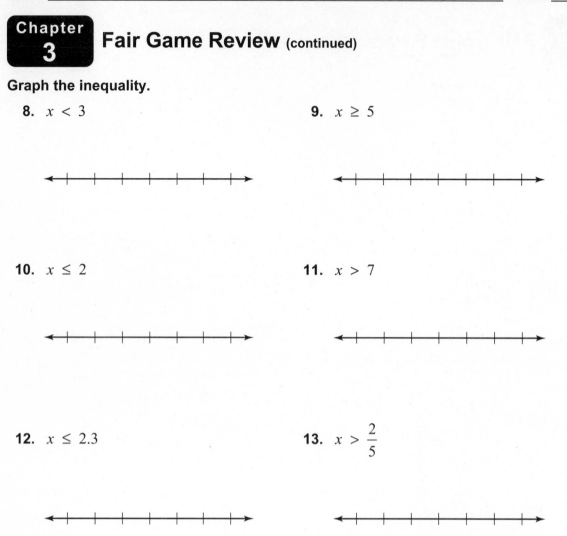

Graph the inequality.

8. $x < 3$

9. $x \geq 5$

10. $x \leq 2$

11. $x > 7$

12. $x \leq 2.3$

13. $x > \dfrac{2}{5}$

14. The deepest free dive by a human in the ocean is 417 feet. The depth humans have been in the ocean can be represented by the inequality $x \leq 417$. Graph the inequality.

Name_____ Date _____

Essential Question How can you use an inequality to describe a real-life statement?

---

1 ACTIVITY: Writing and Graphing Inequalities

Work with a partner. Write an inequality for the statement. Then sketch the graph of all the numbers that make the inequality true.

a. Statement: The temperature t in Minot, North Dakota has never been below $-36°F$.

Inequality: _____

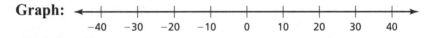

Graph:

```
<---+----+----+----+----+----+----+----+----+--->
   -40  -30  -20  -10   0   10   20   30   40
```

b. Statement: The elevation e in Wisconsin is at most 1951.5 feet above sea level.

Inequality: _____

Graph:

```
<---+------+------+------+------+------+------+--->
  -3000  -2000  -1000    0    1000   2000   3000
```

---

2 ACTIVITY: Writing and Graphing Inequalities

Work with a partner. Write an inequality for the graph. Then, in words, describe all the values of x that make the inequality true.

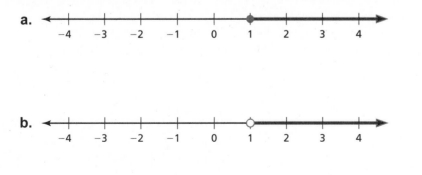

a.
```
<---+----+----+----+----+----●----+----+----+--->
   -4   -3   -2   -1    0    1    2    3    4
```

b.
```
<---+----+----+----+----+----○----+----+----+--->
   -4   -3   -2   -1    0    1    2    3    4
```

3.1 **Writing and Graphing Inequalities** (continued)

c.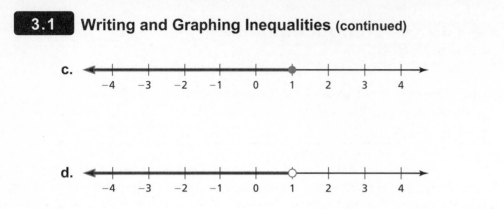

d.

---

3 **ACTIVITY:** Triangle Inequality

Work with a partner. Use 8 to 10 pieces of spaghetti.

- Break one piece of spaghetti into three parts that can be used to form a triangle.

- Form a triangle and use a centimeter ruler to measure each side. Round the side lengths to the nearest tenth.

- Record the side lengths in the table.

- Repeat the process with two other pieces of spaghetti.

Side Lengths That Form a Triangle			
Small	Medium	Large	S + M

- Repeat the experiment by breaking pieces of spaghetti into three pieces that *do not* form a triangle. Record the lengths in a table.

Side Lengths That Do Not Form a Triangle			
Small	Medium	Large	S + M

3.1 **Writing and Graphing Inequalities** (continued)

- **INDUCTIVE REASONING** Write a rule that uses an inequality to compare the lengths of three sides of a triangle.

- Use your rule to decide whether the following triangles are possible. Explain.

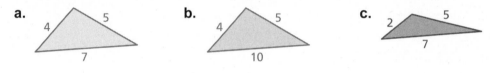

a.
4
5
7

b.
4
5
10

c.
2
5
7

What Is Your Answer?

4. **IN YOUR OWN WORDS** How can you use an inequality to describe a real-life statement? Give two examples of real-life statements that can be represented by inequalities.

Name _____ Date _____

Write the word sentence as an inequality.

1. A number p is no greater than -6.

2. A number n divided by -2 is no less than $\frac{1}{2}$.

Tell whether the given value is a solution of the inequality.

3. $q + 7 \geq 8;\ q = 10$

4. $-12r < -6;\ r = -2$

5. $-2.4k \geq -4;\ k = 0.5$

6. $\frac{x}{4} < x - 9;\ x = 8$

Graph the inequality on a number line.

7. $p \leq 4\frac{1}{2}$

8. $z > -8.3$

$\longleftarrow \!\! + \!\! + \!\! + \!\! + \!\! + \!\! + \!\! + \!\! + \!\! \longrightarrow$

$\longleftarrow \!\! + \!\! + \!\! + \!\! + \!\! + \!\! + \!\! + \!\! + \!\! \longrightarrow$

9. For your birthday, you want to invite some friends to join you at the movies. Movie tickets cost $8. You can spend no more than $35. Write an inequality to represent this situation. Then solve the inequality to find the greatest number of people you can invite.

Name_____ Date_____

3.2 Solving Inequalities Using Addition or Subtraction
For use with Activity 3.2

Essential Question How can you use addition or subtraction to solve an inequality?

1 **ACTIVITY:** Quarterback Passing Efficiency

Work with a partner. The National Collegiate Athletic Association (NCAA) uses the following formula to rank the passing efficiency P of quarterbacks.

$$P = \frac{8.4Y + 100C + 330T - 200N}{A}$$

$Y =$ total length of all completed passes (in **Y**ards)
$C = $ **C**ompleted passes
$T = $ passes resulting in a **T**ouchdown
$N = $ i**N**tercepted passes
$A = $ **A**ttempted passes
$M = $ inco**M**plete passes

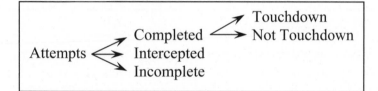

Which of the following equations or inequalities are true relationships among the variables? Explain your reasoning.

   a. $C + N < A$ **b.** $C + N \le A$ **c.** $T < C$ **d.** $T \le C$

   e. $N < A$ **f.** $A > T$ **g.** $A - C \ge M$ **h.** $A = C + N + M$

Name _____ Date _____

2 **ACTIVITY:** Quarterback Passing Efficiency

Work with a partner. Which of the following quarterbacks has a passing efficiency rating that satisfies the inequality $P > 100$? Show your work.

Player	Attempts	Completions	Yards	Touchdowns	Interceptions
A	149	88	1065	7	9
B	400	205	2000	10	3
C	426	244	3105	30	9
D	188	89	1167	6	15

3 **ACTIVITY:** Finding Solutions of Inequalities

Work with a partner. Use the passing efficiency formula to create a passing record that makes the inequality true. Then describe the values of P that make the inequality true.

   a. $P < 0$

Attempts	Completions	Yards	Touchdowns	Interceptions

   b. $P + 100 \geq 250$

Attempts	Completions	Yards	Touchdowns	Interceptions

   c. $180 < P - 50$

Attempts	Completions	Yards	Touchdowns	Interceptions

3.2 **Solving Inequalities Using Addition or Subtraction** (continued)

d. $P + 30 \geq 120$

Attempts	Completions	Yards	Touchdowns	Interceptions

e. $P - 250 > -80$

Attempts	Completions	Yards	Touchdowns	Interceptions

What Is Your Answer?

4. Write a rule that describes how to solve inequalities like those in Activity 3. Then use your rule to solve each of the inequalities in Activity 3.

5. **IN YOUR OWN WORDS** How can you use addition or subtraction to solve an inequality?

6. How is solving the inequality $x + 3 < 4$ similar to solving the equation $x + 3 = 4$? How is it different?

3.2 Practice
For use after Lesson 3.2

Solve the inequality. Graph the solution.

1. $x - 4 < 8$

2. $16 + p \geq 14$

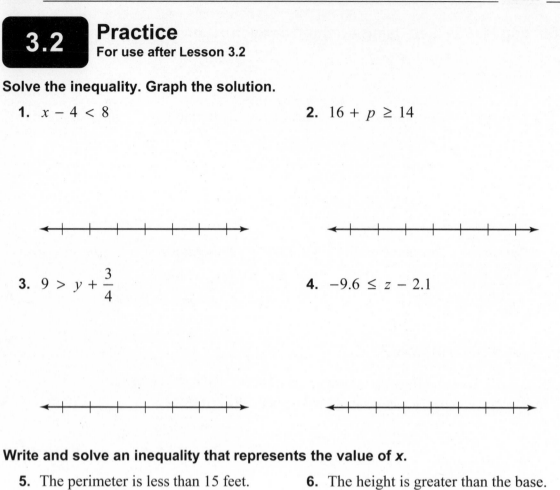

3. $9 > y + \dfrac{3}{4}$

4. $-9.6 \leq z - 2.1$

Write and solve an inequality that represents the value of x.

5. The perimeter is less than 15 feet.

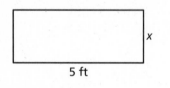

5 ft

6. The height is greater than the base.

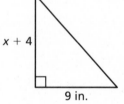

$x + 4$

9 in.

7. Your goal is to sell at least 50 boxes of cookies for your school fundraiser.

   a. Write an inequality that represents your goal.

   b. You sell 26 boxes. Write and solve a new inequality to represent how many boxes you need to sell to reach your goal.

3.3 **Solving Inequalities Using Multiplication or Division**
For use with Activity 3.3

Essential Question How can you use multiplication or division to solve an inequality?

1 **ACTIVITY:** Using a Table to Solve an Inequality

Work with a partner.

- **Complete the table.**
- **Decide which graph represents the solution of the inequality.**
- **Write the solution of the inequality.**

a. $3x \leq 6$

x	−1	0	1	2	3	4	5
3x							
3x $\overset{?}{\leq}$ 6							

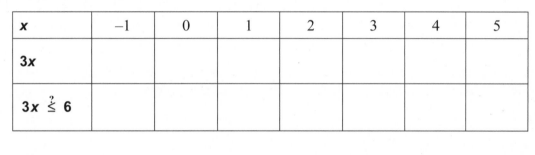

b. $-2x > 4$

x	−5	−4	−3	−2	−1	0	1
−2x							
−2x $\overset{?}{>}$ 4							

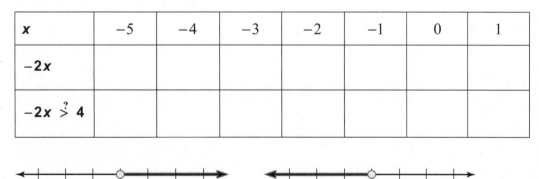

3.3 **Solving Inequalities Using Multiplication or Division** (continued)

2 **ACTIVITY:** Writing a Rule

Work with a partner. Use a table to solve each inequality.

a. $3x > 3$ **b.** $4x \leq 4$ **c.** $-2x \geq 6$ **d.** $-5x < 10$

x									
$3x$									
$4x$									
$-2x$									
$-5x$									

Write a rule that describes how to solve inequalities like those in Activity 1.
Then use your rule to solve each of the four inequalities above.

3 **ACTIVITY:** Using a Table to Solve an Inequality

Work with a partner.

• **Complete the table.**

• **Decide which graph represents the solution of the inequality.**

• **Write the solution of the inequality.**

a. $\dfrac{x}{2} \geq 1$

x	-1	0	1	2	3	4	5
$\dfrac{x}{2}$							
$\dfrac{x}{2} \overset{?}{\geq} 1$							

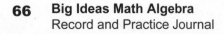

3.3 **Solving Inequalities Using Multiplication or Division** (continued)

b. $\dfrac{x}{-3} < \dfrac{2}{3}$

x	-5	-4	-3	-2	-1	0	1
$\dfrac{x}{-3}$							
$\dfrac{x}{-3} \overset{?}{<} \dfrac{2}{3}$							

4 **ACTIVITY:** Writing a Rule

Work with a partner. Use a table to solve each inequality.

a. $\dfrac{x}{4} \geq 1$ **b.** $\dfrac{x}{2} < \dfrac{3}{2}$ **c.** $\dfrac{x}{-2} > 2$ **d.** $\dfrac{x}{-5} \leq \dfrac{1}{5}$

x										
$\dfrac{x}{4}$										
$\dfrac{x}{2}$										
$\dfrac{x}{-2}$										
$\dfrac{x}{-5}$										

Write a rule that describes how to solve inequalities like those in Activity 3.
Then use your rule to solve each of the four inequalities above.

What Is Your Answer?

5. IN YOUR OWN WORDS How can you use multiplication or division to
solve an inequality?

Name _____ Date _____

Solve the inequality. Graph the solution.

1. $5n < 75$

2. $\dfrac{x}{6} \le -12$

3. $-15t > -60$

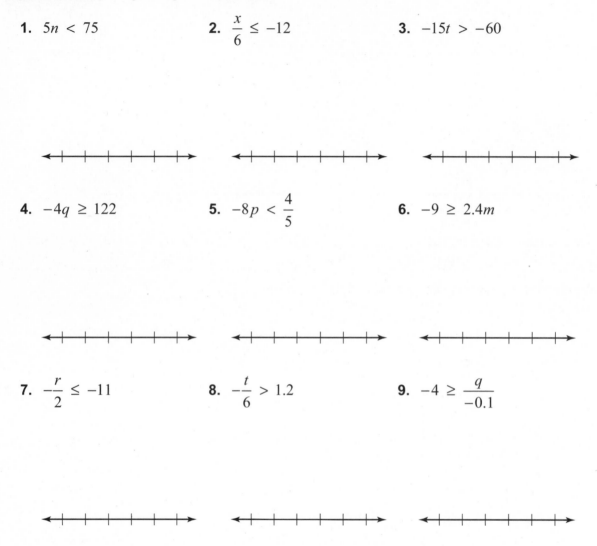

4. $-4q \ge 122$

5. $-8p < \dfrac{4}{5}$

6. $-9 \ge 2.4m$

7. $-\dfrac{r}{2} \le -11$

8. $-\dfrac{t}{6} > 1.2$

9. $-4 \ge \dfrac{q}{-0.1}$

10. To win a trivia game, you need at least 60 points. Each question is worth 4 points. Write and solve an inequality that represents the number of questions you need to answer correctly to win the game.

Name_____ Date_____

Essential Question How can you use an inequality to describe the area and perimeter of a composite figure?

1 **ACTIVITY:** Areas and Perimeters of Composite Figures

Work with a partner.

a. For what values of x will the area of the shaded region be greater than 12 square units?

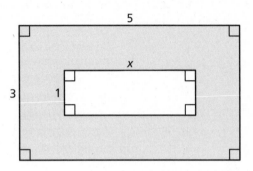

b. For what values of x will the sum of the inner and outer perimeters of the shaded region be greater than 20 units?

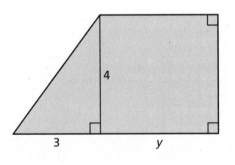

c. For what values of y will the area of the trapezoid be less than or equal to 10 square units?

d. For what values of y will the perimeter of the trapezoid be less than or equal to 16 units?

3.4 **Solving Multi-Step Inequalities** (continued)

e. For what values of *w* will the area of the shaded region be greater than or equal to 36 square units?

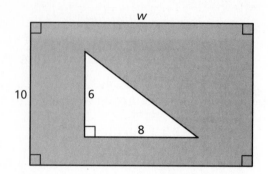

f. For what values of *w* will the sum of the inner and outer perimeters of the shaded region be greater than 47 units?

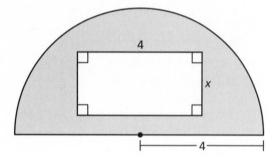

g. For what values of *x* will the area of the shaded region be less than 4π square units?

h. For what values of *x* will the sum of the inner and outer perimeters of the shaded region be less than $4\pi + 20$ units?

---

2 **ACTIVITY:** Volume and Surface Area of a Composite Solid

Work with a partner.

a. For what values of *x* will the volume of the solid be greater than or equal to 42 cubic units?

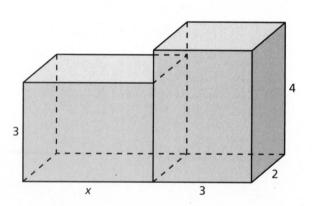

b. For what values of *x* will the surface area of the solid be greater than 72 square units?

Name_____ Date _____

3 **ACTIVITY:** Planning a Budget

Work with a partner.

You are building a patio. You want to cover the patio with Spanish tile that costs $5 per square foot. Your budget for the tile is $1700. How wide can you make the patio without going over your budget?

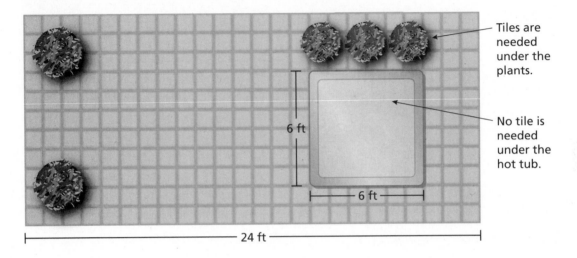

Tiles are needed under the plants.

No tile is needed under the hot tub.

6 ft

6 ft

24 ft

What Is Your Answer?

4. **IN YOUR OWN WORDS** How can you use an inequality to describe the area and perimeter of a composite figure? Give an example. Include a diagram with your example.

Name_____ Date _____

Solve the inequality. Graph the solution, if possible.

1. $9x - 6 > 66$

2. $\dfrac{d}{3} + 7 \le -11$

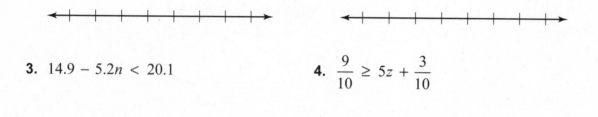

3. $14.9 - 5.2n < 20.1$

4. $\dfrac{9}{10} \ge 5z + \dfrac{3}{10}$

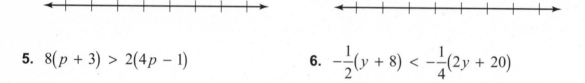

5. $8(p + 3) > 2(4p - 1)$

6. $-\dfrac{1}{2}(y + 8) < -\dfrac{1}{4}(2y + 20)$

7. In the United States music industry, an album is awarded gold certification with at least 500,000 albums sold. A recording artist is selling about 1200 albums each day. The artist has already sold 15,000 albums. About how many more days will it take before the album is awarded gold certification?

Name_____ Date _____

Write the word sentence as an inequality. Graph the inequality.

1. A number q is more than 4 and less than 6.

2. A number r is fewer than -5 and no less than -8.

3. A number s is greater than or equal to 3 and no more than 7.

4. A number t is greater than or equal to 1 or less than -3.

5. Write an inequality to describe the graph.

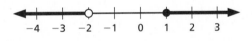

6. Triglycerides are a type of fat in the human bloodstream. Triglyceride levels greater than or equal to 150 milligrams per deciliter and less than 200 milligrams per deciliter are considered borderline high. Write and graph a compound inequality that describes triglyceride levels that are borderline high.

Name _____ Date _____

Solve the inequality. Graph the solution, if possible.

7. $3 < a + 2 < 6$

8. $7 < x + 4 \le 10$

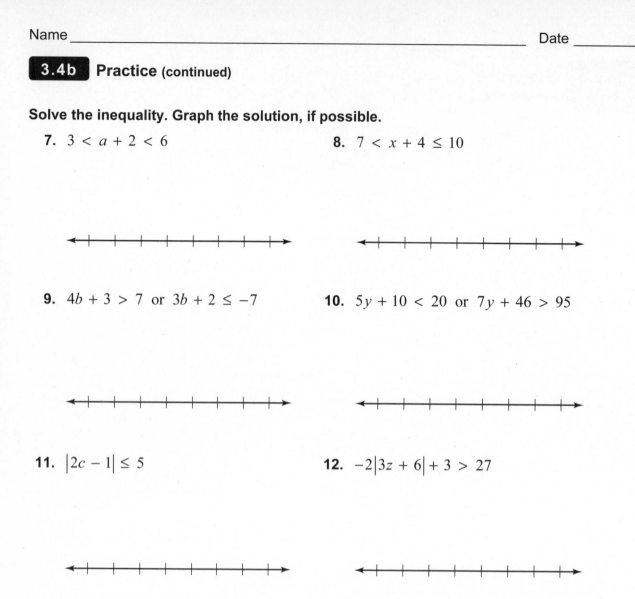

9. $4b + 3 > 7$ or $3b + 2 \le -7$

10. $5y + 10 < 20$ or $7y + 46 > 95$

11. $|2c - 1| \le 5$

12. $-2|3z + 6| + 3 > 27$

13. A country's mint has a rule that the weight of a certain coin must be within 0.02 gram of 3.00 grams to be released into circulation. Use a model to write and solve an absolute value inequality to find the least and greatest weight of a coin that the country's mint will allow to be released into circulation.

3.5 Graphing Linear Inequalities in Two Variables
For use with Activity 3.5

Essential Question   How can you use a coordinate plane to solve problems involving linear inequalities?

1   ACTIVITY: Graphing Inequalities

Work with a partner.

a. Graph $y = x + 1$ in the coordinate plane.

b. Choose three points that lie above the graph of $y = x + 1$. Substitute the values of x and y of each point in the inequality $y > x + 1$. If the substitutions result in true statements, plot the points on the graph.

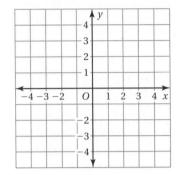

c. Choose three points that lie below the graph of $y = x + 1$. Substitute the values of x and y of each point in the inequality $y > x + 1$. If the substitutions result in true statements, plot the points on the graph.

d. To graph $y > x + 1$, would you choose the points above or below $y = x + 1$?

e. Choose a point that lies on the graph of $y = x + 1$. Substitute the values of x and y in the inequality $y > x + 1$. What do you notice? Do you think the graph of $y > x + 1$ includes the points that lie on the graph of $y = x + 1$? Explain your reasoning.

3.5 Graphing Linear Inequalities in Two Variables (continued)

f. Explain how you could change the inequality so that it includes the points that lie on the graph of $y = x + 1$.

---

2 **ACTIVITY:** Writing and Graphing Inequalities

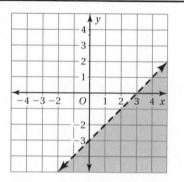

Work with a partner. The graph of a linear inequality in two variables shows all the solutions of the inequality in a coordinate plane. An ordered pair (x, y) is a solution of an inequality if the inequality is true when the values of x and y are substituted into the inequality.

a. Write an equation for the graph of the dashed line.

b. The solutions of the inequality are represented by the shaded region. In words, describe the solutions of the inequality.

c. Write an inequality for the graph. Which inequality symbol did you use? Explain your reasoning.

---

3 **EXAMPLE:** Using a Graphing Calculator

Use a graphing calculator to graph $y \geq \dfrac{1}{4}x - 3$.

a. Enter the equation $y = \dfrac{1}{4}x - 3$ into your calculator.

```
Plot1 Plot2 Plot3
\Y1₿(1/4)X-3
\Y2=
\Y3=
\Y4=
\Y5=
\Y6=
\Y7=
```

3.5 **Graphing Linear Inequalities in Two Variables** (continued)

b. The inequality contains the symbol ≥. So, the region to be shaded is above the graph of $y = \dfrac{1}{4}x - 3$. Adjust your graphing calculator so that the region above the graph will be shaded.

For some calculators, this icon represents the region above the graph.

c. Graph $y \geq \dfrac{1}{4}x - 3$ on your calculator.

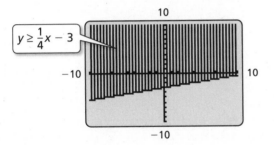

$y \geq \dfrac{1}{4}x - 3$

Some graphing calculators always use a solid line when graphing inequalities. In this case, you will have to decide whether the line should be dashed or solid.

What Is Your Answer?

4. Use a graphing calculator to graph each inequality in a standard viewing window.

a. $y > x + 5$ **b.** $y \leq -\dfrac{1}{2}x + 1$ **c.** $y \geq -x - 4$

5. IN YOUR OWN WORDS How can you use a coordinate plane to solve problems involving linear inequalities? Give an example of a real-life problem that can be represented by an inequality in two variables.

3.5 Practice
For use after Lesson 3.5

Tell whether the ordered pair is a solution of the inequality.

1. $-4x + y > 15$; $(-4, 0)$

2. $-8 - 9y \leq 50$; $(1, -9)$

3. $3x + 2y \geq 7$; $(1, 2)$

4. $5x - 7y < -24$; $(-9, -3)$

Graph the inequality in a coordinate plane.

5. $y \geq -3$

6. $x + y < 2$

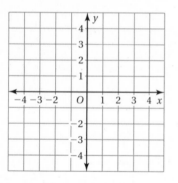

7. You can spend at most $20 on tomatoes and red peppers for a soup. Tomatoes cost $2.50 per pound and red peppers cost $4 per pound.

a. Write and graph an inequality that represents the amounts of tomatoes and red peppers you can buy.

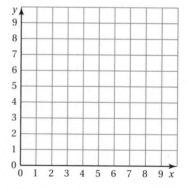

b. Identify and interpret two solutions of the inequality that are on the boundary line.

Chapter 4   Fair Game Review

Solve the equation. Check your solution.

1. $8y - 3 = 13$

2. $4a + 11 - a = 2$

3. $9 = 4(3k - 4) - 7k$

4. $-12 - 5(6 - 2m) = 18$

5. $15 - t + 8t = -13$

6. $5h - 2\left(\dfrac{3}{2}h + 4\right) = 10$

7. The profit P (in dollars) from selling x calculators is $P = 25x - (10x + 250)$. How many calculators are sold when the profit is $425?

Chapter 4 **Fair Game Review** (continued)

Graph the inequality in the coordinate plane.

8. $x \geq -1$

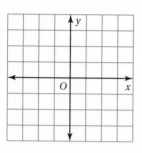

9. $y < 3$

10. $4x - y > 7$

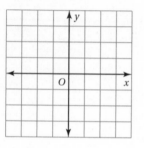

11. $2x + 3y \geq 6$

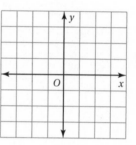

12. Your boat has a weight limit of 1200 pounds. Suppose an average adult weighs 150 pounds and an average child weighs 100 pounds.

a. Use a model to write an inequality that represents this situation.

b. Graph the inequality.

c. There are 4 adults and 5 children on the boat. Is the boat safe? Explain.

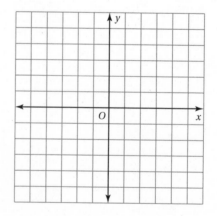

Name_____ Date_____

4.1 Solving Systems of Linear Equations by Graphing
For use with Activity 4.1

Essential Question How can you solve a system of linear equations?

> **1** **ACTIVITY:** Writing a System of Linear Equations

Work with a partner.

Your family starts a bed-and-breakfast. They spend $500 fixing up a bedroom to rent. The cost for food and utilities is $10 per night. Your family charges $60 per night to rent the bedroom.

   a. Write an equation that represents the costs.

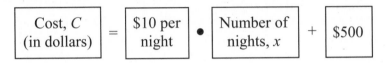

   b. Write an equation that represents the revenue (income).

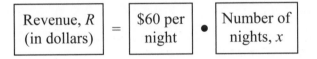

   c. A set of two (or more) linear equations is called a **system of linear equations**. Write the system of linear equations for this problem.

Name _____ Date _____

4.1   **Solving Systems of Linear Equations by Graphing** (continued)

2   **ACTIVITY:** Using a Table to Solve a System

Use the cost and revenue equations from Activity 1 to find how many nights your family needs to rent the bedroom before recovering the cost of fixing up the bedroom. This is the *break-even point*.

a. Complete the table.

x	0	1	2	3	4	5	6	7	8	9	10	11
C												
R												

b. How many nights does your family need to rent the bedroom before breaking even?

3   **ACTIVITY:** Using a Graph to Solve a System

a. Graph the cost equation from Activity 1.

b. In the same coordinate plane, graph the revenue equation from Activity 1.

c. Find the point of intersection of the two graphs. What does this point represent? How does this compare to the break-even point in Activity 2? Explain.

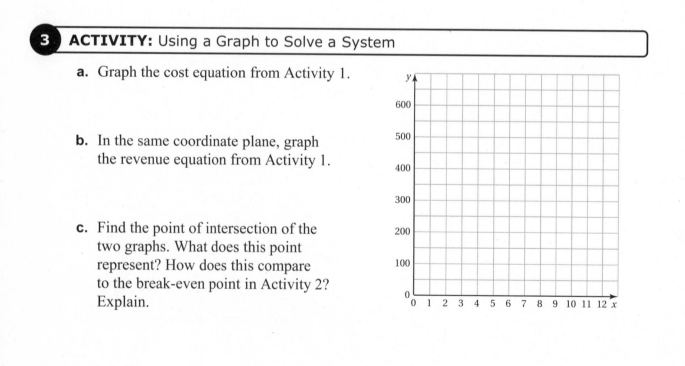

82   **Big Ideas Math Algebra**
Record and Practice Journal

Name_____ Date_____

4 **EXAMPLE:** Using a Graphing Calculator

Use a graphing calculator to solve the system.

$y = 10x + 500$ **Equation 1**

$y = 60x$ **Equation 2**

a. Enter the equations into your calculator. Then graph the equations in an appropriate window.

b. To find the solution, use the *intersect* feature to find the point of intersection. The solution is at $(10, 60)$.

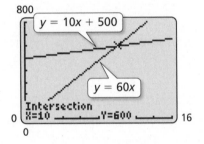

What Is Your Answer?

5. IN YOUR OWN WORDS How can you solve a system of linear equations? How can you check your solution?

6. Solve one of the systems by using a table, another system by sketching a graph, and the remaining system by using a graphing calculator. Explain why you chose each method.

a. $y = 4.3x + 1.2$
$y = -1.7x - 2.4$

b. $y = x$
$y = -2x + 9$

c. $y = -x - 5$
$y = 3x + 1$

Name _____ Date _____

Practice
For use after Lesson 4.1

1. Use the table to find the break-even point. Check your solution.

$C = 25x + 210$

$R = 60x$

x	0	1	2	3	4	5	6	7	8
C									
R									

Solve the system of linear equations by graphing.

2. $y = 3x + 1$

   $y = -2x - 4$

   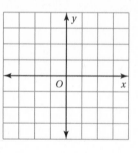

3. $y = -4x + 1$

   $y = 5x - 8$

   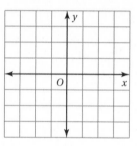

Use a graphing calculator to solve the system of linear equations.

4. $y = \dfrac{2}{3}x + 2$

   $x - y = 4$

5. $y = x - 7$

   $y + x = 3$

6. There are 26 students in your class. There are 4 more girls than boys. Use a system of linear equations to find how many boys are in your class. How many girls are in your class?

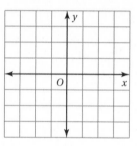

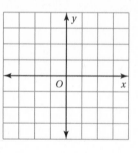

Name_____ Date _____

Essential Question   How can you use substitution to solve a system of linear equations?

1 **ACTIVITY:** Using Substitution to Solve a System

Work with a partner. Solve each system of linear equations using two methods.

Method 1: Solve for x first.

Solve for x in one of the equations. Use the expression for x to find the solution of the system. Explain how you did it.

Method 2: Solve for y first.

Solve for y in one of the equations. Use the expression for y to find the solution of the system. Explain how you did it.

Is the solution the same using both methods?

a. $6x - y = 11$
$2x + 3y = 7$

b. $2x - 3y = -1$
$x - y = 1$

c. $3x + y = 5$
$5x - 4y = -3$

d. $5x - y = 2$
$3x - 6y = 12$

e. $x + y = -1$
$5x + y = -13$

f. $2x - 6y = -6$
$7x - 8y = 5$

4.2 **Solving Systems of Linear Equations by Substitution** (continued)

2 **ACTIVITY:** Writing and Solving a System of Equations

Work with a partner.

a. Roll a pair of number cubes that
have different colors. Then write the
ordered pair shown by the number cubes.
The ordered pair at the right is (3, 4).

x-value

y-value

b. Write a system of linear equations that
has this ordered pair as its solution.

c. Exchange systems with your partner and use one of the methods from
Activity 1 to solve the system.

3 **ACTIVITY:** Solving a Secret Code

Work with a partner. Decode the quote by Archimedes.

___ ___ ___ ___ ___ ___ ___ ___ ___ ___ ___ ___ ___ ___ ___ ___ ___ ___ ___ ___ ,
−8 −7 7 −5 −4 −5 −3 −2 −1 −3 0 −5   1   2   3   1 −3   4   5

___ ___ ___ ___ ___ ___ ___ ___ ___ ___ ___ ___ ___ ___ ___ ___ ___ ___ ___ .
−3 4   5   −7   6 −7 −1 −1 −4   2   7 −5   1   8   −5 −5 −3   9   1   8

Name_____ Date_____

$(\mathbf{A,C})$ $x + y = -3$ $(\mathbf{D,E})$ $x + y = 0$ $(\mathbf{G,H})$ $x + y = 0$

$x - y = -3$ $x - y = 10$ $x - y = -16$

$(\mathbf{I,L})$ $x + 2y = -9$ $(\mathbf{M,N})$ $x + 2y = 4$ $(\mathbf{O,P})$ $x + 2y = -2$

$2x - y = -13$ $2x - y = -12$ $2x - y = 6$

$(\mathbf{R,S})$ $2x + y = 21$ $(\mathbf{T,U})$ $2x + y = -7$ $(\mathbf{V,W})$ $2x + y = 20$

$x - y = 6$ $x - y = 10$ $x - y = 1$

What Is Your Answer?

4. **IN YOUR OWN WORDS** How can you use substitution to solve a system of linear equations?

4.2 Practice
For use after Lesson 4.2

Solve the system of linear equations by substitution. Check your solution.

1. $y = -2x + 4$

   $-x + 3y = -9$

2. $\dfrac{3}{4}x - 5y = 7$

   $x = -4y + 12$

3. $5x - y = 4$

   $2x + 2y = 16$

4. $2x + 3y = 0$

   $8x + 9y = 18$

5. A gas station sells a total of 4500 gallons of regular gas and premium gas in one day. The ratio of gallons of regular gas sold to gallons of premium gas sold is $7 : 2$.

   a. Write a system of linear equations that represents this situation.

   b. How many gallons sold were regular gas? premium gas?

4.3 Solving Systems of Linear Equations by Elimination
For use with Activity 4.3

Essential Question How can you use elimination to solve a system of linear equations?

 1 ACTIVITY: Using Elimination to Solve a System

Work with a partner. Solve each system of linear equations using two methods.

Method 1: Subtract.

Subtract Equation 2 from Equation 1. What is the result? Explain how you can use the result to solve the system of equations.

Method 2: Add.

Add the two equations. What is the result? Explain how you can use the result to solve the system of equations.

Is the solution the same using both methods?

a. $2x + y = 4$
$2x - y = 0$

b. $3x - y = 4$
$3x + y = 2$

c. $x + 2y = 7$
$x - 2y = -5$

2 ACTIVITY: Using Elimination to Solve a System

Work with a partner.

$2x + y = 2$ Equation 1

$x + 5y = 1$ Equation 2

a. Can you add or subtract the equations to solve the system of linear equations? Explain.

4.3 **Solving Systems of Linear Equations by Elimination** (continued)

b. Explain what property you can apply to Equation 1 in the system so that the *y* coefficients are the same.

c. Explain what property you can apply to Equation 2 in the system so that the *x* coefficients are the same.

d. You solve the system in part (b). Your partner solves the system in part (c). Compare your solutions.

e. Use a graphing calculator to check your solution.

3 **ACTIVITY:** Solving a Secret Code

Work with a partner. Solve the puzzle to find the name of a famous mathematician who lived in Egypt around 350 A.D.

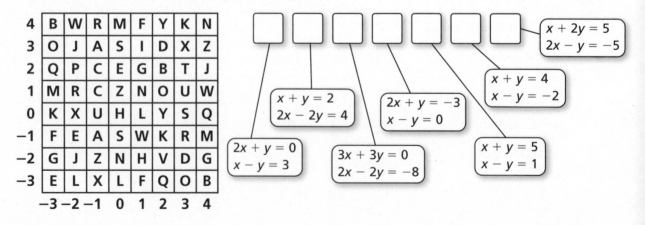

4.3 Solving Systems of Linear Equations by Elimination (continued)

What Is Your Answer?

4. IN YOUR OWN WORDS How can you use elimination to solve a system of linear equations?

5. When can you add or subtract equations in a system to solve the system? When do you have to multiply first? Justify your answers with examples.

6. In Activity 2, why can you multiply the equations in the system by a constant and not change the solution of the system? Explain your reasoning.

4.3 Practice

For use after Lesson 4.3

Solve the system of linear equations by elimination. Check your solution.

1. $x + y = 7$

   $3x - y = 1$

2. $-2x - 5y = -8$

   $-2x + y = 16$

3. $8x - 9y = 7$

   $2x - 3y = -5$

4. $-5x + 3y = -6$

   $9x - 4y = 1$

5. A high school has a total of 850 students. There are 60 more female students than there are male students.

   a. Write a system of linear equations that represents this situation.

   b. How many students are female? male?

Name_____ Date_____

 4.4 **Solving Special Systems of Linear Equations**
For use with Activity 4.4

Essential Question Can a system of linear equations have no solution? Can a system of linear equations have many solutions?

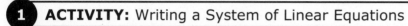
1 **ACTIVITY:** Writing a System of Linear Equations

Work with a partner.

Your cousin is 3 years older than you. Your ages can be represented by two linear equations.

$y = t$ Your age

$y = t + 3$ Your cousin's age

a. Graph both equations in the same coordinate plane.

b. What is the vertical distance between the two graphs? What does this distance represent?

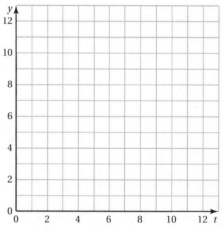

c. Do the two graphs intersect? If not, what does this mean in terms of your age and your cousin's age?

2 **ACTIVITY:** Using a Table to Solve a System

Work with a partner. You invest $500 for equipment to make dog backpacks. Each backpack costs you $15 for materials. You sell each backpack for $15.

a. Complete the table for your cost C and your revenue R.

x	0	1	2	3	4	5	6	7	8	9	10
C											
R											

4.4 **Solving Special Systems of Linear Equations** (continued)

b. When will your company break even? What is wrong?

3 **ACTIVITY:** Using a Graph to Solve a Puzzle

Work with a partner. Let x and y be two numbers. Here are two clues about the values of x and y.

	Words	**Equation**
Clue 1:	The value of y is 4 more than twice the value of x.	$y = 2x + 4$
Clue 2:	The difference of 3y and 6x is 12.	$3y - 6x = 12$

a. Graph both equations in the same coordinate plane.

b. Do the two lines intersect? Explain.

c. What is the solution of the puzzle?

d. Use the equation $y = 2x + 4$ to complete the table.

x	0	1	2	3	4	5	6	7	8	9	10
y											

4.4 **Solving Special Systems of Linear Equations** (continued)

e. Does each solution in the table satisfy *both* clues?

f. What can you conclude? How many solutions does the puzzle have? How can you describe them?

What Is Your Answer?

4. IN YOUR OWN WORDS Can a system of linear equations have no solution? Can a system of linear equations have many solutions? Give examples to support your answers.

Name _____ Date _____

Solve the system of linear equations.

1. $y = 2x - 5$

   $y = 2x + 7$

2. $3x + 4y = -10$

   $y = -\dfrac{3}{4}x - \dfrac{5}{2}$

3. $x - y = 8$

   $2y = 2x - 16$

4. $3y = -6x + 4$

   $2x + y = 9$

5. You start reading a book for your literature class two days before your friend. You both read 10 pages per night. A system of linear equations that represents this situation is $y = 10x + 20$ and $y = 10x$. Will your friend finish the book before you? Justify your answer.

6. You and a friend buy music from different online stores. The system of linear equations represents the total amount spent on x songs and y albums. Both of you buy the same number of albums. Compare the number of songs each of you buy.

   $$0.95x + 10y = 39.5$$
   $$1.9x + 20y = 79$$

Name_____ Date_____

Use a graph to solve the equation. Check your solution.

1. $3x - 4 = -x$

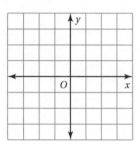

2. $\dfrac{1}{3}x + 3 = 4x - 8$

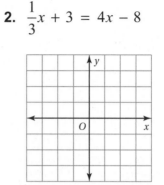

3. $\dfrac{1}{2}x + 4 = -x - 11$

4. $-x + 1 = -\dfrac{1}{4}x - \dfrac{1}{2}$

5. On the first day of your garage sale, you earned $12x + 9$ dollars. The next day you earned $22x$ dollars. Is it possible that you earned the same amount each day? Explain.

4.4b **Practice** (continued)

6. You hike uphill at a rate of 200 feet per minute. Your friend hikes downhill on the same trail at a rate of 250 feet per minute. How long will it be until you meet?

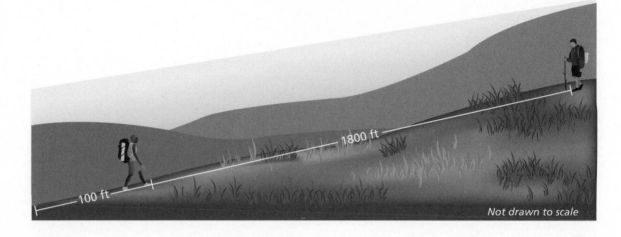

100 ft

1800 ft

Not drawn to scale

7. Two savings accounts earn simple interest. Account A has a beginning balance of $500 and grows by $25 per year. Account B has a beginning balance of $750 and grows by $15 per year.

| Growth rate | • | Years, x | + | Beginning balance | = | Growth rate | • | Years, x | + | Beginning balance |

a. Use the model to write an equation.

b. After how many years x do the accounts have the same balance?

Name_____ Date _____

Essential Question   How can you sketch a graph of a system of linear inequalities?

1 **ACTIVITY:** Graphing Linear Inequalities

Work with a partner. Match the linear inequality with its graph.

$2x + y \leq 4$ Inequality 1
$2x - y \leq 0$ Inequality 2

a.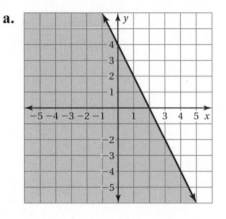

b.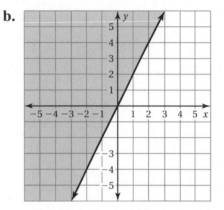

2 **ACTIVITY:** Graphing a System of Linear Inequalities

Work with a partner. Consider the system of linear inequalities given in Activity 1.

$2x + y \leq 4$ Inequality 1
$2x - y \leq 0$ Inequality 2

Use colored pencils to shade the solutions of the two linear inequalities. When you graph both inequalities in the same coordinate plane, what do you get?

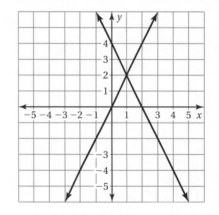

Describe each of the shaded regions in the graph at the right. What does the unshaded region represent?

Name _____ Date _____

3 **ACTIVITY:** Writing a System of Linear Inequalities

Work with a partner. Write a system of 4 linear inequalities whose solution is the traffic sign at the right.

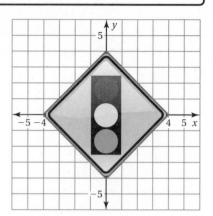

(1) $x + y \leq$ ☐

(2) $x + y \geq$ ☐

(3) $x - y \leq$ ☐

(4) $x - y \geq$ ☐

4 **ACTIVITY:** Representing a State by a Linear System

Two states can be represented as the graph of a system of linear inequalities. Identify the two states. Explain your reasoning.

4.5 **Systems of Linear Inequalities** (continued)

What Is Your Answer?

5. **IN YOUR OWN WORDS** How can you sketch the graph of a system of linear inequalities?

6. When graphing a system of linear inequalities, which region represents the solution of the system? Do you think all systems have a solution? Explain.

Name _____ Date _____

Graph the system of linear inequalities.

1. $y \geq -1$

   $y > 2x + 2$

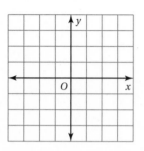

2. $\frac{1}{2}x + y \leq 3$

   $x + y > 4$

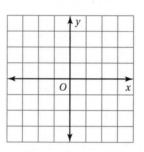

3. $3y - x \leq 0$

   $8x + 3y \leq 12$

4. $y - 4 > 3x$

   $-9x + 3y \leq -2$

5. You have at most 10 hours to study for your math and English finals. You decide to study at least 3 times as much for math as you do for English.

   a. Write and graph a system of linear inequalities that represents this situation.

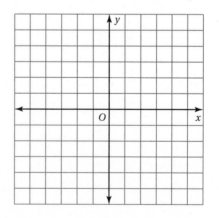

   b. Is it possible to study 7 hours for math and 3 hours for English in this situation? Justify your answer.

Name_____ Date _____

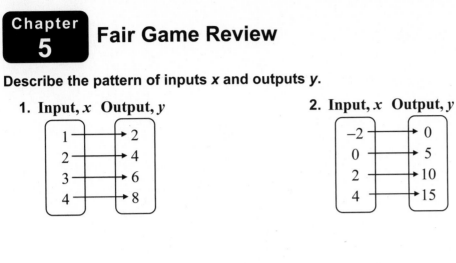

Chapter 5 **Fair Game Review**

Describe the pattern of inputs x and outputs y.

1. Input, x   Output, y

| 1 → 2 |
| 2 → 4 |
| 3 → 6 |
| 4 → 8 |

2. Input, x   Output, y

| −2 → 0 |
| 0 → 5 |
| 2 → 10 |
| 4 → 15 |

3.

Input, x	−3	1	5	9	13
Output, y	−4	−1	2	5	8

4.

Input, x	−2	−1	0	1	2
Output, y	2	−5	−12	−19	−26

5. The table shows the number of customers y in x hours. Describe the inputs and outputs.

Hours, x	0	1	2	3	4
Customers, y	0	15	30	45	60

Chapter 5 **Fair Game Review** (continued)

Draw a mapping diagram for the graph. Then describe the pattern of inputs and outputs.

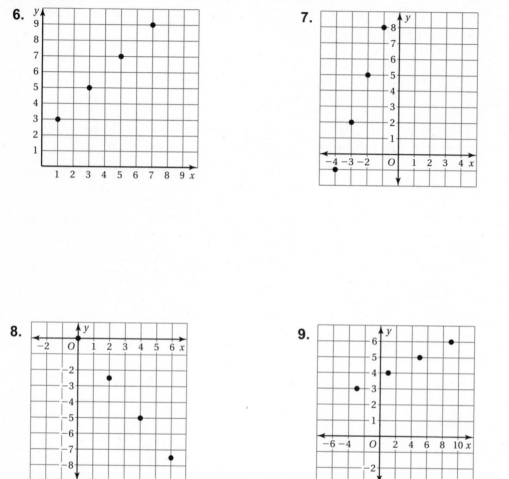

6.

7.

8.

9.

10. In basketball, for each shot you make from inside the three-point circle, you score two points. Draw a mapping diagram for inputs 0, 2, 4, 6, and 8.

Name_____ Date _____

5.1 Domain and Range of a Function
For use with Activity 5.1

Essential Question How can you find the domain and range of a function?

1 ACTIVITY: The Domain and Range of a Function

Work with a partner. In Activity 1 in Section 2.4, you completed the table shown below. The table shows the number of adult and child tickets sold for a school concert.

input ⟶

output ⟶

Number of Adult Tickets, *x*	0	1	2	3	4
Number of Child Tickets, *y*	8	6	4	2	0

The variables *x* and *y* are related by the linear equation $4x + 2y = 16$.

a. Write the equation in *function form* by solving for *y*.

b. The **domain** of a function is the set of all input values. Find the domain of the function represented by the table.

   Domain = _____

   Why is $x = 5$ not in the domain of the function?

   Why is $x = \dfrac{1}{2}$ not in the domain of the function?

c. The **range** of a function is the set of all output values. Find the range of the function represented by the table.

   Range = _____

5.1 **Domain and Range of a Function** (continued)

d. Functions can be described in many ways.

- by an equation
- by an input-output table
- in words
- by a graph
- as a set of ordered pairs

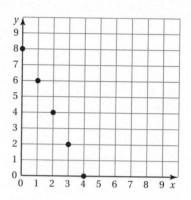

Use the graph to write the function as a set of ordered pairs.

2 **ACTIVITY:** Finding Domains and Ranges

Work with a partner.

- **Complete each input-output table.**
- **Find the domain and range of each function represented by the table.**

a. $y = -3x + 4$

x	−2	−1	0	1	2
y					

b. $y = \dfrac{1}{2}x - 6$

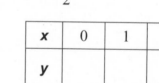

x	0	1	2	3	4
y					

c.

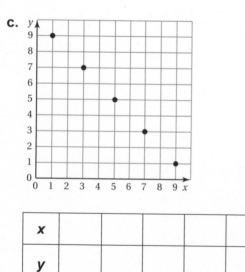

x					
y					

d.

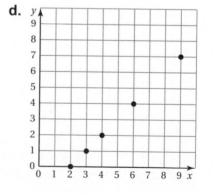

x					
y					

Name_____ Date _____

What Is Your Answer?

3. **IN YOUR OWN WORDS** How can you find the domain and range of a function?

4. **The following are general rules for finding a person's foot length.**

   To find the length y (in inches) of a woman's foot, divide her shoe size x by 3 and add 7.

   To find the length y (in inches) of a man's foot, divide his shoe size x by 3 and add 7.3.

   a. Write an equation for one of the statements.

   b. Make an input-output table for the function in part (a). Use shoe sizes $5\frac{1}{2}$ to 12.

   c. Label the domain and range of the function represented by the table.

Name _____ Date _____

Find the domain and range of the function represented by the graph.

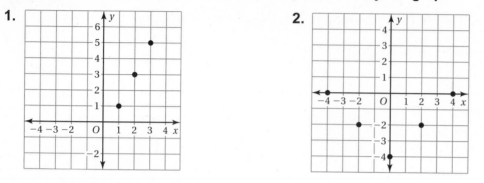

1.

2.

Complete the input-output table for the function. Then find the domain and range of the function represented by the table.

3. $y = 2x - 5$

x	−2	−1	0	1
y				

4. $y = -\dfrac{1}{2}x + 3$

x	0	2	4	6
y				

5. A factory that makes frozen pies produces 300 pies per minute.

   a. Write an equation that represents the number y of pies made each hour x.

   b. Create an input-output table for the equation in part (a). Use inputs 1, 2, 4, 8, and 10.

   c. Find the domain and range of the function represented by the table.

Name_____ Date_____

Determine whether the relation is a function.

1. $(1, -7), (1, -5), (2, -4), (3, -1), (4, 1)$ 2. $(-3, 1), (0, 0), (3, 1), (6, 4), (9, 9)$

3.

Input	Output
6	5
7	1
8	-3

4.

Input	Output
4	1.5
-2	3.0
-2	3.5
0	4.5

5. Input, x Output, y

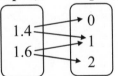

6. Input, x Output, y

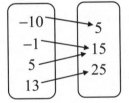

Name _____ Date _____

Determine whether the graph represents a function.

7.

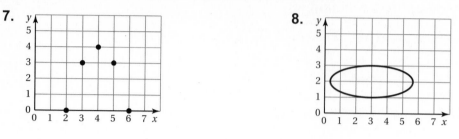

8.

9. Let x represent the number of each month. (For example, $x = 1$ for January.)
   Let y represent the number of days in month x. Do not consider a leap year.

   a. Complete the table.

Input, x												
Output, y												

   b. Does the relation represent a function? Explain.

   c. When you switch the inputs and outputs of this relation, is the resulting
      relation a function?

Name_____ Date _____

5.2 Discrete and Continuous Domains
For use with Activity 5.2

Essential Question How can you decide whether the domain of a function is discrete or continuous?

1 **EXAMPLE:** Discrete and Continuous Domains

In Activities 1 and 2 in Section 2.4, you studied two real-life problems represented by the same equation.

$$4x + 2y = 16 \text{ or } y = -2x + 8$$

a.

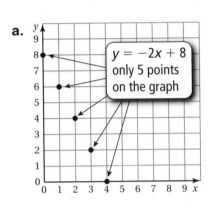

Domain (*x*-values): 0, 1, 2, 3, 4
Range (*y*-values): 8, 6, 4, 2, 0
The domain is **discrete** because it consists of only the numbers 0, 1, 2, 3, and 4.

b.

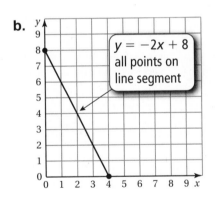

Domain (*x*-values): $0 \leq x \leq 4$
Range (*y*-values): $0 \leq y \leq 8$
The domain is **continuous** because it consists of all numbers from 0 and 4 on the number line.

5.2 **Discrete and Continuous Domains** (continued)

2 **ACTIVITY:** Discrete and Continuous Domains

Work with a partner.

- **Write a function to represent each problem.**

- **Graph each function.**

- **Describe the domain and range of each function. Is the domain discrete or continuous?**

a. You are in charge of reserving hotel rooms for a youth soccer team. Each room costs $69, plus $6 tax, per night. You need each room for two nights. You need 10 to 16 rooms. Write a function for the total hotel cost.

b. The airline you are using for the soccer trip needs an estimate of the total weight of the team's luggage. You determine that there will be 36 pieces of luggage and each piece will weigh from 25 to 45 pounds. Write a function for the total weight of the luggage.

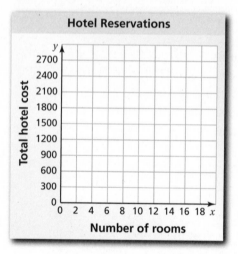

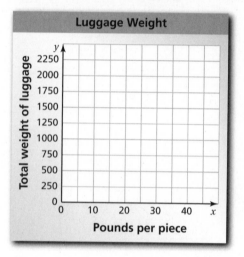

5.2　Discrete and Continuous Domains (continued)

What Is Your Answer?

3. **IN YOUR OWN WORDS** How can you decide whether the domain of a function is discrete or continuous? Describe two real-life examples of functions: one with a discrete domain and one with a continuous domain.

Name _____ Date _____

Graph the function. Is the domain discrete or continuous?

1.

Input Length, x (inches)	Output Area, y (square inches)
2	12
4	24
6	36

2.

Input Shirts, x	Output Cost, y (dollars)
0	0
1	9.25
2	18.50

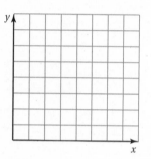

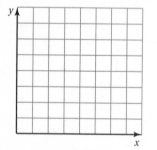

3. The function $c = 20 + 10m$ represents the amount of calories you burn after m minutes of exercising. Graph the function using a domain of 0, 5, 10, and 15. Is the domain discrete or continuous?

4. You buy cards to send to family and friends for their birthdays. The function $y = 2.5x$ represents the cost y of the number of cards x you buy.

   a. Is 8 in the domain? Explain.

   b. Is 40 in the range? Explain.

Name_____ Date _____

Essential Question   How can you use a linear function to describe a linear pattern?

1   ACTIVITY: Finding Linear Patterns

Work with a partner.

- **Plot the points from the table in a coordinate plane.**

- **Write a linear equation for the function.**

a.

x	0	2	4	6	8
y	150	125	100	75	50

b.

x	4	6	8	10	12
y	15	20	25	30	35

c.

x	−4	−2	0	2	4
y	4	6	8	10	12

d.

x	−4	−2	0	2	4
y	1	0	−1	−2	−3

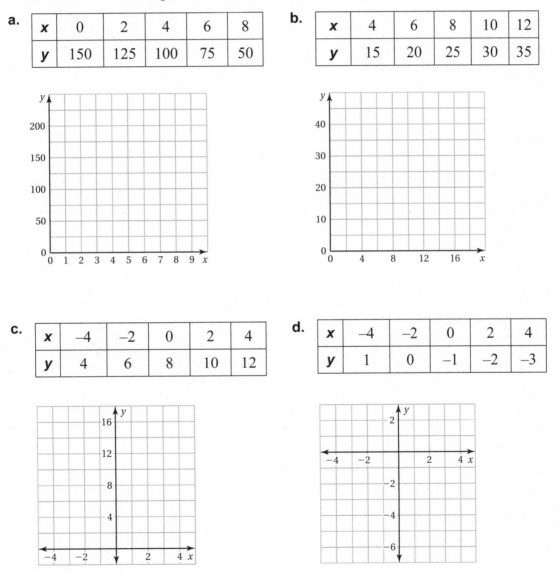

5.3 Linear Function Patterns (continued)

2 ACTIVITY: Finding Linear Patterns

Work with a partner. The table shows a familiar linear pattern from geometry.

- Write a linear function that relates y to x.
- What do the variables x and y represent?
- Graph the linear function.

a.

x	1	2	3	4	5
y	2π	4π	6π	8π	10π

b.

x	1	2	3	4	5
y	10	12	14	16	18

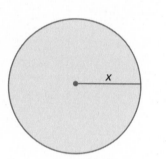

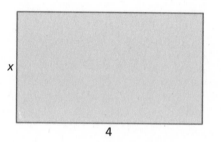

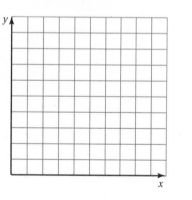

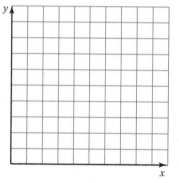

5.3 **Linear Function Patterns** (continued)

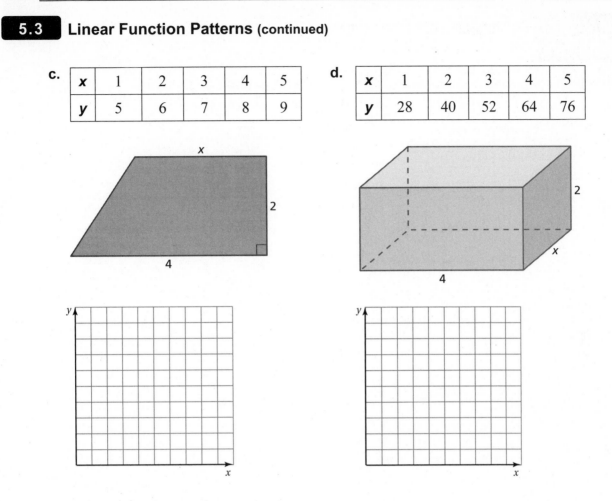

c.

x	1	2	3	4	5
y	5	6	7	8	9

d.

x	1	2	3	4	5
y	28	40	52	64	76

What Is Your Answer?

3. **IN YOUR OWN WORDS** How can you use a linear function to describe a linear pattern?

4. Describe the strategy you used to find the linear functions in Activities 1 and 2.

5.3 Practice

For use after Lesson 5.3

Use the graph or the table to write a linear function that relates *y* to *x*.

1.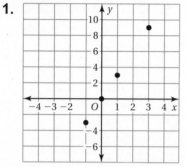

2.

3.

x	0	1	2	3
y	5	7	9	11

4.

x	−2	0	2	4
y	−1	−2	−3	−4

5. The table shows the distance traveled *y* (in miles) after *x* hours.

x	0	2	4	6
y	0	120	240	360

   a. Graph the data. Is the domain discrete or continuous?

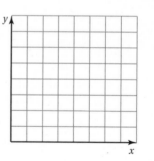

   b. Write a linear function that relates *y* to *x*.

   c. What is the distance traveled after three hours?

Name_____ Date _____

Essential Question How can you use function notation to represent a function?

By naming a function f, you can write the function using **function notation**.

$$f(x) = 2x - 3 \qquad \text{Function notation}$$

This is read as "f of x equals $2x$ minus 3." The notation $f(x)$ is another name for y. When function notation is used, the parentheses do not imply multiplication. You can use letters other than f to name a function. The letters g, h, j, and k are often used to name functions.

---

1 **ACTIVITY:** Matching Functions with Their Graphs

Work with a partner. Match each function with its graph.

a. $f(x) = 2x - 3$

b. $g(x) = -x + 2$

c. $h(x) = x^2 - 1$

d. $f(x) = 2x^2 - 3$

A.
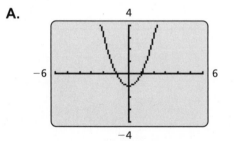

B.
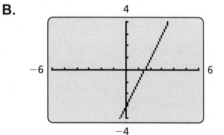

C.
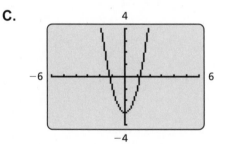

D.
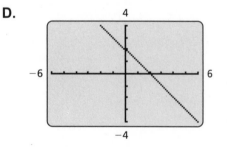

Name _____ Date _____

2 **ACTIVITY:** Evaluating a Function

Work with a partner. Consider the function

$$f(x) = -x + 3.$$

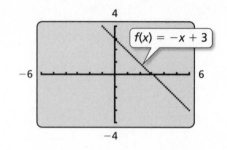

Locate the points $(x, f(x))$ on the graph. Explain how you found each point.

a. $(-1, f(-1))$

b. $(0, f(0))$

c. $(1, f(1))$

d. $(2, f(2))$

3 **ACTIVITY:** Comparing Graphs of Functions

Work with a partner. The graph of a function from trigonometry is shown at the right. Use the graph to sketch the graph of each function. Explain your reasoning.

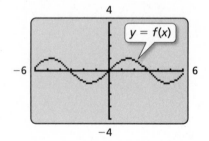

a. $g(x) = f(x) + 2$

b. $g(x) = f(x) + 1$

c. $g(x) = f(x) - 1$

d. $g(x) = f(x) - 2$

5.4 **Function Notation** (continued)

What Is Your Answer?

4. **IN YOUR OWN WORDS** How can you use function notation to represent a function? How are standard notation and function notation similar? How are they different?

Standard Notation	*Function Notation*
$y = 2x + 5$	$f(x) = 2x + 5$

5. Use what you discovered in Activity 3 to write a general observation that compares the graphs of

$$y = f(x) \quad \text{and} \quad y = f(x) + c.$$

Name _____ Date _____

5.4 Practice
For use after Lesson 5.4

Find the value of *x* so that the function has the given value.

1. $g(x) = 8x - 11; g(x) = 5$

2. $v(x) = -2x - 2; v(x) = 12$

3. $k(x) = \dfrac{3}{2}x + 7; k(x) = -2$

4. $j(x) = -4x + 9; j(x) = 8$

Graph the linear function.

5. $f(x) = -3x + 1$

6. $h(x) = \dfrac{1}{4}x - 2$

7. You have $124. You earn $22 each time you mow your neighbor's lawn. The function $s(x) = 22x + 124$ represents your total savings.

   a. What will your savings be after you mow 5 times?

   b. How many times do you have to mow to save a total of $300?

Name_____ Date_____

Graph the function. Describe the domain and range.

1. $y = \begin{cases} x - 1, & \text{if } x \le 0 \\ 2x, & \text{if } x > 0 \end{cases}$

2. $y = \begin{cases} -3, & \text{if } x \le -1 \\ -\dfrac{1}{3}x + 1, & \text{if } x > -1 \end{cases}$

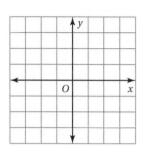

3. $y = \begin{cases} 3, & \text{if } x \le -1 \\ -2x, & \text{if } -1 < x < 1 \\ 3x - 6, & \text{if } x \ge 1 \end{cases}$

4. $y = \begin{cases} -2x - 4, & \text{if } x \le -2 \\ 4x + 1, & \text{if } -2 < x \le 1 \\ x, & \text{if } x > 1 \end{cases}$

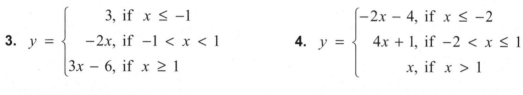

5. Write a piecewise function for the graph.

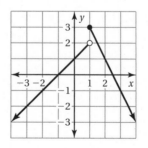

5.4b Practice (continued)

Graph the function. Compare the graph to the graph of $y = |x|$. Describe the domain and range.

6. $y = |x| - 2$

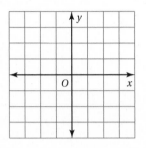

7. $y = |x + 3|$

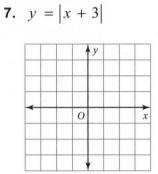

8. $y = -\dfrac{1}{3}|x|$

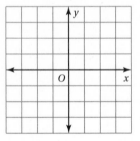

9. $y = |x - 1| - 4$

Write an equation for the given translation of $y = |x|$.

10. 3 units right

11. 2 units down and 8 units left

Name_____ Date_____

Essential Question How can you recognize when a pattern in real life is linear or nonlinear?

1 ACTIVITY: Finding Patterns for Similar Figures

Work with a partner. Complete each table for the sequence of similar rectangles. Graph the data in each table. Decide whether each pattern is linear or nonlinear.

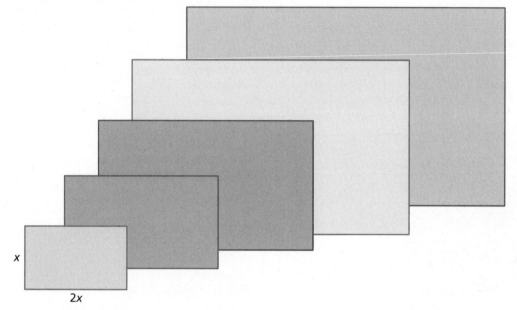

a. Perimeters of Similar Rectangles

x	1	2	3	4	5
P					

b. Areas of Similar Rectangles

x	1	2	3	4	5
A					

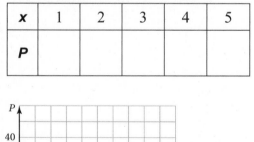

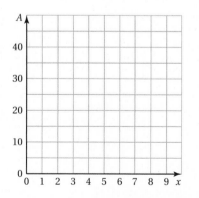

Name _____ Date _____

2 **ACTIVITY:** Comparing Linear and Nonlinear Functions

Work with a partner. The table shows the height h (in feet) of a falling object at t seconds.

- **Graph the data in the table.**

- **Decide whether the graph is linear or nonlinear.**

- **Compare the two falling objects. Which one has an increasing speed?**

a. Falling parachute jumper

t	0	1	2	3	4
h	300	285	270	255	240

b. Falling bowling ball

t	0	1	2	3	4
h	300	284	236	156	44

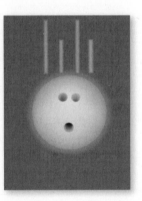

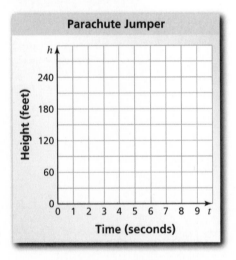

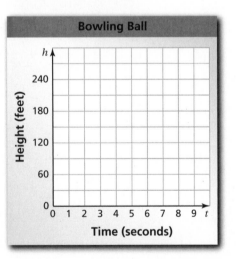

5.5   **Comparing Linear and Nonlinear Functions** (continued)

What Is Your Answer?

3. **IN YOUR OWN WORDS** How can you recognize when a pattern in real life is linear or nonlinear? Describe two real-life patterns: one that is linear and one that is nonlinear. Use patterns that are different from those described in Activities 1 and 2.

Name _____ Date _____

Practice
For use after Lesson 5.5

Graph the data in the table. Decide whether the function is *linear* or *nonlinear*.

1.

x	−2	0	2	4
y	4	0	4	16

2.

x	−1	0	1	2
y	−1	1	3	5

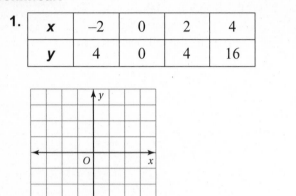

Does the graph represent a *linear* or nonlinear *function*? Explain.

3.

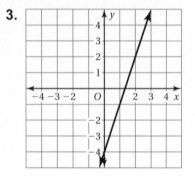

4.

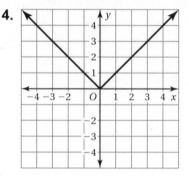

5. The table shows the area of a square with side length *x* inches. Does the table represent a linear or nonlinear function? Explain.

Side Length, x	1	2	3	4
Area, A	1	4	9	16

5.6 Arithmetic Sequences
For use with Activity 5.6

Essential Question   How are arithmetic sequences used to describe patterns?

1   ACTIVITY: Describing a Pattern

Work with a partner.

- **Use the figures to complete the table.**

- **Plot the points in your completed table.**

- **Describe the pattern of the *y*-values.**

a.

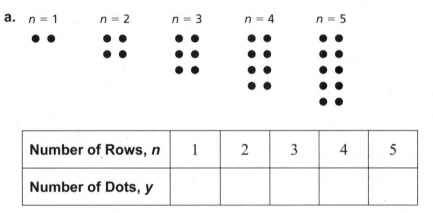

Number of Rows, *n*	1	2	3	4	5
Number of Dots, *y*					

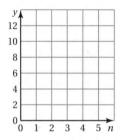

b.   *n* = 1   *n* = 2   *n* = 3   *n* = 4   *n* = 5

Number of Stars, *n*	1	2	3	4	5
Number of Sides, *y*					

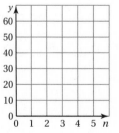

5.6 Arithmetic Sequences (continued)

c.

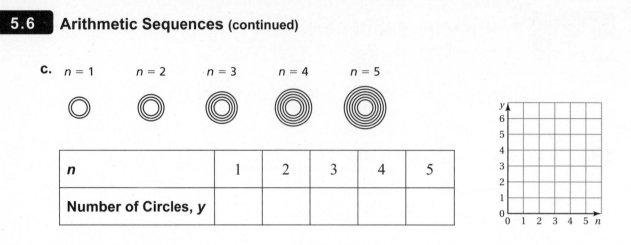

n		1	2	3	4	5
Number of Circles, *y*						

---

2 ACTIVITY: Using a Pattern in Science to Predict

Work with a partner. In chemistry, water is called H_2O because each molecule of water has 2 hydrogen atoms and 1 oxygen atom.

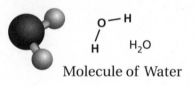

Molecule of Water

- Use the figures to complete the table.

- Describe the pattern of the *y*-values.

- Use your pattern to predict the number of atoms in 23 molecules.

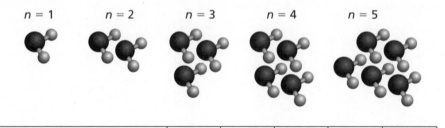

Number of Molecules, *n*	1	2	3	4	5
Number of Atoms, *y*					

5.6 **Arithmetic Sequences** (continued)

3 **ACTIVITY:** Writing a Story

Work with a partner.

- **Describe the pattern in the table.**

- **Write and illustrate a story using the numbers in the table.**

- **Graph the data shown in the table.**

Jan	Feb	Mar	Apr	May	Jun	Jul	Aug	Sep	Oct	Nov	Dec
12	20	28	36	44	52	60	68	76	84	92	100

What Is Your Answer?

4. **IN YOUR OWN WORDS** How are arithmetic sequences used to describe patterns? Give an example from real life.

5.6 **Practice**
For use after Lesson 5.6

Write the next three terms of the arithmetic sequence.

1. First term: 3

   Common difference: 12

2. First term: 5

   Common difference: 1.3

Find the common difference of the arithmetic sequence.

3. 4, 8, 12, 16, …

4. 6.3, 7, 7.7, 8.4, …

5. 200, 500, 800, 1100, …

Write the next three terms of the arithmetic sequence.

6. 1, 10, 19, 28, …

7. $8\frac{2}{3}, 9, 9\frac{1}{3}, 9\frac{2}{3}, \ldots$

8. 10, 25, 40, 55, …

Determine whether the sequence is arithmetic. If so, find the common difference.

9. 3, 6, 12, 24, …

10. $0, \frac{5}{6}, 1\frac{2}{3}, 2\frac{1}{2}, \ldots$

11. An amusement park charges $45 per person for admission. A season pass costs $112 per person.

    a. Write the first five terms of an arithmetic sequence that represents the total cost of admission for the number of visits in a season.

    b. How many times does a person have to visit the park for a season pass to be the better deal? Explain.

Name_____ Date_____

Evaluate the expression.

1. $5^2 \cdot 2 - 1 - 6 \cdot 3^2 + 8$

2. $9 - \left(\dfrac{18}{3}\right) \cdot 2^3 + 20 \cdot 5^{-1}$

3. $4 + 4^2 + (12 - 3 \cdot 2) - 3$

4. $9 + 7(2 - 8) + 5^0 + \left(6^2 - 8\right)$

5. Find $\sqrt{81}$.

6. Find $-\sqrt{25}$.

7. Find $\pm\sqrt{16}$.

8. Find the side length s of the square.

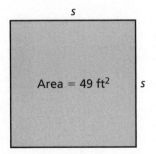

s

Area = 49 ft^2

s

Chapter 6 Fair Game Review (continued)

Write an equation for the *n*th term of the arithmetic sequence.

9. 1, 5, 9, 13, …

10. 1, −11, −23, −35, …

11. 18, 12, 6, 0, …

12. −24, −15, −6, 3, …

13. Your family is driving on the highway. The amount of gas in the tank after 1 hour, 2 hours, and 3 hours is 19.5 gallons, 17 gallons, and 14.5 gallons, respectively.

   a. Write an equation for the amount of gas left after the *n*th hour of driving.

   b. How much gas will be left in the tank after 8 hours?

Name_____ Date _____

6.1 Properties of Square Roots
For use with Activity 6.1

Essential Question How can you multiply and divide square roots?

Recall that when you multiply a number by itself, you square the number.

> Symbol for squaring is 2nd power. → $4^2 = 4 \cdot 4$
> $= 16$

4 squared is 16.

To "undo" this, take the square root of the number.

> Symbol for square root is a radical sign. → $\sqrt{16} = \sqrt{4^2} = 4$

The square root of 16 is 4.

---

1 ACTIVITY: Finding Square Roots

Work with a partner. Use a square root symbol to write the side length of the square. Then find the square root. Check your answer by multiplying.

a. $s = \sqrt{81} = $ _____   **Check:**

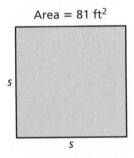

Area = 81 ft²

s

s

The side length of the square is _____.

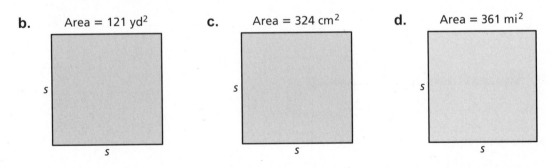

b. Area = 121 yd²

s

s

c. Area = 324 cm²

s

s

d. Area = 361 mi²

s

s

6.1 Properties of Square Roots (continued)

e. Area = 2.89 in.^{2}

s s

f. Area = 6.25 m^2

s s

g. Area = $\frac{16}{25}$ ft^2

s s

2 ACTIVITY: Operations with Square Roots

Work with a partner. When you have an expression that involves two operations, you need to know whether you obtain the same result regardless of the order in which you perform the operations. In each of the following, compare the results obtained by the two orders. What can you conclude?

a. Square Roots and Addition

Is $\sqrt{36} + \sqrt{64}$ equal to $\sqrt{36 + 64}$?

In general, is $\sqrt{a} + \sqrt{b}$ equal to $\sqrt{a + b}$?

Explain your reasoning.

b. Square Roots and Multiplication

Is $\sqrt{4} \cdot \sqrt{9}$ equal to $\sqrt{4 \cdot 9}$?

In general, is $\sqrt{a} \cdot \sqrt{b}$ equal to $\sqrt{a \cdot b}$?

Explain your reasoning.

6.1 **Properties of Square Roots** (continued)

c. Square Roots and Subtraction

Is $\sqrt{64} - \sqrt{36}$ equal to $\sqrt{64 - 36}$?

In general, is $\sqrt{a} - \sqrt{b}$ equal to $\sqrt{a - b}$?

Explain your reasoning.

d. Square Roots and Division

Is $\dfrac{\sqrt{100}}{\sqrt{4}}$ equal to $\sqrt{\dfrac{100}{4}}$?

In general, is $\dfrac{\sqrt{a}}{\sqrt{b}}$ equal to $\sqrt{\dfrac{a}{b}}$?

Explain your reasoning.

What Is Your Answer?

3. **IN YOUR OWN WORDS** How can you multiply and divide square roots? Write a rule for:

   a. The product of square roots

   b. The quotient of square roots

Name_____ Date _____

Practice
For use after Lesson 6.1

Simplify the expression.

1. $\sqrt{44}$

2. $-\sqrt{175}$

3. $-\sqrt{\dfrac{10}{49}}$

4. $\sqrt{\dfrac{54}{81}}$

5. $\dfrac{8 - \sqrt{112}}{4}$

6. $\dfrac{-6 + \sqrt{72}}{18}$

Simplify the expression. Assume all variables are positive.

7. $\sqrt{36xy^2}$

8. $\sqrt{50x^2 yz^3}$

9. A trampoline has an area of 49π square feet. What is the diameter of the trampoline?

6.1b Real Number Operations
For use with Activity 6.1b

A set of numbers is **closed** under an operation when the operation performed on any two numbers in the set results in a number that is also in that set. For example, the set of integers is closed under addition, subtraction, and multiplication. This means that if a and b are two integers, then $a + b$, $a - b$, and ab are also integers.

---

1 ACTIVITY: Sums and Products of Rational Numbers

The table shows several sums and products of rational numbers. Complete the table.

Sum or Product	Answer	Rational or Irrational?
$12 + 5$		
$-4 + 9$		
$\dfrac{4}{5} + \dfrac{2}{3}$		
$0.74 + 2.1$		
3×8		
-4×6		
3.1×0.6		
$\dfrac{3}{4} \times \dfrac{5}{7}$		

6.1b **Real Number Operations** (continued)

2 **ACTIVITY:** Sums of Rational and Irrational Numbers

The table shows several sums of rational and irrational numbers. Complete the table.

Sum	Answer	Rational or Irrational?
$1 + \sqrt{5}$		
$\sqrt{2} + \dfrac{5}{6}$		
$4 + \pi$		
$-8 + \sqrt{10}$		

Practice

1. Using the results in Activity 1, do you think the set of rational numbers is closed under addition? under multiplication? Explain your reasoning.

2. Using the results in Activity 2, what do you notice about the sum of a rational number and an irrational number?

6.1b Real Number Operations (continued)

3 ACTIVITY: Products of Rational and Irrational Numbers

The table shows several products of rational and irrational numbers. Complete the table.

Product	Answer	Rational or Irrational?
$6 \cdot \sqrt{12}$		
$-2 \cdot \pi$		
$\dfrac{2}{5} \cdot \sqrt{3}$		
$0 \times \sqrt{6}$		

4 ACTIVITY: Sums and Products of Irrational Numbers

The table shows several sums and products of irrational numbers. Complete the table.

Sum or Product	Answer	Rational or Irrational?
$3\sqrt{2} + 5\sqrt{2}$		
$\sqrt{12} + \sqrt{27}$		
$\sqrt{7} + \pi$		
$-\pi + \pi$		
$\pi \cdot \sqrt{7}$		
$\sqrt{5} \times \sqrt{2}$		
$4\pi \cdot \sqrt{3}$		
$\sqrt{3} \cdot \sqrt{3}$		

6.1b **Real Number Operations** (continued)

Practice

3. Using the results in Activity 3, is the product of a rational number and an irrational number always irrational? Explain.

4. Using the results in Activity 4, do you think the set of irrational numbers is closed under addition? under multiplication? Explain your reasoning.

5. **CRITICAL THINKING** Is the set of irrational numbers closed under division? If not, find a counterexample. (A *counterexample* is an example that shows that a statement is false.)

6. **STRUCTURE** The set of integers is closed under addition and multiplication. Use this information to show that the sum and product of two rational numbers are always rational numbers.

Name_____ Date _____

Essential Question   How can you use inductive reasoning to observe patterns and write general rules involving properties of exponents?

1   **ACTIVITY:** Writing a Rule for Products of Powers

Work with a partner. Write the product of the two powers as a single power. Then, write a *general rule* for finding the product of two powers with the same base.

a. $\left(3^4\right)\left(3^3\right) =$

b. $\left(2^2\right)\left(2^3\right) =$

c. $\left(4^1\right)\left(4^5\right) =$

d. $\left(5^3\right)\left(5^5\right) =$

e. $\left(x^2\right)\left(x^6\right) =$

2   **ACTIVITY:** Writing a Rule for Quotients of Powers

Work with a partner. Write the quotient of the two powers as a single power. Then, write a *general rule* for finding the quotient of two powers with the same base.

a. $\dfrac{3^4}{3^2} =$

b. $\dfrac{4^3}{4^2} =$

c. $\dfrac{2^5}{2^2} =$

d. $\dfrac{x^6}{x^3} =$

e. $\dfrac{3^4}{3^4} =$

6.2 **Properties of Exponents** (continued)

3 **ACTIVITY:** Writing a Rule for Powers of Powers

Work with a partner. Write the expression as a single power. Then, write a *general rule* **for finding a power of a power.**

   a. $\left(3^2\right)^3 =$

   b. $\left(2^2\right)^4 =$

   c. $\left(7^3\right)^2 =$

   d. $\left(y^3\right)^3 =$

   e. $\left(x^4\right)^2 =$

4 **ACTIVITY:** Writing a Rule for Powers of Products

Work with a partner. Write the expression as the product of two powers. Then, write a *general rule* **for finding a power of a product.**

   a. $(2 \bullet 3)^3 =$

   b. $(2 \bullet 5)^2 =$

   c. $(5 \bullet 4)^3 =$

   d. $(6a)^4 =$

   e. $(3x)^2 =$

Name _____ Date _____

---

5 **ACTIVITY:** Writing a Rule for Powers of Quotients

Work with a partner. Write the expression as the quotient of two powers.
Then, write a *general rule* for finding a power of a quotient.

a. $\left(\dfrac{3}{2}\right)^{4} =$

b. $\left(\dfrac{2}{3}\right)^{2} =$

c. $\left(\dfrac{4}{3}\right)^{3} =$

d. $\left(\dfrac{x}{2}\right)^{3} =$

e. $\left(\dfrac{a}{b}\right)^{4} =$

What Is Your Answer?

6. **IN YOUR OWN WORDS** How can you use inductive reasoning to observe
patterns and write general rules involving properties of exponents?

7. There are 3^3 small cubes in the cube below.
Write an expression for the number of small
cubes in the large cube at the right.

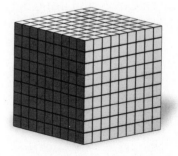

Name_____ Date _____

Simplify. Write your answer using only positive exponents.

1. $m^3 \bullet m^6$

2. $\dfrac{t^2}{t^4}$

3. $\left(3^3\right)^2$

4. $h^6 \bullet h^{-8}$

5. $\left(4p\right)^4$

6. $\left(\dfrac{y}{5}\right)^3$

7. $\left(\dfrac{3}{a}\right)^{-5}$

8. $\left(-2w\right)^{-7}$

9. Write an expression using only positive exponents for the width w of the rectangle.

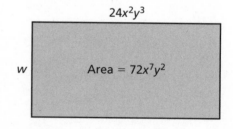

$24x^2y^3$

w Area $= 72x^7y^2$

6.3 Radicals and Rational Exponents
For use with Activity 6.3

Essential Question How can you write and evaluate an *n*th root of a number?

Recall that you cube a number as follows.

> Symbol for cubing is 3rd power.

$$2^3 = 2 \bullet 2 \bullet 2$$
$$= 8$$

2 cubed is 8.

To "undo" this, take the cube root of the number.

> Symbol for cube root is $\sqrt[3]{}$.

$$\sqrt[3]{8} = \sqrt[3]{2^3} = 2$$

The cube root of 8 is 2.

---

1 ACTIVITY: Finding Cube Roots

Work with a partner. Use a cube root symbol to write the side length of the cube. Then find the cube root. Check your answer by multiplying. Which cube is the largest? Which two are the same size? Explain your reasoning.

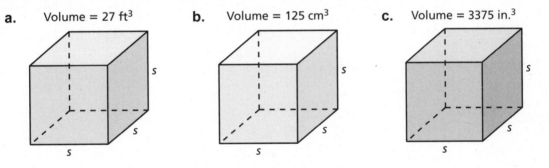

a. Volume = 27 ft³   **b.** Volume = 125 cm³   **c.** Volume = 3375 in.³

Cubes are not drawn to scale.

6.3 Radicals and Rational Exponents (continued)

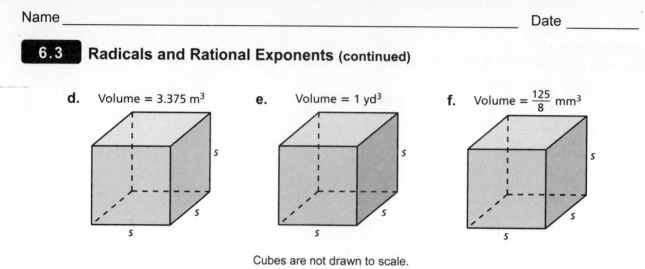

d. Volume = 3.375 m³   **e.** Volume = 1 yd³   **f.** Volume = $\frac{125}{8}$ mm³

Cubes are not drawn to scale.

2 ACTIVITY: Estimating *n*th Roots

Work with a partner. When you raise an *n*th root of a number to the *n*th power, you get the original number.

$$\left(\sqrt[n]{a}\right)^n = a$$

Sample: The 4th root of 16 is 2 because $2^4 = 16$.

$$\sqrt[4]{16} = \underline{\hspace{1.5cm}} \qquad \textbf{Check:} \ \underline{\hspace{5cm}}$$

Match the *n*th root with the point on the number line on the following page. Justify your answer.

a. $\sqrt[4]{25}$ **b.** $\sqrt{0.5}$ **c.** $\sqrt[5]{2.5}$

d. $\sqrt[3]{65}$ **e.** $\sqrt[3]{55}$ **f.** $\sqrt[6]{20,000}$

6.3   **Radicals and Rational Exponents** (continued)

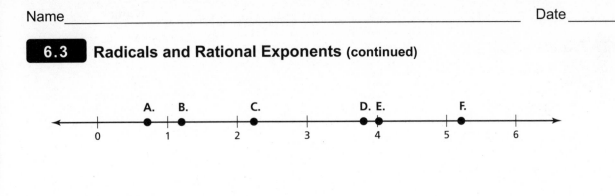

What Is Your Answer?

3. **IN YOUR OWN WORDS** How can you write and evaluate the *n*th root of a number?

4. The body mass *m* (in kilograms) of a dinosaur that walked on two feet can be modeled by

$$m = (0.00016)C^{2.73}$$

where *C* is the circumference (in millimeters) of the dinosaur's femur. The mass of a Tyrannosaurus rex was 4000 kilograms. What was the circumference of its femur?

6.3 Practice
For use after Lesson 6.3

Simplify the expression.

1. $\sqrt[5]{243}$

2. $\sqrt[3]{64}$

3. $144^{1/2}$

4. $729^{1/3}$

5. $1000^{2/3}$

6. $64^{3/2}$

7. $81^{3/4}$

8. $32^{7/5}$

9. The radius r of the base of a cylinder is given by the equation $r = \left(\dfrac{V}{\pi h}\right)^{1/2}$, where V is the volume of the cylinder and h is the height of the cylinder. Find the radius of the cylinder to the nearest inch. Use 3.14 for π.

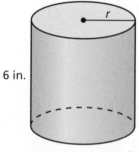

6 in.

Volume = 170 in.³

6.4 Exponential Functions
For use with Activity 6.4

Essential Question   What are the characteristics of an exponential function?

---

1   ACTIVITY: Describing an Exponential Function

Work with a partner. The graph below shows estimates of the population of Earth from 5000 B.C. through 1500 A.D. at 500-year intervals.

   a. Describe the pattern.

   b. Did Earth's population increase by the same *amount* or the same *percent* for each 500-year period? Explain.

   c. Assume the pattern continued. Estimate Earth's population in 2000.

   d. Use the Internet to find Earth's population in 2000. Did the pattern continue? If not, why did the pattern change?

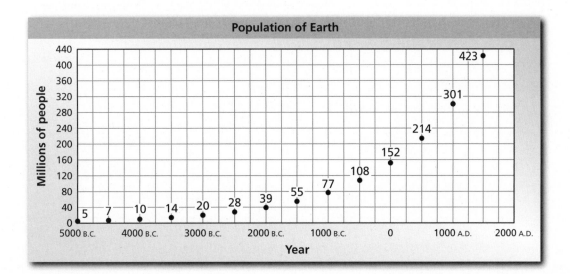

6.4 **Exponential Functions** (continued)

2 **ACTIVITY:** Modeling an Exponential Function

Work with a partner. Use the following exponential function to complete the table. Compare the results with the data in Activity 1.

$$P = 152(1.406)^{t/500}$$

Year	t	Population from Activity 1	P
5000 B.C.	−5000		
4500 B.C.	−4500		
4000 B.C.	−4000		
3500 B.C.	−3500		
3000 B.C.	−3000		
2500 B.C.	−2500		
2000 B.C.	−2000		
1500 B.C.	−1500		
1000 B.C.	−1000		
500 B.C.	−500		
1 B.C.	0		
500 A.D.	500		
1000 A.D.	1000		
1500 A.D.	1500		

6.4 **Exponential Functions** (continued)

What Is Your Answer?

3. **IN YOUR OWN WORDS** What are the characteristics of an exponential function?

4. Sketch the graph of each exponential function. Does the function match the characteristics you described in Question 3? Explain.

   a. $y = 2^x$

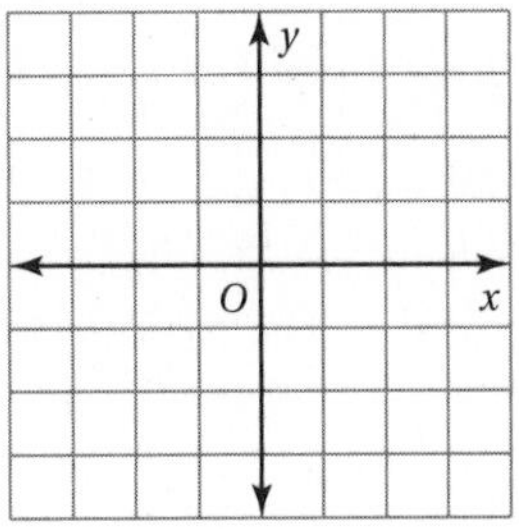

   b. $y = 2(3)^x$

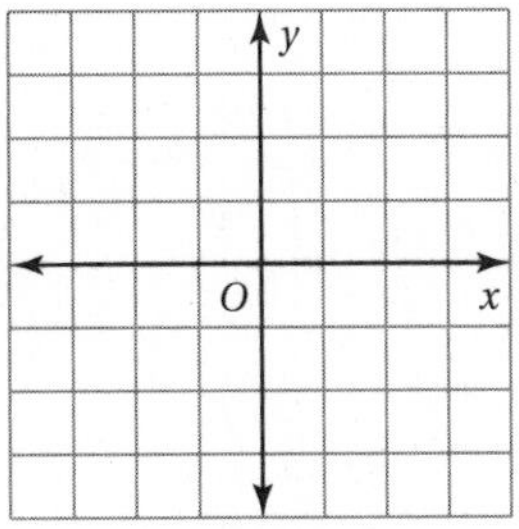

   c. $y = 3(1.5)^x$

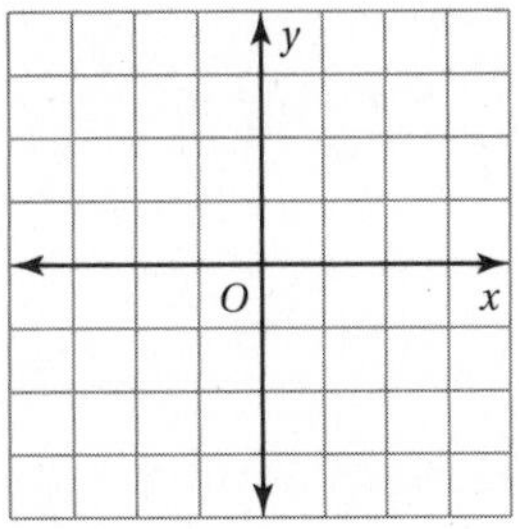

Name _____ Date _____

Evaluate the function for the given value of x.

1. $y = 4^x; x = 2$

2. $f(x) = 2.5(10)^x; x = 4$

3. $f(x) = \frac{1}{4}(2)^x; x = 5$

4. $y = -2(7)^x; x = 3$

Graph the function. Describe the domain and range.

5. $f(x) = 3\left(\frac{1}{2}\right)^x$

6. $y = -\frac{1}{3}(3)^x$

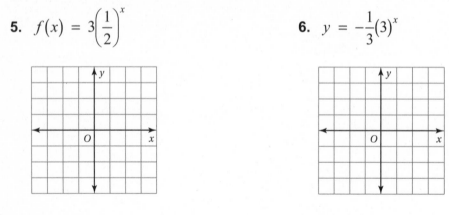

7. The number of visits y to a new website quadruples every day. The function $y = 12(4)^x$ represents the number of visits, where x is the day.

   a. Graph the function. Describe the domain and range.

   b. How many visitors did the website have on the 3rd day?

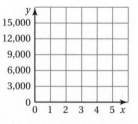

6.4b Practice
For use after Lesson 6.4b

Solve the equation. Check your solution, if possible.

1. $4^x = 64$

2. $\dfrac{1}{125} = 5^x$

3. $3^{3x} = 27^{2x+1}$

4. $7^{x-5} = 7^{x+2}$

5. $243^{2x-6} = 9^{x+1}$

6. $\left(\dfrac{1}{8}\right)^{3-x} = 8^{2x-9}$

Name _____ Date _____

Use a graphing calculator to solve the equation.

7. $5^{x-1} = 18$

8. $0.4 = 3^{4x}$

9. $6^{1-x} = 2$

10. $2^{-5x} = 4^{x+2}$

11. $-2^{x-5} = 3^{2x}$

12. $\left(\dfrac{1}{3}\right)^{3x+4} = 7^{x+3}$

13. Restaurant A opens across the street from restaurant B. Restaurant A begins gaining customers and restaurant B begins losing customers. The equations $A = 4^x$ and $B = 2^{9-x}$ represent the daily number of customers that eat at the respective restaurants.

   a. When do the restaurants have the same number of customers?

   b. Check your answer.

Name_____ Date_____

6.5 Exponential Growth
For use with Activity 6.5

Essential Question What are the characteristics of exponential growth?

---

1 **ACTIVITY:** Comparing Types of Growth

Work with a partner. Describe the pattern of growth for each sequence and graph. How many of the patterns represent exponential growth? Explain your reasoning.

a. 1, 4, 7, 10, 13, 16, 19, 22, 25, 28, 31

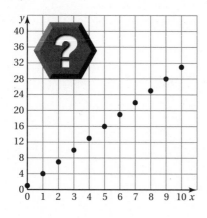

b. 1.0, 1.4, 2.0, 2.7, 3.8, 5.4, 7.5, 10.5, 14.8, 20.7, 28.9

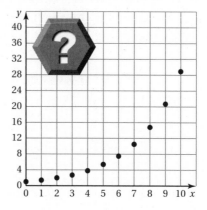

c. 1.0, 1.3, 2.3, 4.0, 6.3, 9.3, 13.0, 17.3, 22.3, 28.0, 34.3

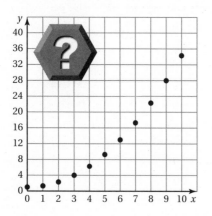

d. 1.0, 1.6, 3.4, 2.4, 4.7, 6.4, 8.7, 11.5, 15.3, 20.2, 26.6

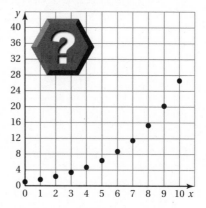

Name _____ Date _____

6.5 Exponential Growth (continued)

2 ACTIVITY: Describing a Growth Pattern

Work with a partner. It is estimated that in 1782 there were about 100,000 nesting pairs of bald eagles in the United States. By the 1960s, this number had dropped to about 500 nesting pairs. This decline was attributed to loss of habitat, loss of prey, hunting, and the use of the pesticide DDT. The 1940 Bald Eagle Protection Act prohibited the trapping and killing of the birds. In 1967, the bald eagle was declared an endangered species in the United States. With protection, the nesting pair population began to increase, as shown in the graph. Finally, in 2007, the bald eagle was removed from the list of endangered and threatened species.

Describe the growth pattern shown in the graph. Is it exponential growth? Assume the pattern continues. When will the population return to the levels of the late 1700s? Explain your reasoning.

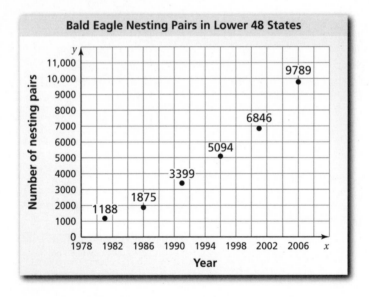

6.5 **Exponential Growth** (continued)

What Is Your Answer?

3. **IN YOUR OWN WORDS** What are the characteristics of exponential growth? How can you distinguish exponential growth from other growth patterns?

4. Which of the following are examples of exponential growth? Explain.

   a. Growth of the balance of a savings account

   b. Speed of the moon in orbit around Earth

   c. Height of a ball that is dropped from a height of 100 feet

6.5 **Practice**
For use after Lesson 6.5

Identify the initial amount *a* and the rate of growth *r* (as a percent) of the exponential function. Evaluate the function when *t* = 4. Round your answer to the nearest tenth.

1. $y = 250(1.01)^t$

2. $f(t) = 14(1.35)^t$

3. $f(t) = 4.2(1.9)^t$

4. $y = 1800(1.059)^t$

5. Credit card debt of $1100 increases by 28% each year. Write and graph a function that represents this situation.

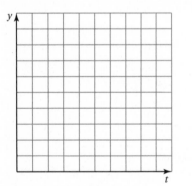

6. You deposit $675 in an account that earns 3.4% annual interest compounded twice a year.

    a. Write a function that represents this situation.

    b. Find the balance in the account after 2.5 years.

6.6 Exponential Decay
For use with Activity 6.6

Essential Question What are the characteristics of exponential decay?

1 ACTIVITY: Comparing Types of Decay

Work with a partner. Describe the pattern of decay for each sequence and graph. How many of the patterns represent exponential decay? Explain your reasoning.

a. 30.0, 24.3, 19.2, 14.7, 10.8, 7.5, 4.8, 2.7, 1.2, 0.3, 0.0

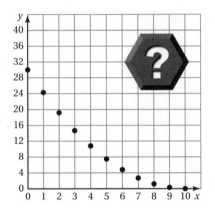

b. 30, 27, 24, 21, 18, 15, 12, 9, 6, 3, 0

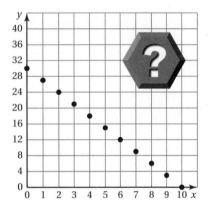

c. 30.0, 24.0, 19.2, 15.4, 12.3, 9.8, 7.9, 6.3, 5.0, 4.0, 3.2

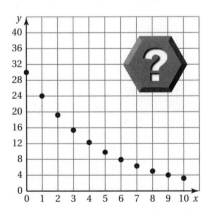

d. 30.0, 29.7, 28.8, 27.3, 25.2, 22.5, 19.2, 15.3, 10.8, 5.7, 0.0

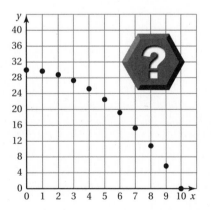

6.6 Exponential Decay (continued)

2 ACTIVITY: Describing a Decay Pattern

Work with a partner. Newton's Law of Cooling states that when an object at one temperature is exposed to air of another temperature, the difference in the two temperatures drops by the same percent each hour.

A forensic pathologist was called to estimate the time of death of a person. At midnight, the body temperature was 80.5°F and the room temperature was 60°F. One hour later, the body temperature was 78.5°F.

a. By what percent did the difference between the body temperature and the room temperature drop during the hour?

b. Assume that the original body temperature was 98.6°F. Use the percent decrease found in part (a) to make a table showing the decreases in body temperature. Use the table to estimate the time of death.

Time	Temperature (°F)
0	98.6
1	
2	
3	
4	
5	
6	
7	
8	
9	
10	

6.6 **Exponential Decay** (continued)

What Is Your Answer?

3. **IN YOUR OWN WORDS** What are the characteristics of exponential decay? How can you distinguish exponential decay from other decay patterns?

4. Sketch a graph of the data from the table in Activity 2. Do the data represent exponential decay? Explain your reasoning.

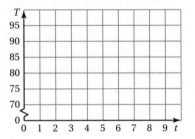

5. Suppose the pathologist arrived at 5:30 A.M. What was the body temperature at 6 A.M.?

Name _____ Date _____

6.6 Practice
For use after Lesson 6.6

Determine whether the table represents an *exponential growth function*, an *exponential decay function*, or *neither*.

1.

x	1	2	3	4
y	216	72	24	8

2.

x	0	1	2	3
y	74	62	50	38

3.

x	1	2	3	4
y	4	28	196	1372

4.

x	0	2	4	6
y	3000	300	30	3

Write the rate of decay of the function as a percent.

5. $f(t) = 40(0.78)^t$

6. $y = 5\left(\dfrac{2}{5}\right)^t$

7. The mass of a radioactive element is 35 milligrams. The mass of the element decreases by 12.9% every year.

   a. Write a function that represents this situation.

   b. Predict the mass of the element in 4 years. Round your answer to the nearest tenth.

Name_____ Date _____

Essential Question How are geometric sequences used to describe patterns?

1 **ACTIVITY:** Describing Calculator Patterns

Work with a partner.

- **Enter the keystrokes on a calculator and record the results in the table.**

- **Describe the pattern.**

a. Step 1   `2` `=`

    Step 2   `×` `2` `=`

    Step 3   `×` `2` `=`

    Step 4   `×` `2` `=`

    Step 5   `×` `2` `=`

Step	1	2	3	4	5
Calculator Display					

b. Step 1   `6` `4` `=`

    Step 2   `×` `.` `5` `=`

    Step 3   `×` `.` `5` `=`

    Step 4   `×` `.` `5` `=`

    Step 5   `×` `.` `5` `=`

Step	1	2	3	4	5
Calculator Display					

c. Use a calculator to make your own sequence. Start with any number and multiply by 3 each time. Record your results in the table.

Step	1	2	3	4	5
Calculator Display					

2 **ACTIVITY:** Folding a Sheet of Paper

Work with a partner. A sheet of paper is about 0.1 mm thick.

a. How thick would it be if you folded it in half once?

b. How thick would it be if you folded it in half a second time?

c. How thick would it be if you folded it in half 6 times?

d. What is the greatest number of times you can fold a sheet of paper in half? How thick is the result?

e. Do you agree with the statement below? Explain your reasoning.

"If it were possible to fold the paper 15 times, it would be taller than you."

6.7 **Geometric Sequences** (continued)

3 **ACTIVITY:** Writing a Story

The King and the Beggar

A king offered a beggar fabulous meals for one week. Instead, the beggar asked for a single grain of rice the first day, 2 grains the second day, and double the amount each day after for one month. The king agreed. But, as the month progressed, he realized that he would lose his entire kingdom.

Work with a partner.

- **Why does the king think he will lose his entire kingdom?**

- **Write your own story about doubling or tripling a small object many times.**

- **Draw pictures for your story.**

- **Include a table to organize the amounts.**

- **Write your story so that one of the characters is surprised by the size of the final number.**

What Is Your Answer?

4. **IN YOUR OWN WORDS** How are geometric sequences used to describe patterns? Give an example from real life.

6.7 Practice
For use after Lesson 6.7

Find the common ratio of the geometric sequence.

1. 5, 15, 45, 135, …

2. 448, −112, 28, −7, …

3. 0.2, 1.6, 12.8, 102.4, …

Write the next three terms of the geometric sequence. Then graph the sequence.

4. $\dfrac{7}{32}, \dfrac{7}{8}, 3\dfrac{1}{2}, 14, \ldots$

5. 3125, 625, 125, 25, …

Tell whether the sequence is *arithmetic, geometric,* or *neither*.

6. 6, 13, 20, 27, …

7. 1, 2, 8, 48, …

8. $144, 24, 4, \dfrac{2}{3}, \ldots$

9. In art class, you are creating a design that uses 1 glass bead in the first row, 3 glass beads in the second row, and 9 glass beads in the third row.

a. Describe the pattern of the design.

b. Write the next three terms of the sequence.

c. Is the sequence *arithmetic, geometric,* or *neither*? Explain.

Name_____ Date _____

Practice
For use after Lesson 6.7b

Write the first six terms of the sequence. Then graph the sequence.

1. $a_1 = 1, a_n = a_{n-1} + 6$

2. $a_1 = 64, a_n = \dfrac{1}{4}a_{n-1}$

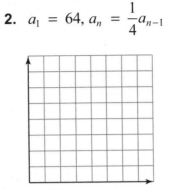

3. $a_1 = -5, a_n = 3a_{n-1}$

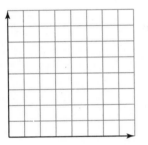

4. $a_1 = 20, a_n = a_{n-1} - 9$

Write a recursive rule for the sequence.

5. $24, 31, 38, 45, 52, \ldots$

6. $-5, 30, -180, 1080, -6480, \ldots$

7. Write a recursive rule for the insect population over time.

Week	1	2	3
Insect Population	200	1400	9800

6.7b **Practice** (continued)

Write an explicit equation for the recursive rule.

8. $a_1 = 54, a_n = \dfrac{1}{3}a_{n-1}$

9. $a_1 = 0, a_n = a_{n-1} + 12$

Write a recursive rule for the explicit equation.

10. $a_n = -25n + 85$

11. $a_n = 16(1.5)^{n-1}$

Write a recursive rule for the sequence. Then write the next 3 terms of the sequence.

12. $3, 8, 11, 19, 30, \ldots$

13. $1, 2, 1, -1, -2, -1, 1, 2, \ldots$

Use a pattern in the products of consecutive terms to write a recursive rule for the sequence. Then write the next 2 terms of the sequence.

14. $1.25, 4, 5, 20, 100, \ldots$

15. $-3, -2, 6, -12, -72, \ldots$

Name_____ Date _____

Simplify the expression.

1. $5y + 6 - 9y$

2. $-2h + 11 + 3h - 4$

3. $8a - 10 - 4a + 6 + a$

4. $7 - 2(m + 8)$

5. $5 - (d + 3) + 4(d - 6)$

6. $16q + 9(-q - 2) + 7$

Write an expression for the perimeter of the figure.

7.

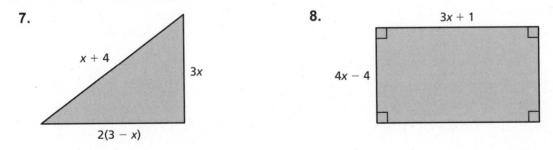

$x + 4$

$3x$

$2(3 - x)$

8.

$3x + 1$

$4x - 4$

Name_____ Date _____

Find the greatest common factor.

9. 12, 33

10. 45, 70

11. 12, 18

12. 48, 80

13. 8, 26

14. −30, 105

15. You and your friend are playing a card game with only one way to score. You have 56 points and your friend has 40 points. What is the greatest number of points you could receive each time you score?

16. You have two pieces of fabric. One piece is 84 centimeters wide and the other piece is 147 centimeters wide. You want to cut both pieces into strips of equal width with no fabric left over. What is the widest you can cut the strips?

7.1 Polynomials
For use with Activity 7.1

Essential Question How can you use algebra tiles to model and classify polynomials?

---

1 ACTIVITY: Meaning of Prefixes

Work with a partner. Think of a word that uses one of the prefixes with one of the base words. Then define the word and write a sentence that uses the word.

Prefix	*Base Word*
Mono	Dactyl
Bi	Cycle
Tri	Ped
Poly	Syllabic

---

2 ACTIVITY: Classifying Polynomials Using Algebra Tiles

Work with a partner. Six different algebra tiles are shown at the right.

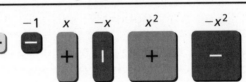

Write the polynomial that is modeled by the algebra tiles. Then classify the polynomial as a monomial, binomial, or trinomial. Explain your reasoning.

a.

b.

7.1 Polynomials (continued)

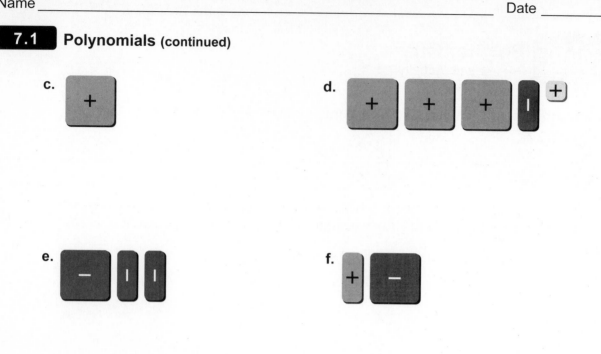

c.

d.

e.

f.

---

3 ACTIVITY: Solving an Algebra Tile Puzzle

Work with a partner. Write the polynomial modeled by the algebra tiles, evaluate the polynomial at the given value, and write the result in the corresponding square of the Sudoku puzzle. Then solve the puzzle.

A3, H7

Value when $x = 2$

A4, B3, E5, G6, I7

Value when $x = 2$

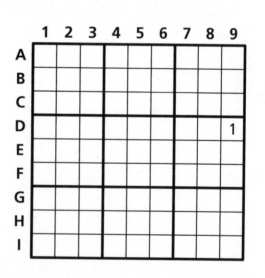

7.1 **Polynomials** (continued)

A6, D7, E2, H5

Value when $x = -3$

B5, F1, H3

Value when $x = -1$

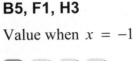

A7, F9, I4

Value when $x = 3$

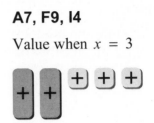

E8, F3, I6

Value when $x = -1$

C4, I3

Value when $x = 3$

B7, D1

Value when $x = -2$

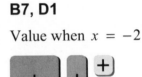

What Is Your Answer?

4. **IN YOUR OWN WORDS** How can you use algebra tiles to model and classify polynomials? Explain why algebra tiles have the dimensions, shapes, and colors that they have.

Name _____ Date _____

Write the polynomial in standard form. Identify the degree and classify the polynomial by the number of terms.

1. $4v^6$

2. $-2c^3 + 1 - 9c$

3. $5t^5 + 8$

4. $\dfrac{3}{2}m^6 + \dfrac{3}{4}m^8$

5. $-\sqrt{12}g^4$

6. $1.8a - a^9 + 3.2a^{12}$

Tell whether the expression is a polynomial. If so, identify the degree and classify the polynomial by the number of terms.

7. $6 - 2d^{2.5}$

8. $-7u - 2u^2 - 2u^{10}$

9. You drop a ball off of a skyscraper. Use the polynomial $-16t^2 + v_0 t + s_0$ to write a polynomial that represents the height of the ball. Then find the height of the ball after 5 seconds.

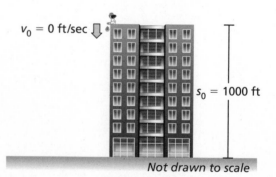

$v_0 = 0$ ft/sec

$s_0 = 1000$ ft

Not drawn to scale

7.2 Adding and Subtracting Polynomials
For use with Activity 7.2

Essential Question How can you add polynomials? How can you subtract polynomials?

---

1 EXAMPLE: Adding Polynomials Using Algebra Tiles

Work with a partner. Six different algebra tiles are shown at the right.

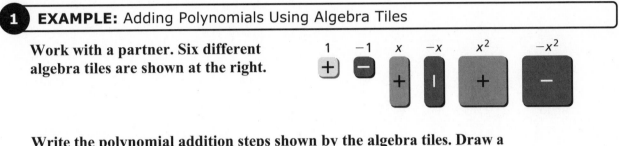

Write the polynomial addition steps shown by the algebra tiles. Draw a sketch for each step.

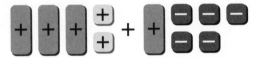

Step 1:   Group like tiles.

Step 2:   Remove zero pairs.

Step 3:   Simplify.

7.2 **Adding and Subtracting Polynomials** (continued)

2 **ACTIVITY:** Adding Polynomials Using Algebra Tiles

Use algebra tiles to find the sum of each polynomial.

a. $\left(x^2 + 2x - 1\right) + \left(2x^2 - 2x + 1\right)$

b. $(4x + 3) + (x - 2)$

c. $\left(x^2 + 2\right) + \left(3x^2 + 2x + 5\right)$

d. $\left(2x^2 - 3x\right) + \left(x^2 - 2x + 4\right)$

e. $\left(x^2 - 3x + 2\right) + \left(x^2 + 4x - 1\right)$

f. $(4x - 3) + (2x + 1) + (-3x + 2)$

g. $\left(-x^2 + 3x\right) + \left(2x^2 - 2x\right)$

h. $\left(x^2 + 2x - 5\right) + \left(-x^2 - 2x + 5\right)$

3 **EXAMPLE:** Subtracting Polynomials Using Algebra Tiles

Write the polynomial subtraction steps shown by the algebra tiles. Draw a sketch for each step.

Step 1:

To subtract, add the opposite.

7.2 **Adding and Subtracting Polynomials** (continued)

Step 2:   Group like tiles.

Step 3:   Remove zero pairs.

Step 4:   Simplify.

4 **ACTIVITY:** Subtracting Polynomials Using Algebra Tiles

Use algebra tiles to find the difference of the polynomials.

a. $\left(x^2 + 2x - 1\right) - \left(2x^2 - 2x + 1\right)$ **b.** $\left(4x + 3\right) - \left(x - 2\right)$

c. $\left(x^2 + 2\right) - \left(3x^2 + 2x + 5\right)$ **d.** $\left(2x^2 - 3x\right) - \left(x^2 - 2x + 4\right)$

What Is Your Answer?

5. **IN YOUR OWN WORDS** How can you add polynomials? Use the results of Activity 2 to summarize a procedure for adding polynomials without using algebra tiles.

6. **IN YOUR OWN WORDS** How can you subtract polynomials? Use the results of Activity 4 to summarize a procedure for subtracting polynomials without using algebra tiles.

Name_____ Date _____

Find the sum.

1. $(2d + 3) + (4d - 6)$

2. $(5m^2 - m + 2) + (3m^2 + 10)$

3. $(2t^2 - 6t - 3) + (-9t^2 + 9t - 5)$

4. $(4c^2 - 8c + 7) + (c^4 + 11c - 3)$

Find the difference.

5. $(3s + 4) - (6s^2 - 2s)$

6. $(9w^2 - 5) - (4w^2 + 9w + 7)$

7. $(y^2 - 6y + 12) - (-3y^2 - 6y + 10)$

8. $(8z^3 + 6z^2 - 9) - (4z^2 - 7z - 4)$

9. You are installing a swimming pool. Write a polynomial that represents the area of the walkway.

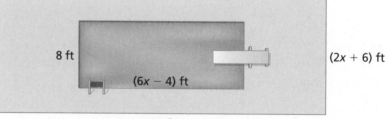

8 ft   (2x + 6) ft

(6x − 4) ft

10x ft

Name_____ Date_____

7.3 Multiplying Polynomials
For use with Activity 7.3

Essential Question How can you multiply two binomials?

1 ACTIVITY: Multiplying Binomials Using Algebra Tiles

Work with a partner. Six different algebra tiles are shown below.

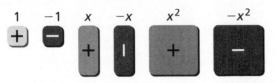

Write the product of the two binomials shown by the algebra tiles.

a. $(x + 3)(x - 2) =$ _____

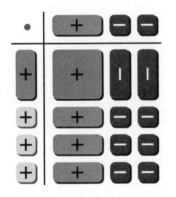

b. $(2x - 1)(2x + 1) =$ _____

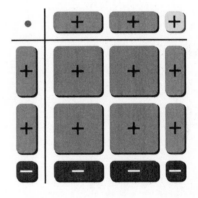

c. $(x + 2)(2x - 1) =$ _____

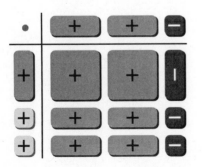

d. $(-x - 2)(x - 3) =$ _____

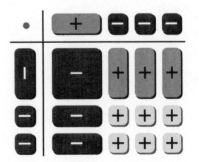

Name _____ Date _____

2 **ACTIVITY:** Multiplying Monomials Using Algebra Tiles

Work with a partner. Write the product. Explain your reasoning.

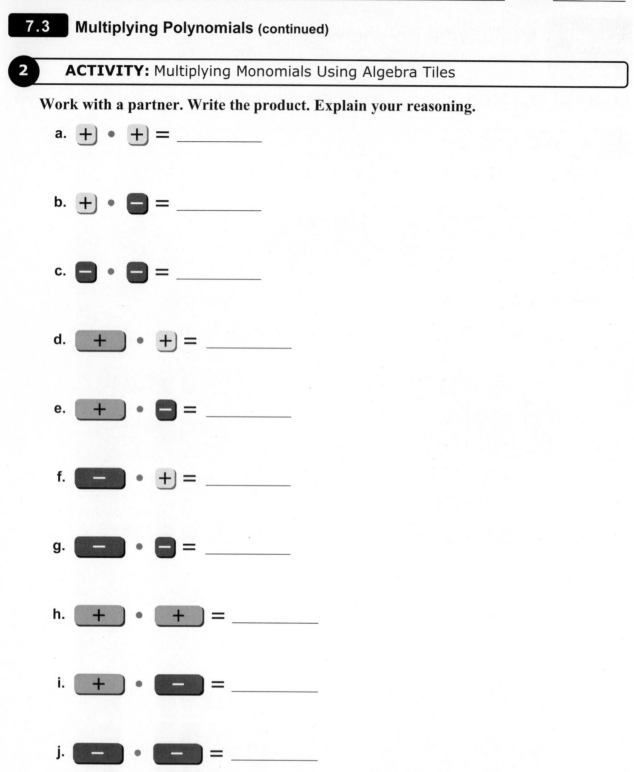

a. $\boxed{+} \cdot \boxed{+} = $ _____

b. $\boxed{+} \cdot \boxed{-} = $ _____

c. $\boxed{-} \cdot \boxed{-} = $ _____

d. $\boxed{+} \cdot \boxed{+} = $ _____

e. $\boxed{+} \cdot \boxed{-} = $ _____

f. $\boxed{-} \cdot \boxed{+} = $ _____

g. $\boxed{-} \cdot \boxed{-} = $ _____

h. $\boxed{+} \cdot \boxed{+} = $ _____

i. $\boxed{+} \cdot \boxed{-} = $ _____

j. $\boxed{-} \cdot \boxed{-} = $ _____

7.3 **Multiplying Polynomials** (continued)

3 **ACTIVITY:** Multiplying Binomials Using Algebra Tiles

Use algebra tiles to find each product.

a. $(2x - 2)(2x + 1)$ **b.** $(4x + 3)(x - 2)$

c. $(-x + 2)(2x + 2)$ **d.** $(2x - 3)(x + 4)$

e. $(3x + 2)(-x - 1)$ **f.** $(2x + 1)(-3x + 2)$

g. $(x - 2x)^2$ **h.** $(2x - 3)^2$

What Is Your Answer?

4. IN YOUR OWN WORDS How can you multiply two binomials? Use the results of Activity 3 to summarize a procedure for multiplying binomials without using algebra tiles.

5. Find two binomials with the given product.

a. $x^2 - 3x + 2$ **b.** $x^2 - 4x + 4$

Name _____ Date _____

Use the Distributive Property to find the product.

1. $(g + 6)(g + 7)$

2. $(3w + 4)(4w - 8)$

Use a table to find the product.

3. $(a - 6)(a - 3)$

4. $(5d - 5)(9d + 2)$

Use the FOIL Method to find the product.

5. $(2x - 8)(x + 9)$

6. $(7 - n)(4 + 3n)$

7. You go to a movie theater $(2t + 3)$ times each year and pay $(t + 7)$ dollars each time, where t is the number of years after 2011.

   a. Write a polynomial that represents your yearly ticket cost.

   b. What is your yearly ticket cost in 2014?

7.4 Special Products of Polynomials
For use with Activity 7.4

Essential Question What are the patterns in the special products $(a + b)(a - b)$, $(a + b)^2$, and $(a - b)^2$?

1 ACTIVITY: Finding a Sum and Difference Pattern

Work with a partner. Six different algebra tiles are shown below.

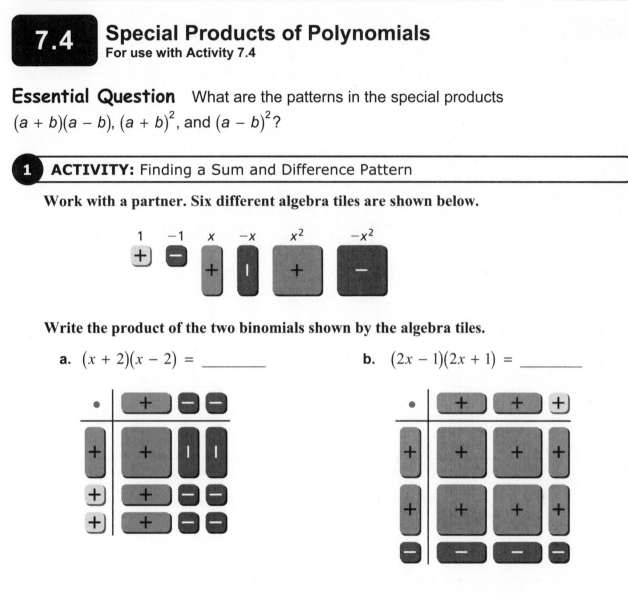

Write the product of the two binomials shown by the algebra tiles.

a. $(x + 2)(x - 2) = $ _____

b. $(2x - 1)(2x + 1) = $ _____

2 ACTIVITY: Describing a Sum and Difference Pattern

Work with a partner.

a. Describe the pattern for the special product: $(a + b)(a - b)$.

7.4 **Special Products of Polynomials** (continued)

b. Use the pattern you described to find each product. Check your answers using algebra tiles.

    i. $(x + 3)(x - 3)$ **ii.** $(x - 4)(x + 4)$ **iii.** $(3x + 1)(3x - 1)$

    iv. $(3y + 4)(3y - 4)$ **v.** $(2x - 5)(2x + 5)$ **vi.** $(z + 1)(z - 1)$

3 **ACTIVITY:** Finding the Square of a Binomial Pattern

Write the product of the two binomials shown by the algebra tiles.

    a. $(x + 2)^2 = $ _____   **b.** $(2x - 1)^2 = $ _____

7.4 **Special Products of Polynomials** (continued)

4 **ACTIVITY:** Describing the Square of a Binomial Pattern

Work with a partner.

a. Describe the pattern for the special product: $(a + b)^2$.

b. Describe the pattern for the special product: $(a - b)^2$.

c. Use the patterns you described to find each product. Check your answers using algebra tiles.

   i. $(x + 3)^2$ **ii.** $(x - 2)^2$ **iii.** $(3x + 1)^2$

   iv. $(3y + 4)^2$ **v.** $(2x - 5)^2$ **vi.** $(z + 1)^2$

What Is Your Answer?

5. IN YOUR OWN WORDS What are the patterns in the special products $(a + b)(a - b)$, $(a + b)^2$, and $(a - b)^2$? Use the results of Activities 2 and 4 to write formulas for these special products.

Name _____ Date _____

Find the product.

1. $(m - 7)(m + 7)$

2. $(p + 10)(p - 10)$

3. $(4s + 8)(4s - 8)$

4. $(9d - 6)(9d + 6)$

5. $(a + 5)^2$

6. $(2k - 4)^2$

7. $(5 - 3r)^2$

8. $(2 + 12f)^2$

9. A garden is extended on two sides.

   a. The area of the garden after the extension is represented by $(x + 11)^2$. Find this product.

   b. Use the polynomial in part (a) to find the area of the garden when $x = 4$. What is the area of the extension?

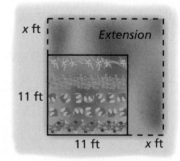

7.5 Solving Polynomial Equations in Factored Form
For use with Activity 7.5

Essential Question   How can you solve a polynomial equation that is written in factored form?

Two polynomial equations are equivalent when they have the same solutions. For instance, the following equations are equivalent because the only solutions of each equation are $x = 1$ and $x = 2$.

Factored Form	Standard Form	Nonstandard Form
$(x - 1)(x - 2) = 0$	$x^2 - 3x + 2 = 0$	$x^2 - 3x = -2$

Check this solution by substituting 1 and 2 for x in each equation.

1   ACTIVITY: Matching Equivalent Forms of an Equation

Work with a partner. Match each factored form of the equation with two other forms of equivalent equations. Notice that an equation is considered to be in factored form only when the product of the factors is equal to 0.

Factored Form		Standard Form		Nonstandard Form	
a.	$(x - 1)(x - 3) = 0$	A.	$x^2 - x - 2 = 0$	1.	$x^2 - 5x = -6$
b.	$(x - 2)(x - 3) = 0$	B.	$x^2 + x - 2 = 0$	2.	$(x - 1)^2 = 4$
c.	$(x + 1)(x - 2) = 0$	C.	$x^2 - 4x + 3 = 0$	3.	$x^2 - x = 2$
d.	$(x - 1)(x + 2) = 0$	D.	$x^2 - 5x + 6 = 0$	4.	$x(x + 1) = 2$
e.	$(x + 1)(x - 3) = 0$	E.	$x^2 - 2x - 3 = 0$	5.	$x^2 - 4x = -3$

2   ACTIVITY: Writing a Conjecture

Work with a partner. Substitute 1, 2, 3, 4, 5, and 6 for x in each equation. Write a conjecture describing what you discovered.

a. $(x - 1)(x - 2) = 0$ b. $(x - 2)(x - 3) = 0$ c. $(x - 3)(x - 4) = 0$

7.5 **Solving Polynomial Equations in Factored Form** (continued)

d. $(x - 4)(x - 5) = 0$ **e.** $(x - 5)(x - 6) = 0$ **f.** $(x - 6)(x - 1) = 0$

3 **ACTIVITY:** Special Properties of 0 and 1

Work with a partner. The numbers 0 and 1 have special properties that are shared by no other numbers. For each of the following, decide whether the property is true for 0, 1, both, or neither. Explain your reasoning.

a. If you add _____ to a number n, you get n.

b. If the product of two numbers is _____, then one or both numbers are 0.

c. The square of _____ is equal to itself.

d. If you multiply a number n by _____, you get n.

e. If you multiply a number n by _____, you get 0.

f. The opposite of _____ is equal to itself.

7.5 Solving Polynomial Equations in Factored Form (continued)

4 **ACTIVITY:** Writing About Solving Equations

Work with a partner. Imagine that you are part of a study group in your algebra class. One of the students in the group makes the following comment.

"I don't see why we spend so much time solving equations that are equal to zero. Why don't we spend more time solving equations that are equal to other numbers?"

Write an answer for this student.

What Is Your Answer?

5. One of the properties in Activity 3 is called the Zero-Product Property. It is one of the most important properties in all of algebra. Which property is it? Explain how it is used in algebra and why it is so important.

6. **IN YOUR OWN WORDS** How can you solve a polynomial equation that is written in factored form?

Name _____ Date _____

Solve the equation.

1. $b(b - 4) = 0$

2. $-8k(k + 3) = 0$

3. $(n - 6)(n + 6) = 0$

4. $(v + 11)(v + 2) = 0$

5. $(h - 9) = 0$

6. $(5 + x)(7 - x) = 0$

7. $(3r - 9)(2r + 2) = 0$

8. $\left(\dfrac{1}{2}p - 8\right)\left(\dfrac{1}{4}p - 1\right) = 0$

9. The arch of a bridge can be modeled by $y = -\dfrac{1}{170}(x - 225)(x + 225)$, where x and y are measured in feet. The x-axis represents the ground. Find the width of the arch of the bridge at ground level.

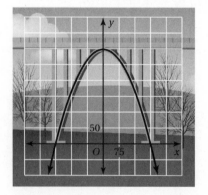

Name_____ Date_____

Essential Question How can you use common factors to write a polynomial in factored form?

1 **ACTIVITY:** Finding Monomial Factors

Work with a partner. Six different algebra tiles are shown below.

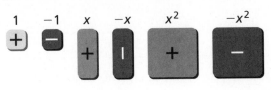

Sample:

Step 1: Look at the rectangular array for $x^2 + 3x$.

Step 2: Use algebra tiles to label the dimensions of the rectangle.

Step 3: Write the polynomial in factored form by finding the dimensions of the rectangle.

Area $= x^2 + 3x =$ _____

Use algebra tiles to write each polynomial in factored form.

a.

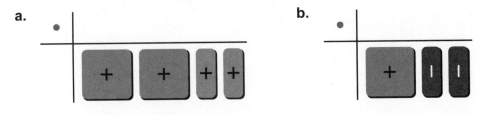

b.

7.6 Factoring Polynomials Using the GCF (continued)

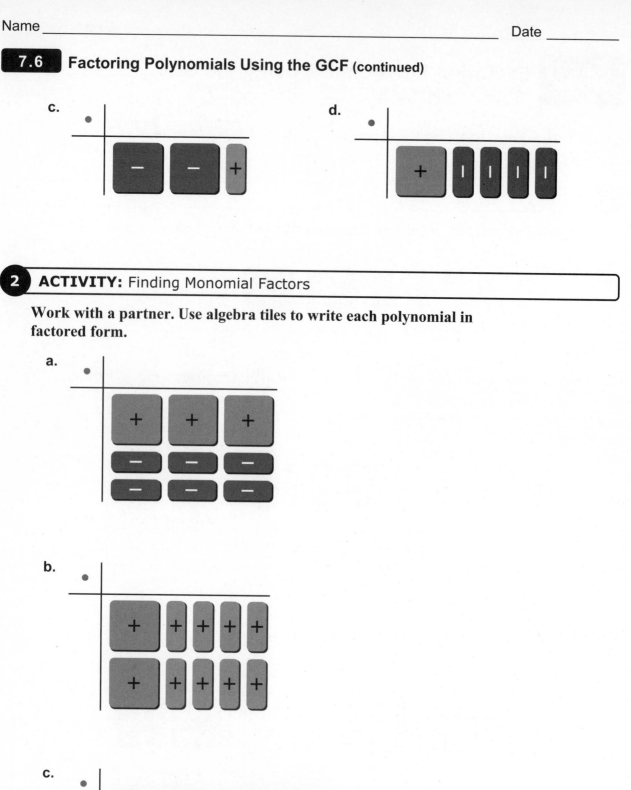

c.

d.

2 ACTIVITY: Finding Monomial Factors

Work with a partner. Use algebra tiles to write each polynomial in factored form.

a.

b.

c.

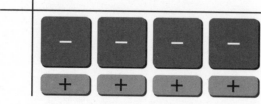

7.6   **Factoring Polynomials Using the GCF** (continued)

3   **ACTIVITY:** Finding Monomial Factors

Work with a partner. Use algebra tiles to model each polynomial as a rectangular array. Then write the polynomial in factored form by finding the dimensions of the rectangle.

    a. $3x^2 - 9x$ **b.** $7x + 14x^2$ **c.** $-2x^2 + 6x$

What Is Your Answer?

   4. Consider the polynomial $4x^2 - 8x$.

      a. What are the terms of the polynomial?

      b. List all the factors that are common to both terms.

      c. Of the common factors, which is the greatest? Explain your reasoning.

   5. **IN YOUR OWN WORDS** How can you use common factors to write a polynomial in factored form?

Name _____ Date _____

Factor the polynomial.

1. $5n^2 - 15n$

2. $6t^3 + 12t^2 - 4t$

Solve the equation.

3. $4a - 16 = 0$

4. $14r^2 + 7r = 0$

5. $-6w^2 = 18w$

6. $14z^2 = 42z$

7. $4x^3 + 36x^2 = 0$

8. $-2p^2 = 9p^3 - 5p^2$

9. The area (in square feet) of the billboard can be represented by $18x^3 + 12x^2$.

    $(3x + 2)$ ft

    a. Write an expression that represents the length of the billboard.

    b. Find the area of the billboard when $x = 2$.

7.7 Factoring $x^2 + bx + c$
For use with Activity 7.7

Essential Question How can you factor the trinomial $x^2 + bx + c$ into the product of two binomials?

1 ACTIVITY: Finding Binomial Factors

Work with a partner. Six different algebra tiles are shown below.

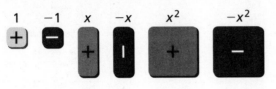

Sample:

Step 1: Arrange the algebra tiles into a rectangular array to model $x^2 + 5x + 6$.

Step 2: Use algebra tiles to label the dimensions of the rectangle.

Step 3: Write the polynomial in factored form by finding the dimensions of the rectangle.

Area $= x^2 + 5x + 6 = $ _____

Use algebra tiles to write each polynomial as the product of two binomials. Check your answer by multiplying.

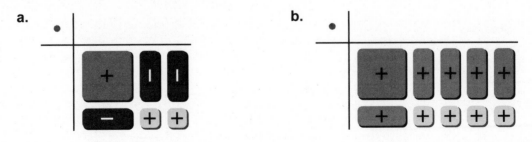

a.

b.

7.7 **Factoring $x^2 + bx + c$** (continued)

2 **ACTIVITY:** Finding Binomial Factors

Work with a partner. Use algebra tiles to write each polynomial as the product of two binomials. Check your answer by multiplying.

a.   b.

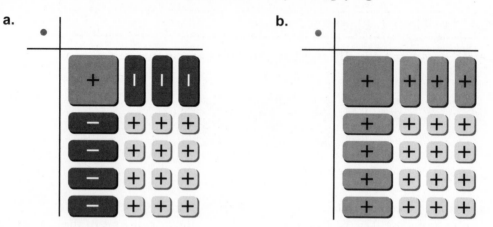

3 **ACTIVITY:** Finding Binomial Factors

Work with a partner. Write each polynomial as the product of two binomials. Check your answer by multiplying.

    a. $x^2 + 6x + 9$ **b.** $x^2 - 6x + 9$ **c.** $x^2 + 6x + 8$

7.7 **Factoring** $x^2 + bx + c$ **(continued)**

d. $x^2 - 6x + 8$ **e.** $x^2 + 6x + 5$ **f.** $x^2 - 6x + 5$

What Is Your Answer?

4. **IN YOUR OWN WORDS** How can you factor the trinomial $x^2 + bx + c$ into the product of two binomials?

    a. Describe a strategy that uses algebra tiles.

    b. Describe a strategy that does not use algebra tiles.

5. Use one of your strategies to factor each trinomial.

    a. $x^2 + 6x - 16$ **b.** $x^2 - 6x - 16$ **c.** $x^2 + 6x - 27$

Name _____ Date _____

7.7 Practice
For use after Lesson 7.7

Factor the polynomial.

1. $w^2 + 8x + 15$

2. $b^2 + 12b + 27$

3. $y^2 - 9y + 18$

4. $h^2 - 15h + 26$

5. $n^2 + n - 42$

6. $k^2 - 5k - 14$

Solve the equation.

7. $t^2 - 14t + 33 = 0$

8. $d^2 - 3d = 54$

9. The area (in square meters) covered by a building can be represented by $x^2 + 7x - 30$.

   a. Write binomials that represent the length and width of the building.

   b. Find the perimeter of the building when $x = 15$ meters.

Name_____ Date _____

 7.8 **Factoring $ax^2 + bx + c$**
For use with Activity 7.8

Essential Question How can you factor the trinomial $ax^2 + bx + c$ into the product of two binomials?

1 ACTIVITY: Finding Binomial Factors

Work with a partner. Six different algebra tiles are shown below.

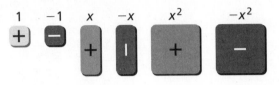

Sample:

Step 1: Arrange the algebra tiles into a rectangular array to model $2x^2 + 5x + 2$.

Step 2: Use algebra tiles to label the dimensions of the rectangles.

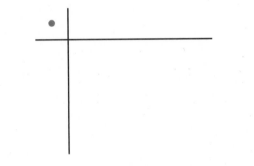

Step 3: Write the polynomial in factored form by finding the dimensions of the rectangle.

Area $= 2x^2 + 5x + 2 = $ _____

Use algebra tiles to write the polynomial as the product of two binomials. Check your answer by multiplying.

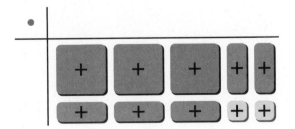

7.8 **Factoring $ax^2 + bx + c$** (continued)

2 **ACTIVITY:** Finding Binomial Factors

Work with a partner. Use algebra tiles to write each polynomial as the product of two polynomials. Check your answer by multiplying.

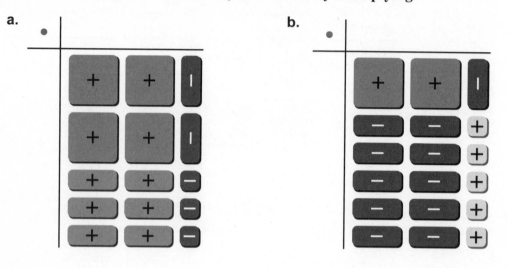

a.

b.

3 **ACTIVITY:** Finding Binomial Factors

Work with a partner. Write each polynomial as the product of two binomials. Check your answer by multiplying.

a. $2x^2 + 5x - 3$ b. $3x^2 + 10x - 8$ c. $4x^2 + 4x - 3$

7.8 **Factoring $ax^2 + bx + c$** (continued)

    d. $2x^2 + 11x + 15$ **e.** $9x^2 - 6x + 1$ **f.** $4x^2 + 11x - 3$

What Is Your Answer?

4. IN YOUR OWN WORDS How can you factor the trinomial $ax^2 + bx + c$ into the product of two binomials?

5. Use your strategy to factor each polynomial.

    a. $4x^2 + 4x + 1$ **b.** $3x^2 + 5x - 2$ **c.** $2x^2 - 13x + 15$

Name _____ Date _____

Factor the polynomial.

1. $5n^2 + 15n + 10$

2. $4h^2 - 20h - 56$

3. $2j^2 + 13j - 45$

4. $9p^2 + 6p - 8$

5. $6b^2 - 7b - 24$

6. $12x^2 - 33x + 18$

Solve the equation.

7. $4y^2 + 8y + 3 = 0$

8. $8d^2 - 4d = 60$

9. The area of the surface of the trampoline is equal to twice its perimeter. Find the dimensions of the trampoline.

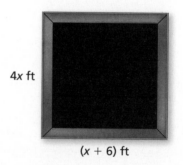

4x ft

(x + 6) ft

7.9 Factoring Special Products
For use with Activity 7.9

Essential Question How can you recognize and factor special products?

---

1 **ACTIVITY:** Factoring Special Products

Work with a partner. Six different algebra tiles are shown below.

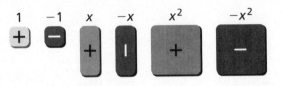

Use algebra tiles to write each polynomial as the product of two binomials. Check your answer by multiplying. State whether the product is a "special product" that you studied in Lesson 7.4.

a.

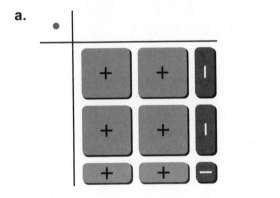

b.

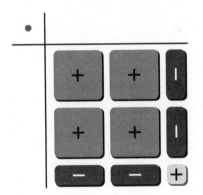

c.

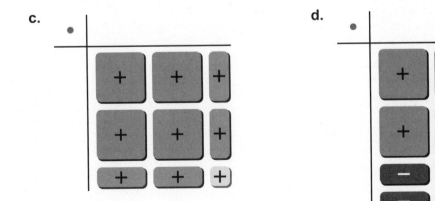

d.

7.9 **Factoring Special Products** (continued)

2 **ACTIVITY:** Factoring Special Products

Work with a partner. Use algebra tiles to complete the rectangular array in three different ways, so that each way represents a different special product. Write each special product in polynomial form and also in factored form.

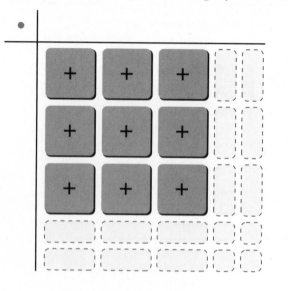

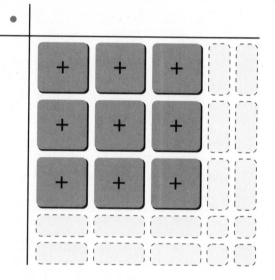

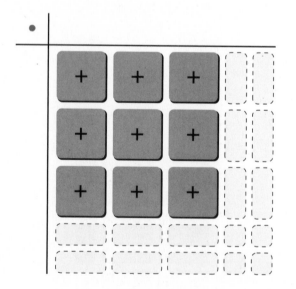

7.9 **Factoring Special Products** (continued)

3 **ACTIVITY:** Finding Binomial Factors

Work with a partner. Write each polynomial as the product of two binomials. Check your answer by multiplying.

    a. $4x^2 - 12x + 9$ **b.** $4x^2 - 9$ **c.** $4x^2 + 12x + 9$

What Is Your Answer?

4. **IN YOUR OWN WORDS** How can you recognize and factor special products? Describe a strategy for recognizing which polynomials can be factored as special products.

5. Use your strategy to factor each polynomial.

    a. $25x^2 + 10x + 1$ **b.** $25x^2 - 10x + 1$ **c.** $25x^2 - 1$

Name_____ Date _____

7.9 **Practice**
For use after Lesson 7.9

Factor the polynomial.

1. $b^2 - 81$

2. $16z^2 - 36$

3. $k^2 - 14k + 49$

4. $f^2 + 22f + 121$

Solve the equation.

5. $x^2 - 100 = 0$

6. $r^2 + 8r + 16 = 0$

7. $25a^2 = 4$

8. $p^2 + 169 = 26p$

9. A pinecone falls from a tree. The pinecone's height y (in feet) after t seconds can be modeled by $64 - 16t^2$. After how many seconds does the pinecone hit the ground?

Name_____ Date _____

Practice
For use after Lesson 7.9b

Factor the polynomial by grouping.

1. $c^3 - 5c^2 + 4c - 20$

2. $3k^3 + k^2 + 9k + 3$

3. $8p^3 - 28p^2 + 2p - 7$

4. $24t^3 - 18t^2 - 8t + 6$

5. $ab + b^2 + 8a + 8b$

6. $3xy + 4y - 18x - 24$

Factor the polynomial completely, if possible.

7. $4d^3 - 32d^2 - 36d$

8. $12n^3 - 48n$

7.9b **Practice** (continued)

9. $h^2 + 4h - 11$

10. $6w^3 + 48w^2 + 96w$

Solve the equation.

11. $q^3 - 6q^2 + 8q = 0$

12. $6r^3 - 54r = 0$

13. $3a^3 + 21a^2 - 90a = 0$

14. $2f^3 - 28f^2 + 98f = 0$

15. A high school soccer field has length x and width y. The field must be resized to comply with new regulations. The new area (in square yards) can be represented by $xy + 8x - 10y - 80$.

    a. Write binomials that represent the length and width of the resized field.

    b. Evaluate the expressions in part (a) when $x = 120$ and $y = 62$.

Name_____ Date_____

Graph the linear equation.

1. $y = x - 2$

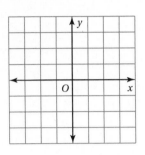

2. $y = -2x + 3$

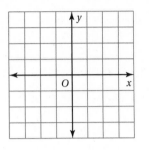

3. $y = -3x - 3$

4. $y = 4x$

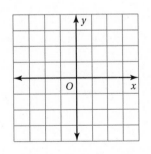

5. $y = -x + 2$

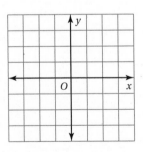

6. $y = 3x + 1$

Name_____ Date _____

Evaluate the expression when $x = 2$.

7. $2x^2 - x + 4$

8. $-x^2 + 3x + 3$

9. $4x^2 - 2x - 5$

10. $-2x^2 + 6x - 7$

Evaluate the expression when $x = -3$.

11. $-x^2 + x + 3$

12. $3x^2 + 5x + 2$

13. $-4x^2 - 3x + 9$

14. $x^2 - 4x - 15$

15. The height (in feet) of a ball thrown off a balcony can be represented by $-16t^2 + 28t + 31$, where t is time in seconds.

    a. Find the height of the ball when $t = 2$.

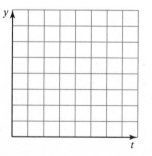

    b. The ball's velocity (in feet per second) can be modeled by $y = -32t + 28$. Graph the linear equation.

Name_____ Date_____

Essential Question What are the characteristics of the graph of the quadratic function $y = ax^2$? How does the value of a affect the graph of $y = ax^2$?

1 ACTIVITY: Graphing a Quadratic Function

Work with a partner.

- Complete the input-output table.
- Plot the points in the table.
- Sketch the graph by connecting the points with a smooth curve.
- What do you notice about the graphs?

a.

x	$y = x^2$
−3	
−2	
−1	
0	
1	
2	
3	

b.

x	$y = -x^2$
−3	
−2	
−1	
0	
1	
2	
3	

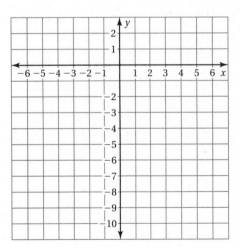

8.1 **Graphing** $y = ax^2$ **(continued)**

2 **ACTIVITY:** Graphing a Quadratic Function

Work with a partner. Graph each function. How does the value of *a* affect the graph of $y = ax^2$**?**

a. $y = 3x^2$

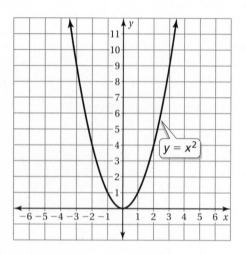

b. $y = -5x^2$

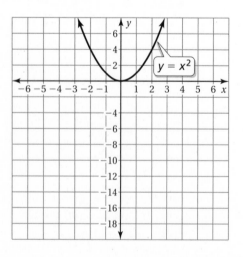

8.1 **Graphing** $y = ax^2$ **(continued)**

c. $y = -0.2x^2$

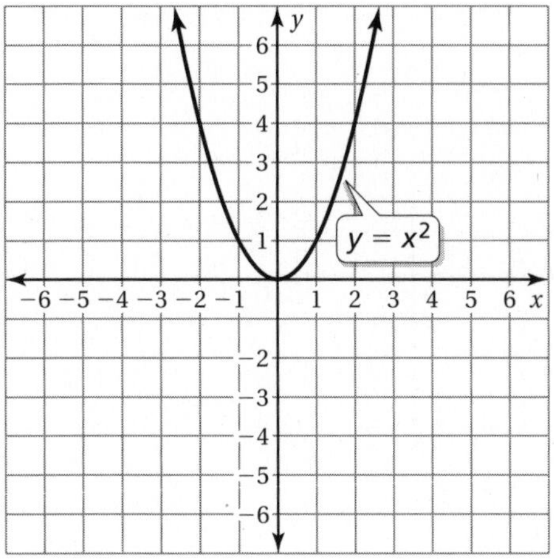

d. $y = \dfrac{1}{10}x^2$

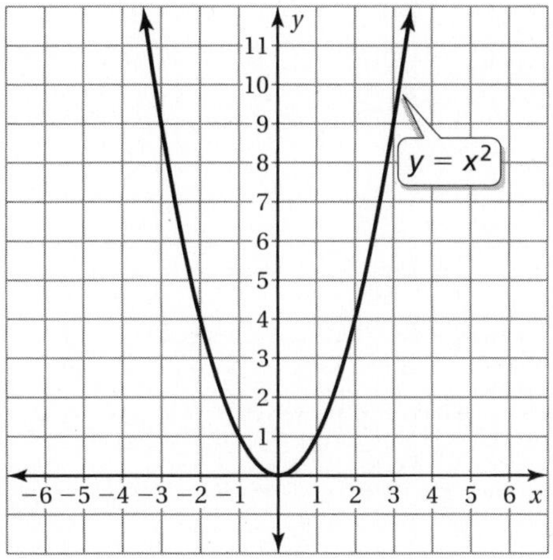

What Is Your Answer?

3. IN YOUR OWN WORDS What are the characteristics of the graph of the quadratic function $y = ax^2$? How does the value of a affect the graph of $y = ax^2$? Consider $a < 0$, $|a| > 1$, and $0 < |a| < 1$ in your answer.

Name_____ Date _____

8.1 **Practice**
For use after Lesson 8.1

Graph the function. Compare the graph to the graph of $y = x^2$.

1. $y = 3x^2$

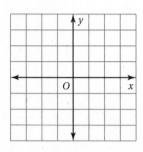

2. $y = \dfrac{2}{3}x^2$

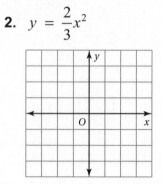

3. $y = \dfrac{6}{5}x^2$

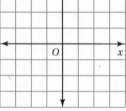
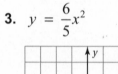
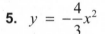

4. $y = -4x^2$

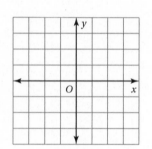

5. $y = -\dfrac{4}{3}x^2$

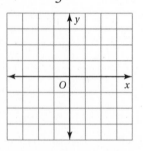

6. $y = -\dfrac{3}{7}x^2$

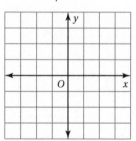

7. The path of a dolphin jumping out of water can be modeled by $y = -0.096x^2$, where x and y are measured in feet. Find the distance and maximum height of the jump.

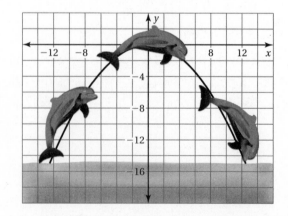

216 **Big Ideas Math Algebra**
Record and Practice Journal

Copyright © Big Ideas Learning, LLC
All rights reserved.

8.2 Focus of a Parabola
For use with Activity 8.2

Essential Question Why do satellite dishes and spotlight reflectors have parabolic shapes?

---

1 ACTIVITY: A Property of Satellite Dishes

Work with a partner. Rays are coming straight down. When they hit the parabola, they reflect off at the same angle at which they entered.

- Draw the outgoing part of each ray so that it intersects the *y*-axis.

- What do you notice about where the reflected rays intersect the *y*-axis?

- Where is the receiver for the satellite dish? Explain.

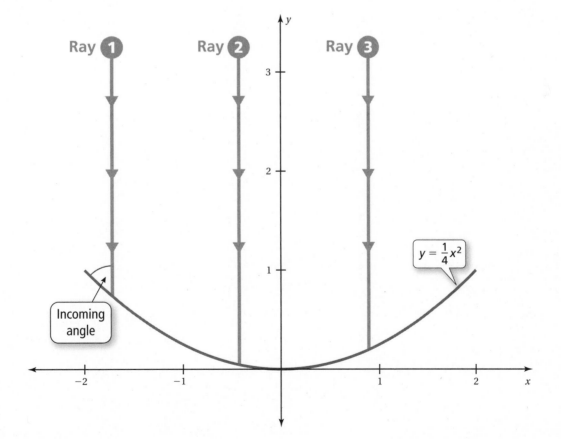

$y = \frac{1}{4}x^2$

Incoming angle

8.2 **Focus of a Parabola** (continued)

2 **ACTIVITY:** A Property of Spotlights

Work with a partner. Beams of light are coming from the bulb in a spotlight. When the beams hit the parabola, they reflect off at the same angle at which they entered.

- Draw the outgoing part of each beam. What do they have in common? Explain.

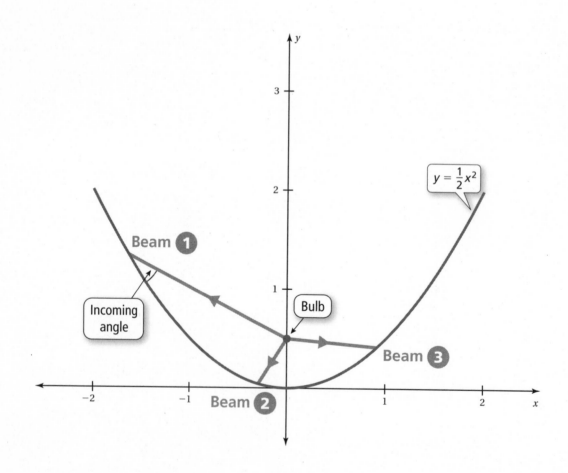

8.2 Focus of a Parabola (continued)

What Is Your Answer?

3. **IN YOUR OWN WORDS** Why do satellite dishes and spotlight reflectors have parabolic shapes?

4. Design and draw a parabolic satellite dish. Label the dimensions of the dish. Label the receiver.

Name _____ Date _____

Graph the function. Identify the focus.

1. $y = -x^2$

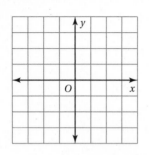

2. $y = \dfrac{3}{2}x^2$

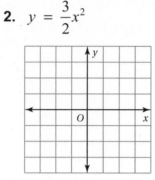

3. $y = \dfrac{1}{8}x^2$

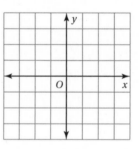

4. $y = -5x^2$

Write an equation of the parabola with a vertex at the origin and the given focus.

5. $(0, 3)$

6. $(0, -0.1)$

7. A metal molding company builds a solar furnace to power its factory. The furnace consists of hundreds of mirrors forming a parabolic dish that reflects the energy of the Sun to a focal point. Write an equation for the cross section of the dish when the receiver is 12 feet from the vertex of the parabola.

Name_____ Date _____

Essential Question How does the value of c affect the graph of
$y = ax^2 + c$?

1 **ACTIVITY:** Graphing $y = ax^2 + c$

Work with a partner. Sketch the graphs of both functions in the same
coordinate plane. How does the value of c affect the graph of $y = ax^2 + c$?

a. $y = x^2$ and $y = x^2 + 2$

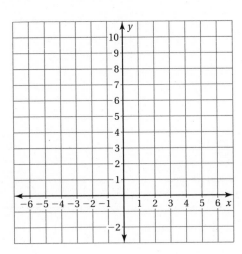

b. $y = 2x^2$ and $y = 2x^2 - 2$

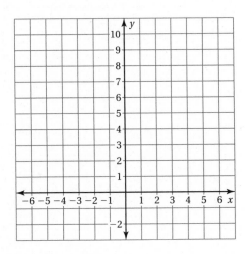

8.3 Graphing $y = ax^2 + c$ (continued)

c. $y = -x^2 + 4$ and $y = -x^2 + 9$

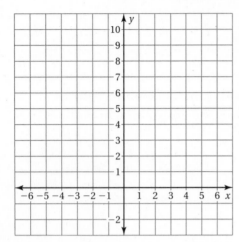

d. $y = \frac{1}{2}x^2$ and $y = \frac{1}{2}x^2 - 8$

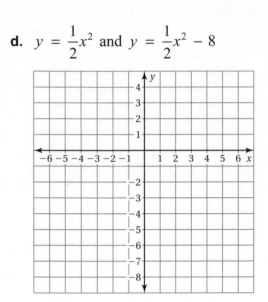

2 ACTIVITY: Finding *x*-Intercepts of Graphs

Work with a partner. Graph each function. Find the *x*-intercepts of the graph. Explain how you found the *x*-intercepts.

a. $y = x^2 - 4$

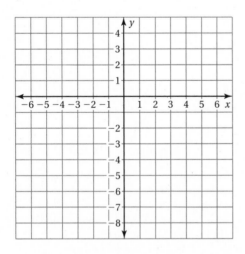

b. $y = 2x^2 - 8$

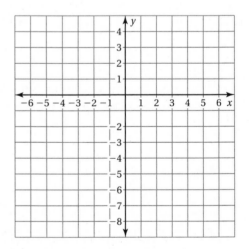

8.3 Graphing $y = ax^2 + c$ (continued)

c. $y = -x^2 + 1$

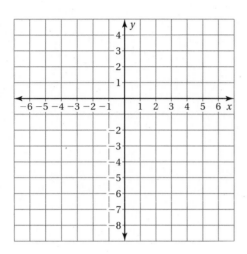

d. $y = \dfrac{1}{3}x^2 - 3$

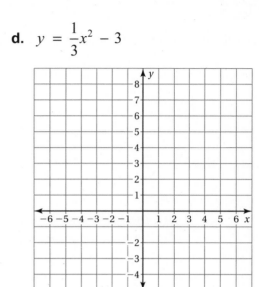

What Is Your Answer?

3. IN YOUR OWN WORDS How does the value of c affect the graph of $y = ax^2 + c$? Use a graphing calculator to verify your conclusions.

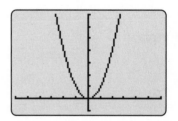

Name _____ Date _____

Graph the function. Compare the graph to the graph of $y = x^2$.

1. $y = x^2 - 6$

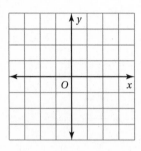

2. $y = x^2 + 3$

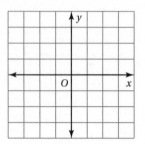

3. $y = -x^2 + 8$

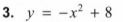

4. $y = \dfrac{1}{3}x^2 - 4$

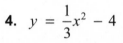

Describe how to translate the graph of $y = x^2 - 3$ to the graph of the given function.

5. $y = x^2 + 5$

6. $y = x^2 - 7$

7. A rock is dropped from a height of 25 feet. The function $h = -16x^2 + 25$ gives the height h of the rock after x seconds. When does it hit the ground?

8.4 Graphing $y = ax^2 + bx + c$

For use with Activity 8.4

Essential Question How can you find the vertex of the graph of
$y = ax^2 + bx + c$?

1 ACTIVITY: Comparing Two Graphs

Work with a partner.

- Sketch the graphs of $y = 2x^2 - 8x$ and $y = 2x^2 - 8x + 6$.

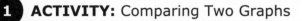

$$y = 2x^2 - 8x \qquad\qquad\qquad y = 2x^2 - 8x + 6$$

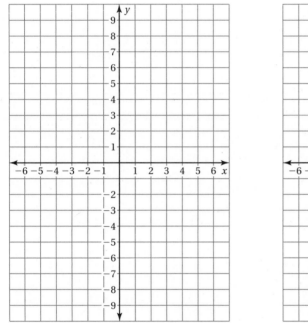 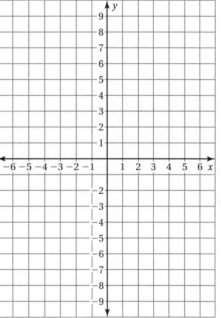

- What do you notice about the x-value of the vertex of each graph?

8.4 **Graphing** $y = ax^2 + bx + c$ (continued)

2 **ACTIVITY:** Comparing x-Intercepts with the Vertex

Work with a partner.

- Use the graph in Activity 1 to find the x-intercepts of the graph of $y = 2x^2 - 8x$. Verify your answer by solving $0 = 2x^2 - 8x$.

- Compare the location of the vertex to the location of the x-intercepts.

3 **ACTIVITY:** Finding Intercepts

Work with a partner.

- Solve $0 = ax^2 + bx$ by factoring.

- What are the x-intercepts of the graph of $y = ax^2 + bx$?

- Complete the table to verify your answer.

x	$y = ax^2 + bx$
0	
$-\dfrac{b}{a}$	

8.4 Graphing $y = ax^2 + bx + c$ (continued)

---

4 ACTIVITY: Deductive Reasoning

Work with a partner. Complete the following logical argument.

> The x-intercepts of the graph of $y = ax^2 + bx$ are 0 and $-\dfrac{b}{a}$.

> The vertex of the graph of $y = ax^2 + bx$ occurs when $x =$ _____.

> The vertices of the graphs of $y = ax^2 + bx$ and $y = ax^2 + bx + c$ have the same x-value.

> The vertex of $y = ax^2 + bx + c$ occurs when $x =$ _____.

What Is Your Answer?

5. **IN YOUR OWN WORDS** How can you find the vertex of the graph of $y = ax^2 + bx + c$?

6. Without graphing, find the vertex of the graph of $y = x^2 - 4x + 3$. Check your result by graphing.

Name _____ Date _____

Find (a) the axis of symmetry and (b) the vertex of the graph of the function.

1. $y = 6x^2 - 12x + 1$

2. $y = -\dfrac{4}{3}x^2 - 8x$

Graph the function. Describe the domain and range.

3. $y = -2x^2 + 16x - 18$

4. $y = \dfrac{1}{3}x^2 + 4x + 5$

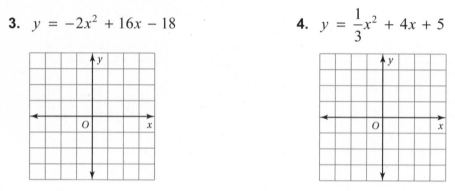

Tell whether the function has a minimum or a maximum value. Then find the value.

5. $y = \dfrac{1}{5}x^2 + 6x - 1$

6. $y = -5x^2 - 20x + 9$

7. The entrance of a tunnel can be modeled by $y = -\dfrac{1}{18}x^2 + 2x - 2$, where x and y are measured in feet. What is the height of the tunnel?

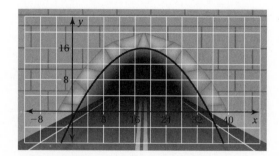

8.4b Practice

For use after Lesson 8.4b

Graph the function. Compare the graph to the graph of $y = x^2$ **. Use a graphing calculator to check your answer.**

1. $y = (x - 2)^2$

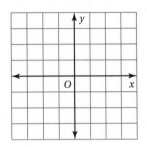

2. $y = (x + 4)^2$

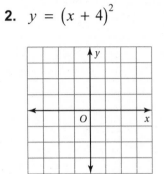

3. $y = (x + 7)^2$

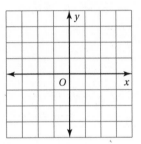

4. $y = (x - 3.5)^2$

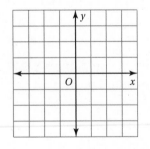

5. $y = (x + 6)^2 + 3$

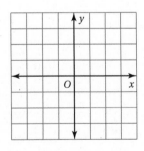

6. $y = (x - 5)^2 + 1$

8.4b **Practice** (continued)

7. $y = (x + 2)^2 - 8$

8. $y = 2(x - 1)^2 - 4$

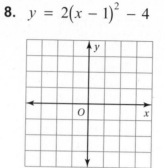

9. $y = -3(x - 4)^2 + 2$

10. $y = \frac{1}{3}(x + 5)^2 - 6$

Describe how the graph of g(x) compares to the graph of f(x).

11. $g(x) = f(x - 9)$

12. $g(x) = 4f(x) + 5$

13. The profit (in millions) of company A can be modeled by
$A = -(t - 8)^2 + 10$ and the profit (in millions) of company B
can be modeled by $B = -(t - 13)^2 + 9$, where t is time in years.

a. How much greater is company A's maximum profit than
company B's maximum profit?

b. How many years after company A reached its maximum profit
did company B reach its maximum profit?

8.5 Comparing Linear, Exponential, and Quadratic Functions For use with Activity 8.5

Essential Question How can you compare the growth rates of linear, exponential, and quadratic functions?

1 ACTIVITY: Comparing Speeds

Work with a partner. Three cars start traveling at the same time. The distance traveled in t minutes is y miles.

- Complete each table and sketch all three graphs in the same coordinate plane.

t	$y = t$
0	
0.2	
0.4	
0.6	
0.8	
1.0	

t	$y = 2^t - 1$
0	
0.2	
0.4	
0.6	
0.8	
1.0	

t	$y = t^2$
0	
0.2	
0.4	
0.6	
0.8	
1.0	

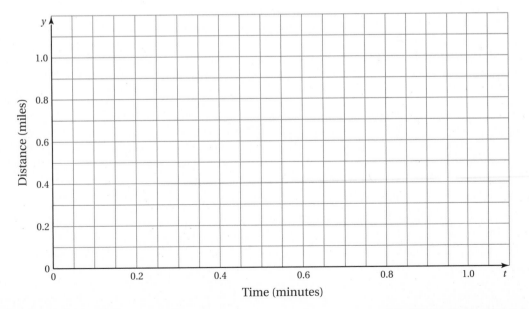

8.5 Comparing Linear, Exponential, and Quadratic Functions (continued)

- Compare the speeds of the three cars. Which car has a constant speed? Which car is accelerating the most? Explain your reasoning.

2 ACTIVITY: Comparing Speeds

Work with a partner. Analyze the speeds of the three cars over the given time periods. The distance traveled t minutes is y miles. Which car eventually overtakes the others?

a.

t	$y = t$
1	
2	
3	
4	

t	$y = 2^t - 1$
1	
2	
3	
4	

t	$y = t^2$
1	
2	
3	
4	

8.5 **Comparing Linear, Exponential, and Quadratic Functions** (continued)

b.

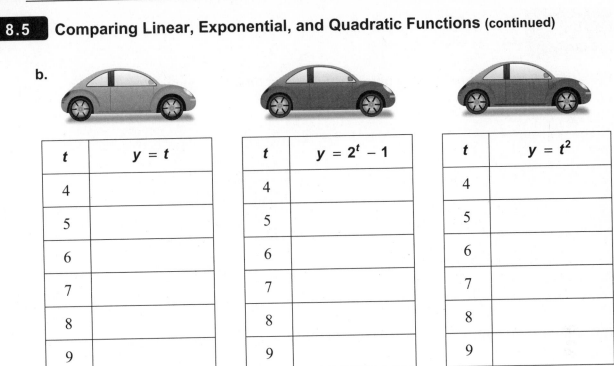

t	$y = t$
4	
5	
6	
7	
8	
9	

t	$y = 2^t - 1$
4	
5	
6	
7	
8	
9	

t	$y = t^2$
4	
5	
6	
7	
8	
9	

What Is Your Answer?

3. **IN YOUR OWN WORDS** How can you compare the growth rates of linear, exponential, and quadratic functions? Which type of growth eventually leaves the other two in the dust? Explain your reasoning.

Name_____ Date _____

Plot the points. Tell whether the points represent a *linear*, an *exponential*, or a *quadratic* function.

1. $\left(-3, \dfrac{1}{9}\right), \left(-2, \dfrac{1}{3}\right), (-1, 1), (0, 3), (1, 9)$ **2.** $(0, -1), (1, 2), (2, 3), (3, 2), (4, -1)$

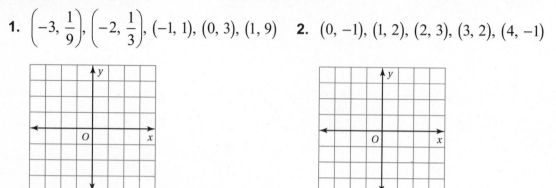

Tell whether the table of values represents a *linear*, an *exponential*, or a *quadratic* function.

3.

x	−5	−4	−3	−2	−1
y	0	−1	0	3	8

4.

x	−2	−1	0	1	2
y	−5	−3.5	−2	−0.5	1

Tell whether the data values represent a *linear*, an *exponential*, or a *quadratic* function. Then write an equation for the function using the form $y = mx + b$, $y = ab^x$, or $y = ax^2$.

5. $(-3, 12), (-2, 7), (-1, 2), (0, -3), (1, -8)$

6. $(-1, 0.5), (0, 2), (1, 8), (2, 32), (3, 128)$

7. The table shows the shipping cost c (in dollars) by weight w (in pounds) for items from an online store.

Weight, w	1	2	3	4
Cost, c	8.5	11	13.5	16

   a. Does a *linear*, an *exponential*, or a *quadratic* function represent this situation?

   b. How much does it cost to ship a 6-pound item?

8.5b Comparing Graphs of Functions
For use with Activity 8.5b

You have already learned that the average rate of change (or slope) between any two points on a line is the change in y divided by the change in x. You can find the average rate of change between two points of a nonlinear function using the same method.

1 ACTIVITY: Rates of Change of a Quadratic Function

In Example 4 on page 428 of your textbook, the function $f(t) = -16t^2 + 80t + 5$ gives the height (in feet) of a water balloon t seconds after it is launched.

a. Complete the table for $f(t)$.

t	0	0.5	1	1.5	2	2.5	3	3.5	4	4.5	5
$f(t)$											

b. Graph the ordered pairs from part (a). Then draw a smooth curve through the points.

c. For what values is the function increasing?

For what values is the function decreasing?

d. Complete the tables to find the average rate of change for each interval.

Time Interval	0 to 0.5 sec	0.5 to 1 sec	1 to 1.5 sec	1.5 to 2 sec	2 to 2.5 sec
Average Rate of Change (ft/sec)					

Time Interval	2.5 to 3 sec	3 to 3.5 sec	3.5 to 4 sec	4 to 4.5 sec	4.5 to 5 sec
Average Rate of Change (ft/sec)					

8.5b **Comparing Graphs of Functions** (continued)

Practice

1. Compared to the average rate of change of a linear function, what do you notice about the average rate of change in part (d) of Activity 1?

2. Is the average rate of change increasing or decreasing from 0 to 2.5 seconds? How can you use the graph to justify your answer?

3. What do you notice about the average rate of change when the function is increasing and when the function is decreasing?

4. In Example 4 on page 419 of your textbook, the function $f(t) = -16t^2 + 64$ gives the height of an egg t seconds after it is dropped.

   a. Complete the table for $f(t)$.

t	0	0.5	1	1.5	2
$f(t)$					

   b. Graph the ordered pairs and draw a smooth curve through the points.

   c. Describe where the function is increasing and decreasing.

   d. Find the average rate of change for each interval in the table. What do you notice?

Name_____ Date _____

2 **ACTIVITY:** Rates of Change of Different Functions

The graphs show the number y of videos on three video-sharing websites x hours after the websites are launched.

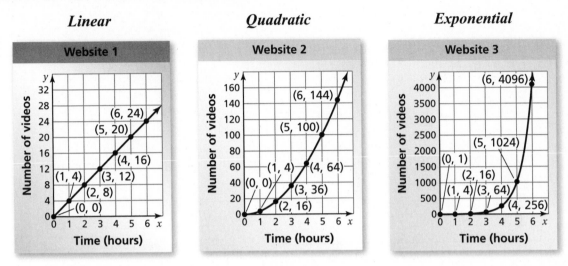

Linear *Quadratic* *Exponential*

a. Do the three websites ever have the same number of videos?

b. Complete the table for each function.

Linear

Time Interval	0 to 1 h	1 to 2 h	2 to 3 h	3 to 4 h	4 to 5 h	5 to 6 h
Average Rate of Change (videos/hour)						

Quadratic

Time Interval	0 to 1 h	1 to 2 h	2 to 3 h	3 to 4 h	4 to 5 h	5 to 6 h
Average Rate of Change (videos/hour)						

Exponential

Time Interval	0 to 1 h	1 to 2 h	2 to 3 h	3 to 4 h	4 to 5 h	5 to 6 h
Average Rate of Change (videos/hour)						

8.5b **Comparing Graphs of Functions** (continued)

    c. What do you notice about the average rate of change of the linear function?

    d. What do you notice about the average rate of change of the quadratic function?

    e. What do you notice about the average rate of change of the exponential function?

    f. Which average rate of change increases more quickly, the quadratic function or the exponential function?

Practice

    5. REASONING How does a quantity that is increasing exponentially compare to a quantity that is increasing linearly or quadratically?

    6. REASONING Explain why the average rate of change of a linear function is constant and the average rate of change of a quadratic or exponential function is not constant.

Name_____ Date_____

Find the square root(s).

1. $-\sqrt{36}$

2. $\sqrt{121}$

3. $\sqrt{\dfrac{4}{49}}$

4. $\pm\sqrt{2.25}$

Find the side length of the square.

5.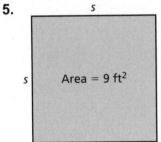

6.

Area = 9 ft² (square, side s)

Area = 0.25 m² (square, side s)

7. Simplify $\sqrt{20}$.

8. Simplify $\sqrt{63}$.

9. Simplify $\sqrt{108}$.

10. Simplify $\sqrt{288}$.

Chapter 9 | Fair Game Review (continued)

Find the side length of the square.

11.

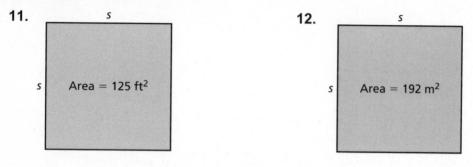

s

s   Area = 125 ft²

12.

s

s   Area = 192 m²

Factor the trinomial.

13. $y^2 - 6y + 9$

14. $b^2 + 18b + 81$

15. $n^2 + 28n + 196$

16. $h^2 - 16h + 64$

17. The surface area (in square inches) of a square card table can be represented by $x^2 - 50x + 625$.

   a. Write an expression that represents the side length of the table.

   b. Write an expression for the perimeter of the table.

Name_____ Date _____

Essential Question How can you use a graph to solve a quadratic equation in one variable?

Earlier in the book, you learned that the x-intercept of the graph of

$$y = ax + b \qquad \text{2 variables}$$

is the same as the solution of

$$ax + b = 0. \qquad \text{1 variable}$$

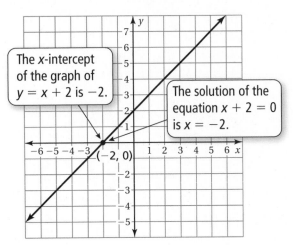

The x-intercept of the graph of $y = x + 2$ is -2.

The solution of the equation $x + 2 = 0$ is $x = -2$.

$(-2, 0)$

---

1 ACTIVITY: Solving a Quadratic Equation by Graphing

Work with a partner.

a. Sketch the graph of $y = x^2 - 2x$.

b. What is the definition of an x-intercept of a graph? How many x-intercepts does this graph have? What are they?

c. What is the definition of a solution of an equation in x? How many solutions does the equation $x^2 - 2x = 0$ have? What are they?

d. Explain how you can verify that the x-values found in part (c) are solutions of $x^2 - 2x = 0$.

9.1 **Solving Quadratic Equations by Graphing** (continued)

2 **ACTIVITY:** Solving Quadratic Equations by Graphing

Work with a partner. Solve each equation by graphing.

a. $x^2 - 4 = 0$

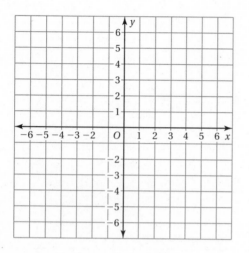

b. $x^2 + 3x = 0$

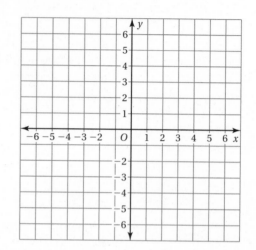

c. $-x^2 + 2x = 0$

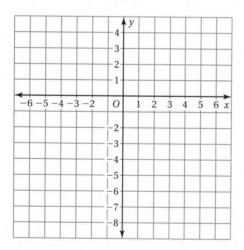

d. $x^2 - 2x + 1 = 0$

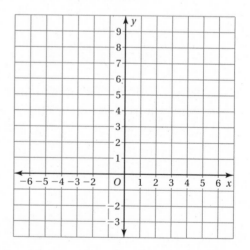

Name_____ Date_____

What Is Your Answer?

3. **IN YOUR OWN WORDS** How can you use a graph to solve a quadratic equation in one variable?

4. After you find a solution graphically, how can you check your result algebraically? Use your solutions in Activity 2 as examples.

9.1 Practice

For use after Lesson 9.1

Solve the equation by graphing. Check your solution(s).

1. $2x^2 + 8x = 0$

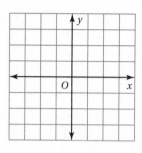

2. $x^2 + 2x + 1 = 0$

3. $x^2 - 4x + 5 = 0$

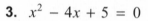
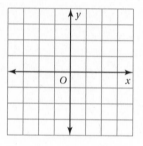

4. $x^2 - 5x + 6 = 0$

5. $-x^2 - 10x - 25 = 0$

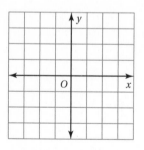

6. $-x^2 - 2x + 3 = 0$

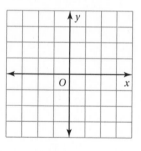

7. The height h (in feet) of a javelin thrown at a track and field competition can be modeled by $h = -16t^2 + 50t + 6$, where t is time in seconds. After how many seconds is the javelin 30 feet above the ground?

9.2 Solving Quadratic Equations Using Square Roots
For use with Activity 9.2

Essential Question How can you determine the number of solutions of a quadratic equation of the form $ax^2 + c = 0$?

---

1 ACTIVITY: The Number of Solutions of $ax^2 + c = 0$

Work with a partner. Solve each equation by graphing. Explain how the number of solutions of

$$ax^2 + c = 0 \qquad \text{Quadratic equation}$$

relates to the graph of

$$y = ax^2 + c. \qquad \text{Quadratic function}$$

a. $x^2 - 4 = 0$

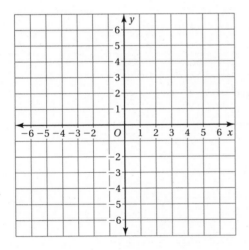

b. $2x^2 + 5 = 0$

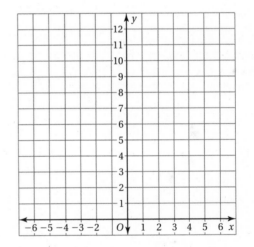

9.2 **Solving Quadratic Equations Using Square Roots** (continued)

c. $x^2 = 0$

d. $x^2 - 5 = 0$

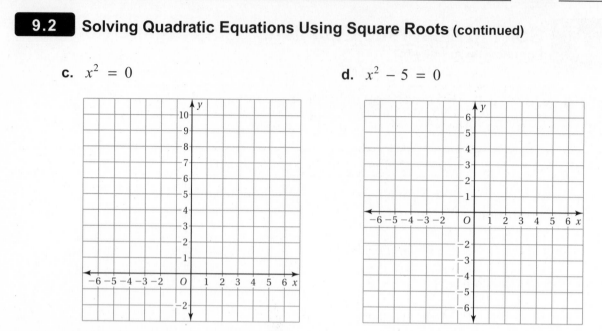

2 ACTIVITY: Estimating Solutions

Work with a partner. Complete each table. Use the completed tables to estimate the solutions of $x^2 - 5 = 0$. Explain your reasoning.

a.

x	$x^2 - 5$
2.21	
2.22	
2.23	
2.24	
2.25	
2.26	

b.

x	$x^2 - 5$
−2.21	
−2.22	
−2.23	
−2.24	
−2.25	
−2.26	

Name_____ Date_____

9.2 Solving Quadratic Equations Using Square Roots (continued)

3 ACTIVITY: Using Technology to Estimate Solutions

Work with a partner. Two equations are equivalent when they have the same solutions.

a. Are the equations $x^2 - 5 = 0$ and $x^2 = 5$ equivalent? Explain your reasoning.

b. Use the square root key on a calculator to estimate the solutions of $x^2 - 5 = 0$. Describe the accuracy of your estimates.

c. Write the *exact* solutions of $x^2 - 5 = 0$.

What Is Your Answer?

4. **IN YOUR OWN WORDS** How can you determine the number of solutions of a quadratic equation of the form $ax^2 + c = 0$?

5. Write the exact solutions of each equation. Then use a calculator to estimate the solutions.

a. $x^2 - 2 = 0$ b. $3x^2 - 15 = 0$ c. $x^2 = 8$

9.2 Practice
For use after Lesson 9.2

Solve the equation using square roots.

1. $x^2 - 64 = 0$

2. $x^2 + 18 = 0$

3. $x^2 - 11 = -11$

4. $3x^2 - 75 = 0$

5. $2x^2 + 12 = 9$

6. $-6x^2 + 4 = 4$

Solve the equation using square roots. Use a graphing calculator to check your solution(s).

7. $(x - 4)^2 = 49$

8. $16(x + 3)^2 = 36$

9. The volume of a shed is 972 cubic feet. Find the width x of the shed.

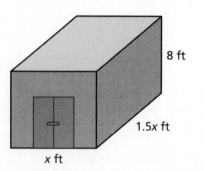

8 ft

1.5x ft

x ft

9.3 Solving Quadratic Equations by Completing the Square For use with Activity 9.3

Essential Question How can you use "completing the square" to solve a quadratic equation?

---

1 **EXAMPLE:** Solving by Completing the Square

Work with a partner. Five different algebra tiles are shown at the right. Solve $x^2 + 4x = -2$ by completing the square.

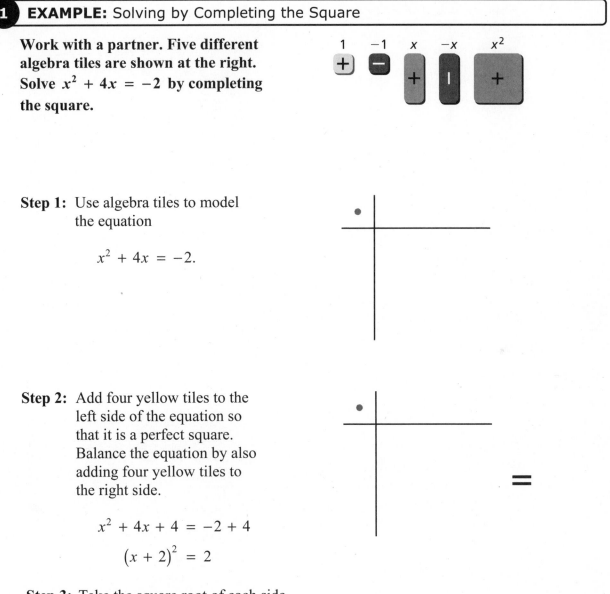

Step 1: Use algebra tiles to model the equation

$$x^2 + 4x = -2.$$

Step 2: Add four yellow tiles to the left side of the equation so that it is a perfect square. Balance the equation by also adding four yellow tiles to the right side.

$$x^2 + 4x + 4 = -2 + 4$$

$$(x + 2)^2 = 2$$

Step 3: Take the square root of each side of the equation and simplify.

9.3 **Solving Quadratic Equations by Completing the Square** (continued)

2 **ACTIVITY:** Solving by Completing the Square

Work with a partner.

- Write the equation modeled by the algebra tiles.

- Use algebra tiles to complete the square.

- Write the solutions of the equation.

- Check each solution.

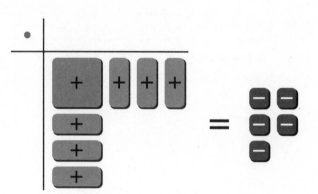

3 **ACTIVITY:** Writing a Rule

Work with a partner.

- What does this group of tiles represent?

- How is the coefficient of x for this group of tiles related to the coefficient of x in the equation from Activity 2?

- How is it related to the number of tiles you add to each side when completing the square?

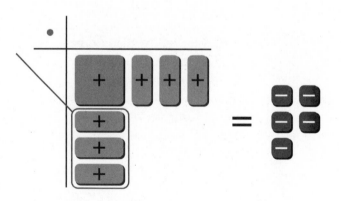

9.3 **Solving Quadratic Equations by Completing the Square** (continued)

- **WRITE A RULE** Fill in the blanks.

  To complete the square, take _____ of the

  coefficient of the x-term and _____ it.

  _____ this number to each side of the equation.

What Is Your Answer?

4. **IN YOUR OWN WORDS** How can you use "completing the square" to solve a quadratic equation?

5. Solve each quadratic equation by completing the square.

   a. $x^2 - 2x = 1$ **b.** $x^2 - 4x = -1$ **c.** $x^2 + 4x = -3$

9.3 Practice
For use after Lesson 9.3

Complete the square for the expression. Then factor the trinomial.

1. $x^2 + 8x$

2. $x^2 - 6x$

3. $x^2 - 20x$

4. $x^2 + 7x$

Solve the equation by completing the square.

5. $x^2 - 2x = 8$

6. $x^2 + 12x + 9 = -5$

7. $x^2 + 5x + 13 = 1$

8. $2x^2 - 6x + 3 = 11$

9. Your backyard is rectangular and has an area of 760 square meters. The length of the yard is 18 meters more than the width. Find the length and width of the backyard.

9.4 Solving Quadratic Equations Using the Quadratic Formula For use with Activity 9.4

Essential Question How can you use the disciminant to determine the number of solutions of a quadratic equation?

1 **ACTIVITY:** Deriving the Quadratic Formula

Work with a partner. The following steps show one method of solving
$ax^2 + bx + c = 0$**. Explain what was done in each step.**

$$ax^2 + bx + c = 0$$ **1.** Write the equation.

$$4a^2x^2 + 4abx + 4ac = 0$$ **2.** _____

$$4a^2x^2 + 4abx + 4ac + b^2 = b^2$$ **3.** _____

$$4a^2x^2 + 4abx + b^2 = b^2 - 4ac$$ **4.** _____

$$(2ax + b)^2 = b^2 - 4ac$$ **5.** _____

$$2ax + b = \pm\sqrt{b^2 - 4ac}$$ **6.** _____

$$2ax = -b \pm \sqrt{b^2 - 4ac}$$ **7.** _____

Quadratic Formula: $x = \dfrac{-b \pm \sqrt{b^2 - 4ac}}{2a}$ **8.** _____

9.4 **Solving Quadratic Equations Using the Quadratic Formula** (continued)

---

2 ACTIVITY: Deriving the Quadratic Formula by Completing the Square

- Solve $ax^2 + bx + c = 0$ by completing the square. (*Hint:* Subtract c from each side, divide each side by a, and then proceed by completing the square.)

- Compare this method with the method in Activity 1. Explain why you think $4a$ and b^2 were chosen in Steps 2 and 3 of Activity 1.

---

3 ACTIVITY: Writing a Rule

Work with a partner. In the quadratic formula in Activity 1, the expression under the radical sign, $b^2 - 4ac$, is called the discriminant. For each graph, decide whether the corresponding discriminant is equal to 0, is greater than 0, or is less than 0. Explain your reasoning.

a. 1 rational solution

b. 2 rational solutions

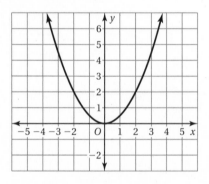

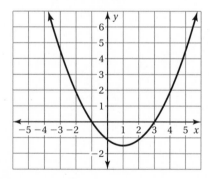

9.4 Solving Quadratic Equations Using the Quadratic Formula (continued)

c. 2 irrational solutions

d. no real solutions

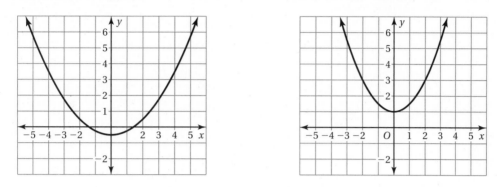

What Is Your Answer?

4. **IN YOUR OWN WORDS** How can you use the discriminant to determine the number of solutions of a quadratic equation?

5. Use the quadratic formula to solve each quadratic equation.

  a. $x^2 + 2x - 3 = 0$ **b.** $x^2 - 4x + 4 = 0$ **c.** $x^2 + 4x + 5 = 0$

6. Use the Internet to research *imaginary numbers*. How are they related to quadratic equations?

9.4 | **Practice**
For use after Lesson 9.4

Solve the equation using the quadratic formula. Round to the nearest tenth, if necessary.

1. $x^2 + 3x - 18 = 0$

2. $x^2 + 8x + 16 = 0$

3. $x^2 - 5x + 7 = 0$

4. $3x^2 - 10x - 8 = 0$

5. $4x^2 - 12x = -9$

6. $4x - 3 = 2x^2$

7. $x^2 + 2x - 6 = 0$

8. $-2x^2 - 11x = -5$

9. The deer population in a forest from 2000 to 2010 can be modeled by $y = -0.1x^2 + 1.1x + 3$, where y is hundreds of deer and x is the number of years since 2000.

    a. When was the deer population about 500?

    b. Do you think this model can be used for future years? Explain your reasoning.

Use the discriminant to determine the number of real solutions of the equation.

10. $x^2 + 8x + 13 = 0$ **11.** $2x^2 - 6x = -9$ **12.** $9x^2 + 4 = 12x$

9.4b Practice
For use after Lesson 9.4b

Solve the equation using two different methods.

1. $x^2 - 7x - 18 = 0$

2. $x^2 + 5x - 3 = 0$

3. $2x^2 + 2 = 4x$

4. $4x^2 + 11x - 3 = 0$

Solve the equation using any method. Explain your choice of method.

5. $x^2 - x - 20 = 0$

6. $3x^2 = 27$

7. $x^2 + 4x = -4$

8. $x^2 + 5x + 8 = 0$

9.4b **Practice** (continued)

9. $x^2 - 12x + 22 = -13$

10. $6x^2 + 2x = 9$

11. $-2x^2 - 10x - 12 = 4$

12. $2x^2 - 1 = 9x + 17$

13. The height h (in feet) of an arrow shot from a bow can be modeled by $h = -16t^2 + 96t + 5$, where t is time in seconds.

    a. When will the arrow hit the ground?

    b. After how many seconds is the arrow 133 feet in the air?

14. The area of the parking lot is 247 square yards. Find the dimensions of the parking lot.

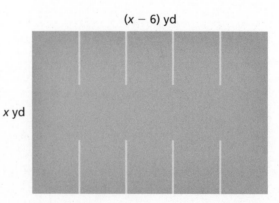

$(x - 6)$ yd

x yd

Name_____ Date_____

9.5 **Solving Systems of Linear and Quadratic Equations**
For use with Activity 9.5

Essential Question How can you solve a system of two equations when one is linear and the other is quadratic?

1 **ACTIVITY:** Solving a System of Equations

Work with a partner. Solve the system of equations using the given strategy. Which strategy do you prefer? Why?

System of Equations:

$y = x + 2$ Linear

$y = x^2 + 2x$ Quadratic

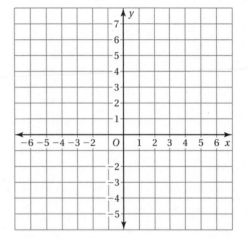

a. Solve by Graphing

Graph each equation and find the points of intersection of the line and the parabola.

b. Solve by Substitution

Substitute the expression for y from the quadratic equation into the linear equation to obtain

$$x^2 + 2x = x + 2.$$

Solve this equation and substitute each x-value into the linear equation $y = x + 2$ to find the corresponding y-value.

c. Solve by Elimination

Eliminate y by subtracting the linear equation from the quadratic equation to obtain

$$y = x^2 + 2x$$
$$\underline{y = x + 2}$$
$$0 = x^2 + x - 2.$$

Solve this equation and substitute each x-value into the linear equation $y = x + 2$ to find the corresponding y-value.

9.5 **Solving Systems of Linear and Quadratic Equations** (continued)

2 ACTIVITY: Analyzing Systems of Equations

Work with a partner. Match each system of equations with its graph. Then solve the system of equations.

a. $y = x^2 - 4$
   $y = -x - 2$

b. $y = x^2 - 2x + 2$
   $y = 2x - 2$

c. $y = x^2 + 1$
   $y = x - 1$

d. $y = x^2 - x - 6$
   $y = 2x - 2$

A.

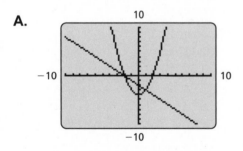

B.

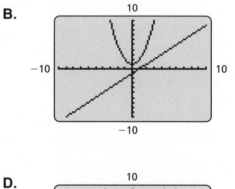

C.

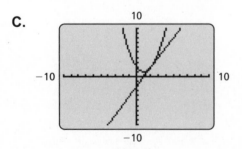

D.

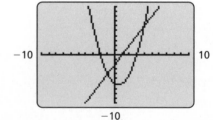

9.5 Solving Systems of Linear and Quadratic Equations (continued)

What Is Your Answer?

3. **IN YOUR OWN WORDS** How can you solve a system of two equations when one is linear and the other is quadratic?

4. Summarize your favorite strategy for solving a system of two equations when one is linear and the other is quadratic.

5. Write a system of equations (one linear and one quadratic) that has the following number of solutions.

   a. no solutions   **b.** one solution   **c.** two solutions

   Your systems should be different from those in the activities.

9.5 Practice
For use after Lesson 9.5

Solve the system by substitution. Check your solution(s).

1. $y = x^2 + 5x - 4$
$y = 3x - 1$

2. $y = 4x + 2$
$y = x^2 + 6$

3. $y = -3x^2$
$y - 1 = 2x$

4. $y - x = 2x^2 - 5$
$y = x + 3$

Solve the system by elimination. Check your solution(s).

5. $y = 4 - 2x$
$y = -x^2 + 2x$

6. $y = x^2 + 5x + 8$
$y = -2x + 2$

7. $y + 6x = 7$
$y = -2x^2 + 9x$

8. $y - 4 = x^2 + 5x$
$y = 3x - 2$

9. The weekly profit y (in dollars) for two street vendors can be modeled by the following equations, where x is the number of weeks since the beginning of the year.

$$y = -x^2 + 9x + 100$$
$$y = 5x + 103$$

When is the weekly profit for each vendor the same?

Name_____ Date _____

Evaluate the expression.

1. $-2\sqrt{9} + 4$

2. $5 + 4\sqrt{36}$

3. $-\sqrt{\dfrac{81}{9}} + 11$

4. $2\sqrt{\dfrac{100}{4}} - 23$

5. $5\left(\sqrt{49} - 3\right)$

6. $-3\left(6 + 2\sqrt{25}\right)$

7. $-4\left(\sqrt{\dfrac{36}{16}} - 5\right)$

8. $9\left(1 - 2\sqrt{\dfrac{16}{144}}\right)$

9. The number of visits to a website can be modeled by $y = \left(\dfrac{x}{4} + 3\right)^2$, where y is hundreds of visits and x is the number of days since the website was launched. When did the website have 4900 visits?

Chapter 10 **Fair Game Review** (continued)

Factor the polynomial.

10. $v^2 - 12v + 32$

11. $d^2 + 9d + 18$

12. $k^2 + 2k - 63$

13. $m^2 - 10m - 24$

14. $t^2 - t - 90$

15. $f^2 + 6f - 27$

16. $a^2 + 16a + 55$

17. $q^2 - 21q + 68$

18. A swimming pool has a shallow end and a deep end. The total area (in square feet) of the swimming pool can be represented by $x^2 + 20x + 36$. Write a binomial that represents the width w of the swimming pool.

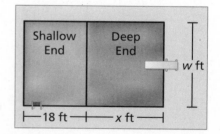

Name_____ Date_____

Essential Question How can you sketch the graph of a square root function?

1 ACTIVITY: Graphing Square Root Functions

Work with a partner.

- Make a table of values for the function.

- Use the table to sketch the graph of the function.

- Describe the domain of the function.

- Describe the range of the function.

a. $y = \sqrt{x}$

b. $y = \sqrt{x} + 2$

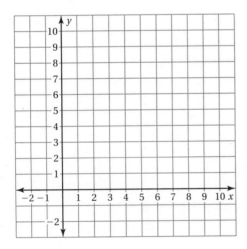

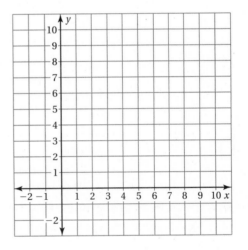

Name_____ Date _____

c. $y = \sqrt{x+1}$

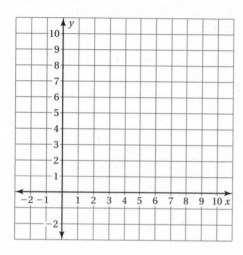

d. $y = -\sqrt{x}$

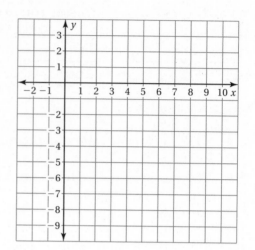

---

2 ACTIVITY: Writing Square Root Functions

Work with a partner. Write a square root function, $y = f(x)$, that has the given values. Then use the function to complete the table.

a.

x	f(x)
−4	0
−3	1
−2	
−1	
0	2
1	

b.

x	f(x)
−4	1
−3	2
−2	
−1	
0	3
1	

10.1 **Graphing Square Root Functions** (continued)

3 **ACTIVITY:** Writing a Square Root Function

Work with a partner. Write a square root function, $y = f(x)$, that has the given points on its graph. Explain how you found your function.

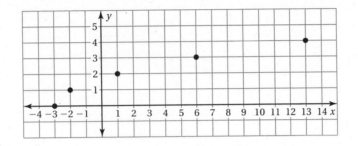

What Is Your Answer?

4. **IN YOUR OWN WORDS** How can you sketch the graph of a square root function? Summarize a procedure for sketching the graph. Then use your procedure to sketch the graph of each function.

    a. $y = 2\sqrt{x}$

    b. $y = \sqrt{x} - 1$

    c. $y = \sqrt{x - 1}$

    d. $y = -2\sqrt{x}$

Name _____ Date _____

Find the domain of the function.

1. $y = 3\sqrt{x}$

2. $y = \sqrt{x - 5}$

3. $y = 2\sqrt{-x + 1}$

Graph the function. Describe the domain and range. Compare the graph to the graph of $y = \sqrt{x}$.

4. $y = \sqrt{x} - 3$

5. $y = \sqrt{x + 2}$

6. $y = \sqrt{x - 4} + 1$

7. $y = -\sqrt{x + 3} + 4$

8. The radius of a sphere is given by $r = \dfrac{1}{2}\sqrt{\dfrac{S}{\pi}}$, where S is the surface area of the sphere.

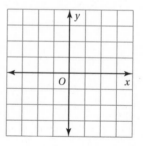

   a. Find the domain of the function. Use a graphing calculator to graph the function.

   b. Use the *trace* feature to approximate the surface area of a sphere with a radius of 2 centimeters.

Name_____ Date _____

Simplify the expression.

1. $\sqrt{\dfrac{1}{26}}$

2. $\dfrac{\sqrt{5}}{\sqrt{3}}$

3. $\sqrt{\dfrac{35}{6}}$

4. $\sqrt{\dfrac{8}{11}}$

5. $\sqrt{\dfrac{32}{24}}$

6. $\dfrac{2}{\sqrt{7}} + \dfrac{12}{\sqrt{7}}$

7. $\dfrac{3}{\sqrt{18}} + \sqrt{2}$

8. $6 - \sqrt{\dfrac{27}{10}}$

Name _____ Date _____

Simplify the expression.

9. $\dfrac{4}{2 - \sqrt{2}}$

10. $\dfrac{1}{\sqrt{6} + 4}$

11. $\dfrac{8}{1 - \sqrt{5}}$

12. $\dfrac{5}{\sqrt{3} + 2}$

13. $\dfrac{9}{\sqrt{5} + \sqrt{8}}$

14. $\dfrac{-2}{\sqrt{12} - \sqrt{6}}$

15. The distance d (in kilometers) that you can see to the horizon with your eye level h meters above the water is given by $d = \sqrt{13h}$. How far can you see when your eye level is $\dfrac{2}{3}$ meter above the water?

Name_____ Date _____

Essential Question How can you solve an equation that contains square roots?

1 **ACTIVITY:** Analyzing a Free-Falling Object

Work with a partner. The table shows the time *t* (in seconds) that it takes a free-falling object (with no air resistance) to fall *d* feet.

a. Sketch the graph of *t* as a function of *d*.

b. Use your graph to estimate the time it takes for a free-falling object to fall 240 feet.

c. The relationship between *d* and *t* is given by the function

$$t = \sqrt{\dfrac{d}{16}}.$$

Use this function to check the estimate you obtained from the graph.

d feet	t seconds
0	0.00
32	1.41
64	2.00
96	2.45
128	2.83
160	3.16
192	3.46
224	3.74
256	4.00
288	4.24
320	4.47

d. Consider a free-falling object that takes 5 seconds to hit the ground. How far did it fall? Explain your reasoning.

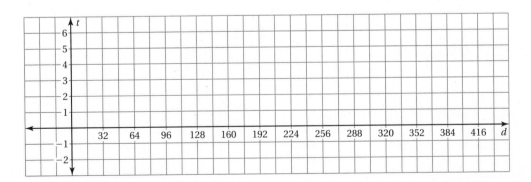

10.2 Solving Square Root Equations (continued)

2 **ACTIVITY:** Solving a Square Root Equation

Work with a partner. Sketch the graph of each function. Then find the value of x such that $f(x) = 2$. Explain your reasoning.

a. $f(x) = \sqrt{x} - 2$

b. $f(x) = \sqrt{x} - 1$

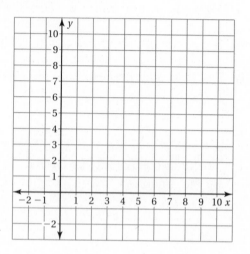

3 **ACTIVITY:** Solving a Square Root Function

Work with a partner. The speed s (in feet per second) of the free-falling object in Activity 1 is given by the function

$$s = \sqrt{64d}.$$

Find the distance traveled for each speed.

a. $s = 8$ ft/sec

b. $s = 16$ ft/sec

c. $s = 24$ ft/sec

10.2 Solving Square Root Equations (continued)

What Is Your Answer?

4. **IN YOUR OWN WORDS** How can you solve an equation that contains square roots? Summarize a procedure for solving a square root equation. Then use your procedure to solve each equation.

   a. $\sqrt{x} + 2 = 3$

   b. $4 - \sqrt{x} = 1$

   c. $5 = \sqrt{x + 20}$

   d. $-3 = -2\sqrt{x}$

Name _____ Date _____

Solve the equation. Check your solution.

1. $\sqrt{x} + 4 = 9$

2. $-2 = 6 - \sqrt{x}$

3. $7 = 1 + 2\sqrt{x + 4}$

4. $\sqrt{5x - 11} - 3 = 5$

5. $\sqrt{4x - 3} = \sqrt{x + 6}$

6. $\sqrt{8x + 1} = \sqrt{7x + 7}$

7. $x = \sqrt{12x - 32}$

8. $\sqrt{4x + 13} = x - 2$

9. The formula $\dfrac{S}{8} = \sqrt{df}$ relates the speed S (in feet per second), drag factor f, and distance d (in feet) it takes for a car to come to a stop after the driver applies the brakes. A car travels at 80 feet per second and the drag factor is $\dfrac{2}{3}$. What distance does it take for the car to stop once the driver applies the brakes?

Name_____ Date _____

Essential Question How are the lengths of the sides of a right triangle related?

Pythagoras was a Greek mathematician and philosopher who discovered one of the most famous rules in mathematics. In mathematics, a rule is called a **theorem**. So, the rule that Pythagoras discovered is called the Pythagorean Theorem.

Pythagoras
(c. 570 B.C.–c. 490 B.C.)

1 ACTIVITY: Discovering the Pythagorean Theorem

Work with a partner.

a. On grid paper, draw any right triangle. Label the lengths of the two shorter sides (the **legs**) a and b.

b. Label the length of the longest side (the **hypotenuse**) c.

c. Draw squares along each of the three sides. Label the areas of the three squares a^2, b^2, and c^2.

d. Cut out the three squares. Make eight copies of the right triangle and cut them out. Arrange the figures to form two identical larger squares.

e. What does this tell you about the relationship among a^2, b^2, and c^2?

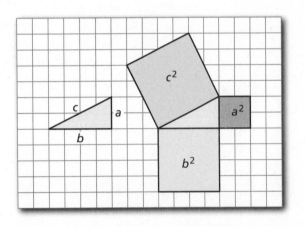

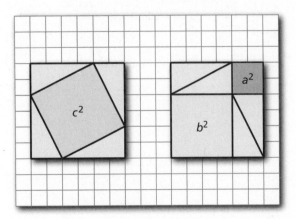

10.3 The Pythagorean Theorem (continued)

2 ACTIVITY: Finding the Length of the Hypotenuse

Work with a partner. Use the result of Activity 1 to find the length of the hypotenuse of each right triangle.

a.

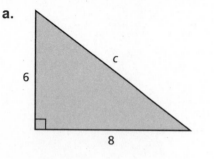

b.

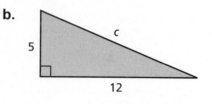

c.

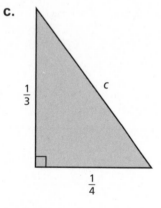

d.

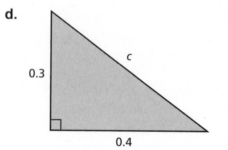

10.3 **The Pythagorean Theorem** (continued)

3 **ACTIVITY:** Finding the Length of a Leg

Work with a partner. Use the result of Activity 1 to find the length of the leg of each right triangle.

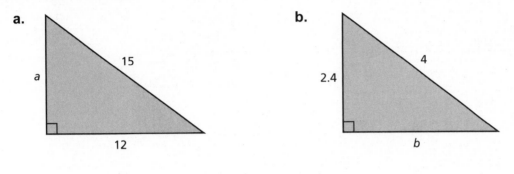

a.

15

a

12

b.

4

2.4

b

What Is Your Answer?

4. **IN YOUR OWN WORDS** How are the lengths of the sides of a right triangle related? Give an example using whole numbers.

10.3 Practice

For use after Lesson 10.3

Find the missing length of the triangle.

1.

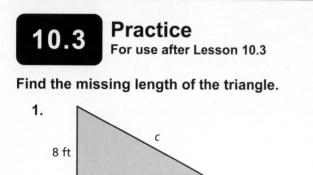

2.

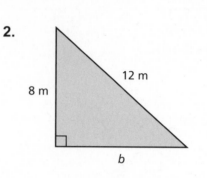

3.

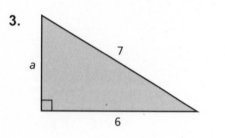

4.

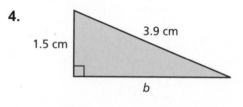

5.

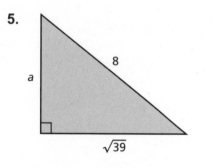

6.

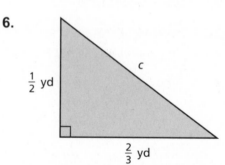

7. The figure shows the location of the eight ball and cue ball in a game of pool. How many inches from the bottom left corner pocket is the eight ball?

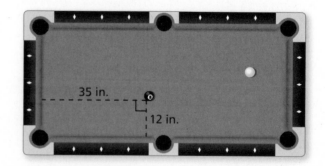

10.4 Using the Pythagorean Theorem
For use with Activity 10.4

Essential Question In what other ways can you use the Pythagorean Theorem?

The *converse* of a statement switches the hypothesis and the conclusion.

Statement:	Converse of the statement:
If p, then q.	If q, then p.

1 ACTIVITY: Analyzing Converses of Statements

Work with a partner. Write the converse of the true statement. Determine whether the converse is true or false. If it is false, give a counterexample.

a. If $a = b$, then $a^2 = b^2$.

Converse:_____

b. If two nonvertical lines have the same slope, then the lines are parallel.

Converse:_____

c. If a sequence has a common difference, then it is an arithmetic sequence.

Converse:_____

d. If a and b are rational numbers, then $a + b$ is a rational number.

Converse:_____

Is the converse of a true statement always true? always false? Explain.

10.4 **Using the Pythagorean Theorem** (continued)

2 **ACTIVITY:** The Converse of the Pythagorean Theorem

Work with a partner. The converse of the Pythagorean Theorem states: "If the equation $a^2 + b^2 = c^2$ is true of the side lengths of a triangle, then the triangle is a right triangle."

   a. Do you think the converse of the Pythagorean Theorem is true or false? How could you use deductive reasoning to support your answer?

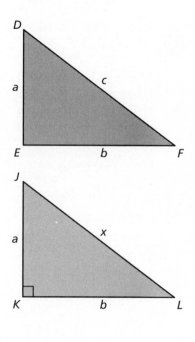

   b. Consider $\triangle DEF$ with side lengths a, b, and c, such that $a^2 + b^2 = c^2$. Also consider $\triangle JKL$ with leg lengths a and b, where $\angle K = 90°$.

   • What does the Pythagorean Theorem tell you about $\triangle JKL$?

   • What does this tell you about c and x?

   • What does this tell you about $\triangle DEF$ and $\triangle JKL$?

   • What does this tell you about $\angle E$?

   • What can you conclude?

Name_____Date_____

3 **ACTIVITY:** Developing the Distance Formula

Work with a partner. Follow the steps below to write a formula that you can use to find the distance between and two points in a coordinate plane.

Step 1: Choose two points in the coordinate plane that do not lie on the same horizontal or vertical line. Label the points (x_1, y_1) and (x_2, y_2).

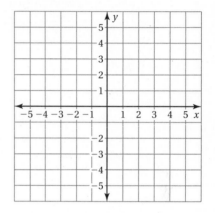

Step 2: Draw a line segment connecting the points. This will be the hypotenuse of a right triangle.

Step 3: Draw horizontal and vertical line segments from the points to form the legs of the right triangle.

Step 4: Use the x-coordinates to write an expression for the length of the horizontal leg.

Step 5: Use the y-coordinates to write an expression for the length of the vertical leg.

Step 6: Substitute the expressions for the lengths of the legs into the Pythagorean Theorem.

Step 7: Solve the equation in Step 6 for the hypotenuse c.

What does the length of the hypotenuse tell you about the two points?

What Is Your Answer?

4. **IN YOUR OWN WORDS** In what other ways can you use the Pythagorean Theorem?

5. What kind of real-life problems do you think the converse of the Pythagorean Theorem can help you solve?

Name _____ Date _____

Tell whether the triangle with the given side lengths is a right triangle.

1.

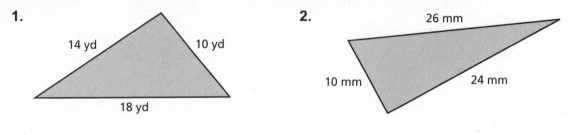

14 yd
10 yd
18 yd

2.

26 mm
10 mm
24 mm

3. 4 m, 4.2 m, 5.8 m

4. 31 in., 35 in., 16 in.

Find the distance between the two points.

5. $(2, 1), (-3, 6)$

6. $(-6, -4), (2, 2)$

7. $(1, -7), (4, -5)$

8. $(-9, 3), (-5, -8)$

9. The cross-section of a wheelchair ramp is shown. Does the ramp form a right triangle?

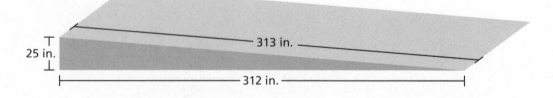

25 in.
313 in.
312 in.

Name_____ Date _____

Evaluate the expression.

1. $\dfrac{2}{3} + \dfrac{5}{3}$

2. $\dfrac{7}{8} - \dfrac{3}{4}$

3. $\dfrac{1}{10} - \dfrac{4}{5}$

4. $\dfrac{11}{6} + \dfrac{5}{12}$

5. $\dfrac{3}{4} \bullet \dfrac{1}{6}$

6. $\dfrac{5}{16} \bullet \dfrac{4}{3}$

7. $\dfrac{1}{3} \div \dfrac{5}{9}$

8. $\dfrac{8}{3} \div \dfrac{4}{15}$

9. You plan to jog $\dfrac{3}{4}$ of a mile tomorrow and $\dfrac{7}{8}$ of a mile the next day. How far will you jog over the next two days?

10. A recipe makes $\dfrac{9}{2}$ cups. A serving is $\dfrac{3}{4}$ cup. How many servings does the recipe make?

Name _____ Date _____

Solve the proportion.

11. $\dfrac{2}{4} = \dfrac{d}{8}$

12. $\dfrac{2}{6} = \dfrac{5}{m}$

13. $\dfrac{12}{a} = \dfrac{4}{9}$

14. $\dfrac{8}{k} = \dfrac{5}{2}$

15. $\dfrac{35}{19} = \dfrac{21}{x}$

16. $\dfrac{17}{28} = \dfrac{c}{21}$

17. It costs $136 for 16 students to visit a museum. How much does it cost for 25 students?

Name_____ Date _____

Essential Question How can you recognize when two variables vary directly? How can you recognize when they vary inversely?

1 **ACTIVITY:** Recognizing Direct Variation

Work with a partner. You hang different weights from the same spring.

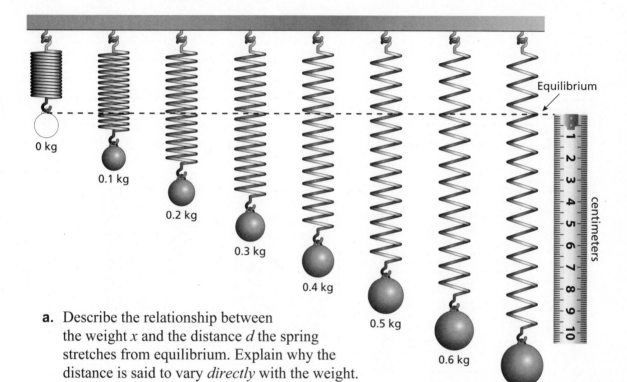

0 kg

0.1 kg

0.2 kg

0.3 kg

0.4 kg

0.5 kg

0.6 kg

0.7 kg

Equilibrium

centimeters

a. Describe the relationship between the weight x and the distance d the spring stretches from equilibrium. Explain why the distance is said to vary *directly* with the weight.

b. Graph the relationship between x and d. What are the characteristics of the graph?

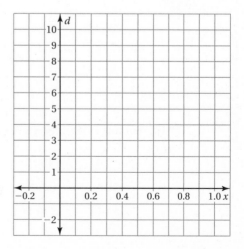

11.1 **Direct and Inverse Variation** (continued)

    c. Write an equation that represents d as a function of x.

    d. In physics, the relationship between d and x is described by Hooke's Law. How would you describe Hooke's Law?

2 **ACTIVITY:** Recognizing Inverse Variation

Work with a partner. The area of each rectangle is 64 square inches.

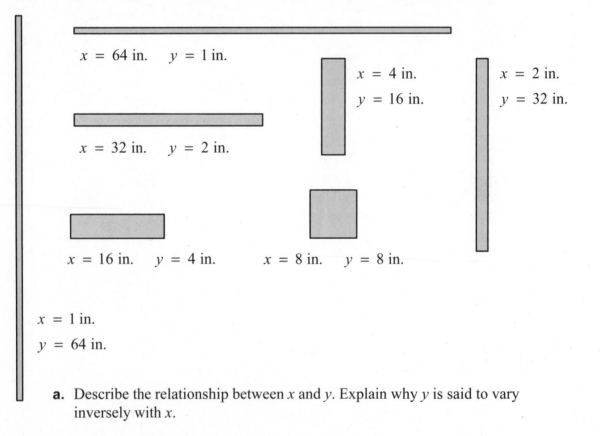

    $x = 64$ in. $y = 1$ in.

                                                                        $x = 4$ in. $x = 2$ in.

                                                                        $y = 16$ in. $y = 32$ in.

    $x = 32$ in. $y = 2$ in.

    $x = 16$ in. $y = 4$ in. $x = 8$ in. $y = 8$ in.

$x = 1$ in.

$y = 64$ in.

    a. Describe the relationship between x and y. Explain why y is said to vary inversely with x.

11.1 **Direct and Inverse Variation** (continued)

    b. Graph the relationship between x and y. What are the characteristics of the graph?

    c. Write an equation that represents y as a function of x.

What Is Your Answer?

    3. IN YOUR OWN WORDS How can you recognize when two variables vary directly? How can you recognize when they vary inversely?

    4. Does the flapping rate of a bird's wings vary directly or inversely with the length of its wings? Explain your reasoning.

11.1 Practice
For use after Lesson 11.1

Tell whether x and y show *direct variation*, *inverse variation*, or *neither*. Explain your reasoning.

1.

x	1	2	3	4
y	7	14	21	28

2. $2xy = 10$

The variable y varies directly with x. Write and graph a direct variation equation that relates x and y.

3. When $x = 3$, $y = 15$.

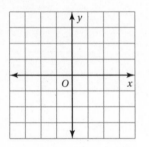

4. When $x = 8$, $y = 2$.

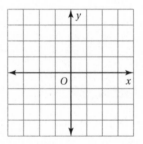

The variable y varies inversely with x. Write and graph an inverse variation equation that relates x and y.

5. When $x = 5$, $y = 8$.

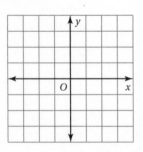

6. When $x = 9$, $y = -4$.

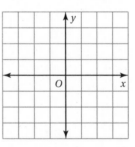

7. An airplane makes a 3000 mile flight. The average flying speed r (in miles per hour) is given by $r = \dfrac{3000}{t}$, where t is the time (in hours) it takes for the flight. Graph the function. Make a conclusion from the graph.

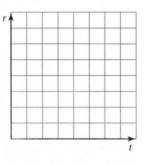

Name_____ Date_____

 11.2 **Graphing Rational Functions**
For use with Activity 11.2

Essential Question What are the characteristics of the graph of a rational function?

1 **ACTIVITY:** Graphing a Rational Function

Work with a partner. As a fundraising project, your math club is publishing an optical illusion calendar. The cost of the art, typesetting, and paper is $850. In addition to this one-time cost, the unit cost of printing each calendar is $3.25.

a. Let A represent the average cost of each calendar. Write a rational function that gives the average cost of printing x calendars.

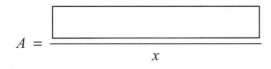

$$A = \frac{}{x}$$

b. Make a table showing the average costs for several different production amounts. Then use the table to graph the average cost function.

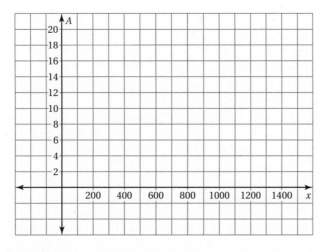

11.2 Graphing Rational Functions (continued)

2 **ACTIVITY:** Analyzing the Graph of a Rational Function

Work with a partner. Use the graph in Activity 1.

    a. What is the *greatest* average cost of a calendar? Explain your reasoning.

    b. What is the *least* average cost of a calendar? Explain your reasoning.

        What characteristic of the graph is associated with the least average cost?

3 **ACTIVITY:** Analyzing Profit and Revenue

Work with a partner. Consider the calendar project in Activity 1. Suppose your club sells 1400 calendars for $10 each.

    a. Find the revenue your club earns from the calendars.

    b. How much profit does your club earn? Explain your reasoning.

Name_____ Date_____

11.2 **Graphing Rational Functions** (continued)

What Is Your Answer?

4. **IN YOUR OWN WORDS** What are the characteristics of the graph of a rational function? Illustrate your answer with the graphs of the following rational functions.

a. $y = \dfrac{x+1}{x}$ **b.** $y = \dfrac{x+2}{x}$ **c.** $y = \dfrac{x+3}{x}$

Name _____ Date _____

Find the excluded value of the function.

1. $y = \dfrac{3}{x - 8}$

2. $y = \dfrac{1}{2x + 6}$

Graph the function. Identify the asymptotes of the graph of the function. Describe the domain and range.

3. $y = -\dfrac{5}{x} + 2$

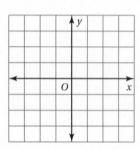

4. $y = \dfrac{2}{x + 4} - 3$

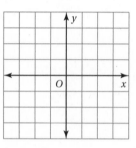

Graph the function. Compare the graph to the graph of $y = \dfrac{1}{x}$.

5. $y = \dfrac{1}{x - 1} - 6$

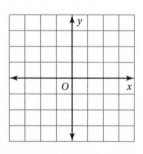

6. $y = \dfrac{-1}{x + 5} + 4$

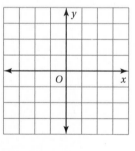

7. A high school football team is taking a trip to an NFL game. Tickets cost \$82 and a charter bus costs \$350. The function

$$y = \dfrac{350}{x + 6} + 82$$ represents the cost y (in dollars) per player

when x players and 6 coaches go on the trip. Graph the function. How many players must go on the trip for the cost per player to be about \$90?

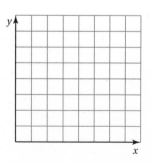

11.2b Practice
For use after Lesson 11.2b

Find the inverse of each relation.

1. $(-2, -1), (-1, 2), (0, 5), (1, 8), (2, 11)$

2. $(-3, 8), (-1, 0), (0, -1), (1, 0), (3, 8)$

3. $(1, 3), (3, 5), (4, 6), (6, 7), (6, 10)$

4.

Input	−4	−2	0	2	4
Output	2	3	4	5	6

5.

Input	−3	−2	−1	0	1
Output	−1	0	−1	−4	−3

6.

Input	−8	−4	−4	0	8
Output	12	8	4	6	4

11.2b Practice (continued)

Find the inverse of the function. Graph the inverse function.

7. $f(x) = \dfrac{1}{2}x + 1$

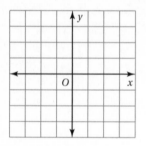

8. $f(x) = -4x - 6$

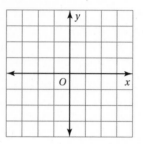

9. $f(x) = x^2 - 5$, where $x \geq 0$

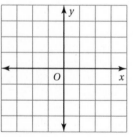

10. $f(x) = \dfrac{1}{3}x^2$, where $x \geq 0$

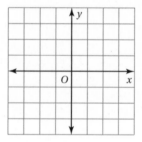

11. $f(x) = \dfrac{1}{x + 4}$

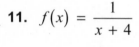

12. $f(x) = \dfrac{1}{x} - 3$

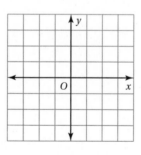

13. Suppose f and g are inverse functions and $f(8) = -3$. What is the value of $g(-3)$?

Name_____ Date _____

Essential Question How can you simplify a rational expression? What are the excluded values of a rational expression?

1 **ACTIVITY:** Simplifying a Rational Expression

Work with a partner.

Sample: You can see that the rational expressions

$$\frac{x^2 + 3x}{x^2} \text{ and } \frac{x + 3}{x}$$

are equivalent by graphing the related functions

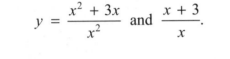

Both functions have the same graph.

Match each rational expression with its equivalent rational expression. Use a graphing calculator to check your answers.

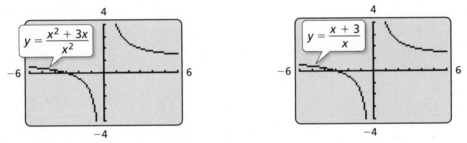

a. $\dfrac{x^2 + x}{x^2}$ **b.** $\dfrac{x^2}{x^2 + x}$ **c.** $\dfrac{x + 1}{x^2 - 1}$ **d.** $\dfrac{x + 1}{x^2 + 2x + 1}$ **e.** $\dfrac{x^2 + 2x + 1}{x + 1}$

A. $\dfrac{1}{x + 1}$ **B.** $x + 1$ **C.** $\dfrac{x + 1}{x}$ **D.** $\dfrac{1}{x - 1}$ **E.** $\dfrac{x}{x + 1}$

11.3 **Simplifying Rational Expressions** (continued)

2 **ACTIVITY:** Finding Excluded Values

Work with a partner. Are the graphs of

$$y = \frac{x^2 + x}{x} \text{ and } y = x + 1$$

exactly **the same? Explain your reasoning.**

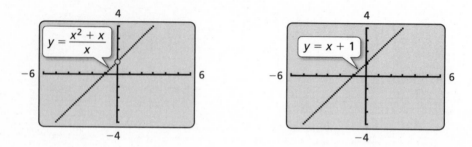

3 **ACTIVITY:** Simplifying and Finding Excluded Values

Work with a partner. Simplify each rational expression, if possible. Then compare the excluded value(s) of the original expression with the excluded value(s) of the simplified expression.

a. $\dfrac{x^2 + 2x}{x^2}$

b. $\dfrac{x^2}{x^2 + 2x}$

c. $\dfrac{x^2}{x}$

11.3 **Simplifying Rational Expressions** (continued)

d. $\dfrac{x^2 + 4x + 4}{x + 2}$ e. $\dfrac{x - 2}{x^2 - 4}$ f. $\dfrac{1}{x^2 + 1}$

What Is Your Answer?

4. **IN YOUR OWN WORDS** How can you simplify a rational expression? What are the excluded values of a rational expression? Include the following rational expressions in your answer.

a. $\dfrac{x(x + 1)}{x}$ b. $\dfrac{x^2 + 3x + 2}{x + 2}$ c. $\dfrac{x + 3}{x^2 - 9}$

Name_____ Date _____

Simplify the rational expression, if possible. State the excluded value(s).

1. $\dfrac{20y^2}{5y}$

2. $\dfrac{18t^2}{12t^4}$

3. $\dfrac{2d}{d-1}$

4. $\dfrac{27a^2b^2}{36a^3b}$

5. $\dfrac{m^3 - 9m^2}{5m^2 - 45m}$

6. $\dfrac{h^2 + 7}{6 - 2h}$

7. $\dfrac{24x - 6x^2}{x^2 - 3x - 4}$

8. $\dfrac{p^2 - 7p - 18}{2p^3 + 10p^2 + 12p}$

9. The shapes shown have the same area. Write and simplify an expression for the height h of the trapezoid.

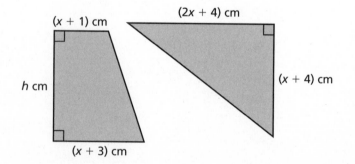

Name_____ Date _____

11.4 Multiplying and Dividing Rational Expressions
For use with Activity 11.4

Essential Question How can you multiply and divide rational expressions?

---

1 ACTIVITY: Matching Quotients and Products

Work with a partner. Match each quotient with a product and then with a simplified expression. Explain your reasoning.

Quotient of Two Rational Expressions	*Product of Two Rational Expressions*	*Simplified Expression*

a. $\dfrac{2x^2}{5} \div \dfrac{14x}{10}$ **A.** $\dfrac{5x^2}{2} \cdot \dfrac{10}{14x}$ **1.** $\dfrac{25x}{14}$

b. $\dfrac{2x^2}{5} \div \dfrac{10}{14x}$ **B.** $\dfrac{2x^2}{5} \cdot \dfrac{10}{14x}$ **2.** $\dfrac{7x^3}{2}$

c. $\dfrac{5x^2}{2} \div \dfrac{14x}{10}$ **C.** $\dfrac{5x^2}{2} \cdot \dfrac{14x}{10}$ **3.** $\dfrac{14x^3}{25}$

d. $\dfrac{5x^2}{2} \div \dfrac{10}{14x}$ **D.** $\dfrac{2x^2}{5} \cdot \dfrac{14x}{10}$ **4.** $\dfrac{2x}{7}$

e. $\dfrac{x^2-1}{x+2} \div \dfrac{x+1}{x^2-4}$ **E.** $\dfrac{x^2-1}{x-2} \cdot \dfrac{x^2-4}{x+1}$ **5.** $x^2 - x - 2$

f. $\dfrac{x^2-1}{x-2} \div \dfrac{x+1}{x^2-4}$ **F.** $\dfrac{x^2-1}{x-2} \cdot \dfrac{x^2-4}{x-1}$ **6.** $x^2 - 3x + 2$

g. $\dfrac{x^2-1}{x-2} \div \dfrac{x-1}{x^2-4}$ **G.** $\dfrac{x^2-1}{x+2} \cdot \dfrac{x^2-4}{x-1}$ **7.** $x^2 + x - 2$

h. $\dfrac{x^2-1}{x+2} \div \dfrac{x-1}{x^2-4}$ **H.** $\dfrac{x^2-1}{x+2} \cdot \dfrac{x^2-4}{x+1}$ **8.** $x^2 + 3x + 2$

11.4 Multiplying and Dividing Rational Expressions (continued)

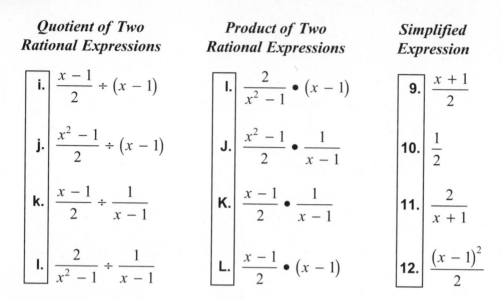

Quotient of Two Rational Expressions

i. $\dfrac{x-1}{2} \div (x-1)$

j. $\dfrac{x^2-1}{2} \div (x-1)$

k. $\dfrac{x-1}{2} \div \dfrac{1}{x-1}$

l. $\dfrac{2}{x^2-1} \div \dfrac{1}{x-1}$

Product of Two Rational Expressions

I. $\dfrac{2}{x^2-1} \cdot (x-1)$

J. $\dfrac{x^2-1}{2} \cdot \dfrac{1}{x-1}$

K. $\dfrac{x-1}{2} \cdot \dfrac{1}{x-1}$

L. $\dfrac{x-1}{2} \cdot (x-1)$

Simplified Expression

9. $\dfrac{x+1}{2}$

10. $\dfrac{1}{2}$

11. $\dfrac{2}{x+1}$

12. $\dfrac{(x-1)^2}{2}$

---

2 **ACTIVITY:** Solving a Math Crossword Puzzle

Work with a partner. Solve the crossword puzzle. Use the clues from the next page.

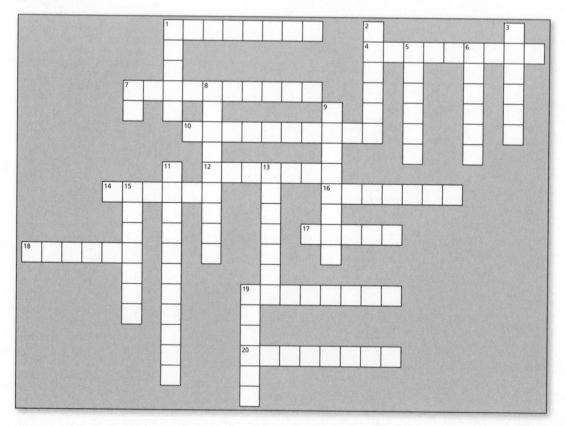

11.4 Multiplying and Dividing Rational Expressions (continued)

Across

1. Inverse of subtraction

4. △ or △

7. Greek mathematician

10. Longest side of a right triangle

12. $x(x + 1)$

14. $y = kx$

16. $y = \dfrac{k}{x}$

17. ∠

18. 3 ft^3

19. $\dfrac{2}{3}$ or $\dfrac{4}{5}$

20. △

Down

1. $30°$

2. C of this is $2\pi r$

3. Dimension of □

5. $120°$

6. Is the same as

7. About 3.14

8. Graph approaches $x = h$

9. $\dfrac{x}{x + 1}$

11. Two numbers whose product is 1

13. x in $\dfrac{1}{x}$

15. $-1, 0, 1$, etc.

19. x in $x(x + 1)$

What Is Your Answer?

3. **IN YOUR OWN WORDS** How can you multiply and divide rational expressions? Include the following in your answer.

a. $\dfrac{x + 3}{x} \cdot \dfrac{1}{x + 3}$

b. $\dfrac{x + 3}{x} \div \dfrac{1}{x}$

Name _____ Date _____

11.4 Practice
For use after Lesson 11.4

Find the product.

1. $\dfrac{8k^2}{7} \cdot \dfrac{k-5}{2k^4}$

2. $\dfrac{8}{w+6} \cdot \dfrac{3w^2+18w}{2}$

3. $\dfrac{2b^3}{b^2-2b-15} \cdot \dfrac{b-5}{6b}$

4. $\dfrac{4n^2-8n}{n^2+9n+14} \cdot \dfrac{n^2-4}{4n}$

Find the quotient.

5. $\dfrac{g+3}{4g^2} \div \dfrac{g+3}{12g}$

6. $\dfrac{y}{-5y^2-20y} \div \dfrac{y^2}{y^2+2y-8}$

7. $\dfrac{a^2-64}{a} \div \left(3a^3+24a^2\right)$

8. $\dfrac{r^2-7r}{3} \div \left(r^2+r-56\right)$

9. Two distinct prairie dog populations, P_1 and P_2 can be modeled by

$P_1 = \dfrac{100x^2}{x+1}$ and $P_2 = \dfrac{100x^2}{x+3}$, where x is the number of years since 2000.

a. Write a function that models the ratio of Population 1 to Population 2, that is $\dfrac{P_1}{P_2}$.

b. Find the ratio of Population 1 to Population 2 in 2004.

11.5 Dividing Polynomials
For use with Activity 11.5

Essential Question How can you divide one polynomial by another polynomial?

1 ACTIVITY: Dividing Polynomials

Work with a partner. Six different algebra tiles are shown below.

Step 1: Arrange tiles to model

$$(x^2 + 5x + 4) \div (x + 1)$$

in a rectangular pattern.

Step 2: Complete the pattern.

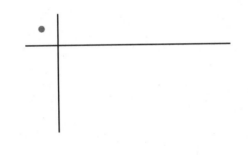

Step 3: Use the completed pattern to write

$$(x^2 + 5x + 4) \div (x + 1) = \underline{\hspace{3cm}}.$$

Dividend ÷ Divisor = Quotient

11.5 Dividing Polynomials (continued)

Complete the pattern and write the division problem.

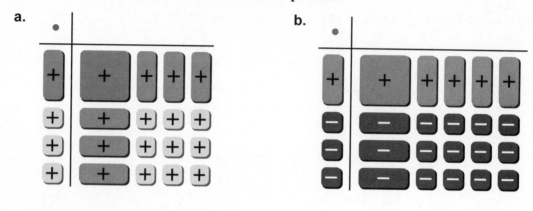

a.

b.

---

2 ACTIVITY: Dividing Polynomials

Work with a partner. Write two different polynomial division problems that can be associated with the given algebra tile pattern. Check your answers by multiplying.

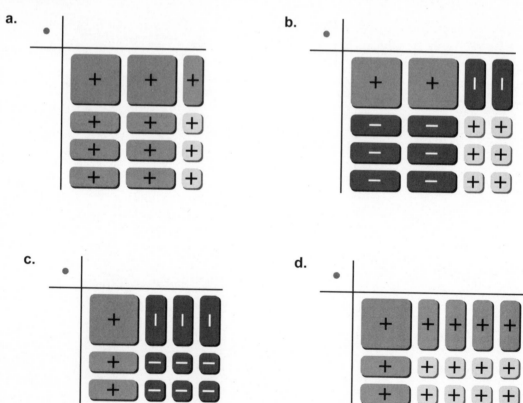

a.

b.

c.

d.

11.5 Dividing Polynomials (continued)

3 ACTIVITY: Dividing Polynomials

Work with a partner. Solve each polynomial division problem.

a. $\left(3x^2 - 8x - 3\right) \div (x - 3)$

b. $\left(8x^2 - 2x - 3\right) \div (4x - 3)$

What Is Your Answer?

4. **IN YOUR OWN WORDS** How can you divide one polynomial by another polynomial? Include the following in your answer.

a. $\left(3x^2 + 20x - 7\right) \div (x + 7)$

b. $\left(4x^2 - 4x - 3\right) \div (2x - 3)$

11.5 Practice
For use after Lesson 11.5

Find the quotient.

1. $\left(b^2 + 11b + 18\right) \div (b + 2)$

2. $\left(n^2 - n - 30\right) \div (n + 5)$

3. $\left(4w^2 + 9w - 3\right) \div (w + 3)$

4. $\left(5c^2 - 10 - 2c\right) \div (c - 1)$

5. $\left(21 + 8x^2 - 26x\right) \div (4x - 7)$

6. $\left(15h - 4 + 6h^2\right) \div (2h + 9)$

7. $\left(r^2 - 12\right) \div (r + 8)$

8. $\left(12y^2 + 8y\right) \div (3y - 4)$

9. The volume of the triangular prism is $x^3 + 6x^2 + 11x + 6$. Write an expression for the height of the prism.

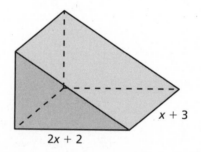

$x + 3$

$2x + 2$

11.6 Adding and Subtracting Rational Expressions
For use with Activity 11.6

Essential Question How can you add and subtract rational expressions?

---

1 ACTIVITY: Adding Rational Expressions

Work with a partner. You and a friend have a summer job mowing lawns. Working alone it takes you 40 hours to mow all of the lawns. Working alone it takes your friend 60 hours to mow all of the lawns.

a. Write a rational expression that represents the portion of the lawns you can mow in t hours.

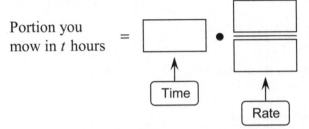

Portion you mow in t hours =

b. Write a rational expression that represents the portion of the lawns your friend can mow in t hours.

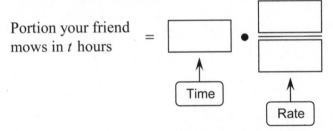

Portion your friend mows in t hours =

c. Add the two expressions to write a rational expression for the portion of the lawns that the two of you working together can mow in t hours.

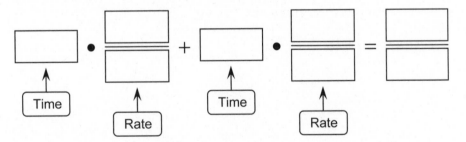

d. Use the expression in part (c) to find the total time it takes both of you working together to mow all of the lawns. Explain your reasoning.

11.6 **Adding and Subtracting Rational Expressions** (continued)

2 **ACTIVITY:** Adding Rational Expressions

Work with a partner. You are hang gliding. For the first 10,000 feet, you travel *x* feet per minute. You then enter a valley in which the wind is greater, and for the next 6000 feet, you travel 2*x* feet per minute.

a. Use the formula $d = rt$ to write a rational expression that represents the time it takes you to travel the first 10,000 feet.

Time to travel
first 10,000 feet $=$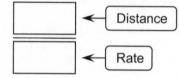

b. Use the formula $d = rt$ to write a rational expression that represents the time it takes you to travel the next 6000 feet.

Time to travel
next 6000 feet $=$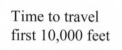

c. Add the two expressions to write a rational expression that represents the total time it takes you to travel 16,000 feet.

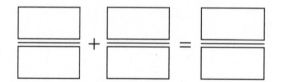

d. Use the expression in part (c) to find the total time it takes you to travel 16,000 feet when your rate during the first 10,000 feet is 2000 feet per minute.

Name_____ Date_____

What Is Your Answer?

    3. IN YOUR OWN WORDS How can you add and subtract rational expressions? Include the following in your answer.

a. $\dfrac{x}{5} + \dfrac{x}{10}$ **b.** $\dfrac{3}{x} + \dfrac{4}{x}$ **c.** $\dfrac{9}{x} + \dfrac{2}{3x}$

d. $\dfrac{x}{2} - \dfrac{x}{4}$ **e.** $\dfrac{x+1}{3} - \dfrac{1}{3}$ **f.** $\dfrac{1}{x} - \dfrac{1}{x^2}$

Name_____ Date _____

Find the sum or difference.

1. $\dfrac{3}{5g} + \dfrac{6}{5g}$

2. $\dfrac{1}{2v + 3} + \dfrac{4}{2v + 3}$

3. $\dfrac{11m}{4m - 2} - \dfrac{3m + 2}{4m - 2}$

4. $\dfrac{y^2}{y^2 + y - 6} - \dfrac{9}{y^2 + y - 6}$

5. $\dfrac{3a + 1}{4a} + \dfrac{a - 2}{6a}$

6. $\dfrac{k^2 + 8}{k - 5} - k$

7. $\dfrac{4x^2 - x}{3x - 12} + \dfrac{x^2 + 4}{4 - x}$

8. $\dfrac{6}{d + 5} - \dfrac{3d - 7}{d^2 + 2d - 15}$

9. You drive 45 miles from home to a relative's house and 45 miles back home. Due to construction, your speed on the way back is only 60% of your speed on the way there. Let r be your speed (in miles per hour) while driving to your relative's house. Write an expression that represents the amount of time you spend driving on your trip.

Name_____ Date_____

Essential Question How can you solve a rational equation?

1 **ACTIVITY:** Solving Rational Equations

Work with a partner. A hockey goalie faces 799 shots and saves 707 of them.

a. What is his save percentage?

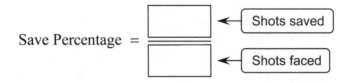

Save Percentage = □/□ ← Shots saved / Shots faced

b. Suppose the goalie has x additional consecutive saves. Write an expression for his new save percentage.

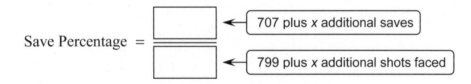

Save Percentage = □/□ ← 707 plus x additional saves / 799 plus x additional shots faced

c. Complete the table showing the goalie's save percentage as x increases.

Additional Saves, x	0	20	40	60	80	100	120	140
Save Percentage								

d. The goalie wants to end the season with a save percentage of .900. How many additional consecutive saves must he have to achieve this? Justify your answer by solving an equation.

11.7 **Solving Rational Equations** (continued)

2 **ACTIVITY:** Solving Rational Equations

Work with a partner. A baseball player has been at bat 47 times and has 8 hits.

a. What is his batting average?

Batting Average $=$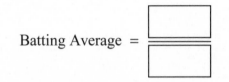

b. Suppose the player has x additional consecutive hits. Write an expression for his new batting average.

Batting Average $=$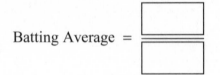

c. Complete the table showing the player's batting average as x increases.

Additional Hits, x	0	1	2	3	4	5	6	7
Batting Average								

d. The player wants to end the season with a batting average of .250. How many additional consecutive hits must he have to achieve this? Justify your answer by solving an equation.

Name_____ Date_____

Solving Rational Equations (continued)

What Is Your Answer?

3. **IN YOUR OWN WORDS** How can you solve a rational equation? Include
   the following in your answer.

a. $\dfrac{x-6}{6} = \dfrac{2}{3}$ b. $\dfrac{x+56}{6} = \dfrac{1}{2}$ c. $\dfrac{x}{4} + \dfrac{x}{2} = \dfrac{2x}{3}$

11.7 Practice
For use after Lesson 11.7

Solve the equation. Check your solution.

1. $\dfrac{4}{h-3} = \dfrac{8}{h}$

2. $\dfrac{6}{q-2} = \dfrac{5}{q-1}$

3. $\dfrac{m}{m+3} = \dfrac{5}{m+7}$

4. $\dfrac{c-3}{5c-6} = \dfrac{c}{c-3}$

5. $\dfrac{6}{z-3} - \dfrac{3}{z} = \dfrac{6}{z}$

6. $\dfrac{4}{k} + \dfrac{14}{k+5} = \dfrac{8}{k+5}$

7. $\dfrac{d}{d+3} + \dfrac{1}{d-1} = \dfrac{4}{d^2+2d-3}$

8. $\dfrac{t}{t-7} - \dfrac{5}{t-4} = \dfrac{3t+3}{t^2-11t+28}$

9. An academic challenge team has 24 members, 9 of which are boys. The team is required to have 50% boys and 50% girls for a competition. How many boys does the team need to add to reach this proportion?

Name_____ Date_____

Use the data in the table to create a circle graph.

1.

Fabric	Percent
Polyester	68%
Rayon	28%
Spandex	4%

2.

Budget	Dollars
Bills	200
Food	100
Savings	50
Other	50

3.

Type of Lunch	Students
Sandwich	24
Pasta	16
Pizza	28
Chicken Nuggets	19
Other	13

4.

Hobbies	Students
Music	12
Collecting	4
Reading	5
Games	15
Other	9

5. You conduct a survey asking students which instrument they play. Organize the results in a circle graph.

Instruments Played	Students
Trumpet	7
Piano	15
Trombone	5
Flute	9
Saxophone	4
Drums	10
None	5

Chapter 12 Fair Game Review (continued)

Use the data in the table to create a histogram.

6.

Concerts attended	Students
0–4	18
5–9	9
10–14	2

7.

Number of Puppies in Litter	Litters
0–2	1
3–5	7
6–8	12
9–11	3

8.

Boxes of Scout Cookies Sold	Scouts
0–4	9
5–9	12
10–14	20
15–19	32
20–24	28

9.

Money Raised	Students
0–19	4
20–39	6
40–59	9
60–79	8
80–99	5

10. You conduct a survey asking students how many siblings they have. Organize the results in a histogram.

Number of Siblings	Students
0–1	11
2–3	15
4–5	5
6–7	2
8–9	1

Name_____ Date_____

12.1 Measures of Central Tendency
For use with Activity 12.1

Essential Question How can you use measures of central tendency to distribute an amount evenly among a group of people?

> **1 ACTIVITY:** Exploring Mean, Median, and Mode

Work with a partner. Forty-five coins are arranged in nine stacks.

5   4   3   6   2   5   8   7   5

a. Record the number of coins in each stack in a table.

Stack	1	2	3	4	5	6	7	8	9
Coins									

b. Find the mean, median, and mode of the data.

c. By moving coins from one stack to another, can you change the mean? the median? the mode? Explain.

d. Is it possible to arrange the coins in stacks so that the median is 6? 8? Explain.

12.1 **Measures of Central Tendency** (continued)

2 EXAMPLE: Drawing a Dot Plot

Work with a partner.

a. Use the number line below. Label the tick marks from 1 to 10.

b. Place each stack of coins in Activity 1 above the number of coins in the stack.

c. Draw a • above each number to represent each coin in the stack. This graph is called a *dot plot*.

Number of Coins

3 ACTIVITY: Fair and Unfair Distributions

Work with a partner.

A distribution of coins to nine people is considered *fair* if each person has the same number of coins.

- Distribute the 45 coins into 9 stacks using a fair distribution. How is this distribution related to the mean?

- Draw a dot plot for each distribution. Which distributions seem most fair? Which distributions seem least fair? Explain your reasoning.

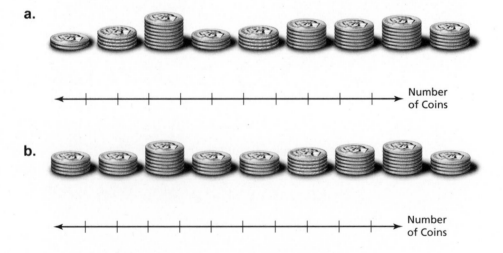

a.

Number of Coins

b.

Number of Coins

12.1 **Measures of Central Tendency** (continued)

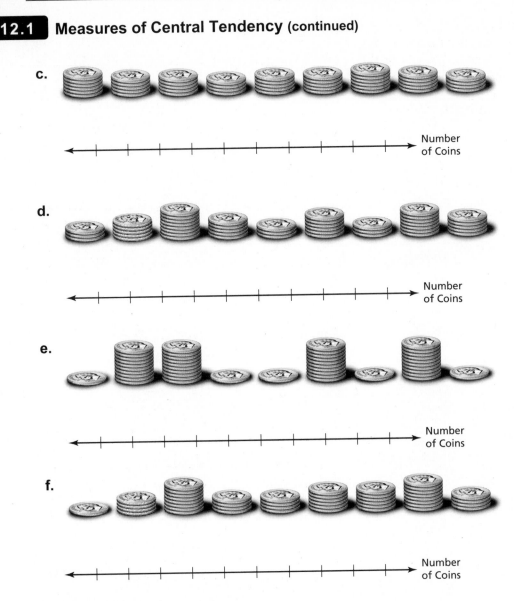

c.

Number of Coins

d.

Number of Coins

e.

Number of Coins

f.

Number of Coins

What Is Your Answer?

4. **IN YOUR OWN WORDS** How can you use measures of central tendency to distribute an amount evenly among a group of people?

5. Use the Internet or some other reference to find examples of mean or median incomes of groups of people. Describe possible distributions that could produce the given means or medians.

Name _____ Date _____

 Practice
12.1 For use after Lesson 12.1

Find the mean, median, and mode of the data.

1.

Song Lengths (minutes)		
2.6	3.25	4.15
2.52	3.67	3.1
3.78	4.9	3.8

2.

Number of Books Read in a Week

Find the value of x.

3. Mean is 20; 6, 22, *x*, 7, 36

4. Median is 28; 16, 24, *x*, 48

5. A statistician records the winning scores of five basketball teams.
105, 98, 92, 108, 70

   a. Identify the outlier.

   b. Which measure of central tendency will be most affected by removing the outlier?

   c. Calculate the mean and median with and without the outlier.

Name_____ Date _____

Essential Question How can you measure the dispersion of a data set?

1 ACTIVITY: Measuring the Dispersion of Data

Work with a partner. The histogram shows the weights of 53 players on the Chicago Bears football team in 2011.

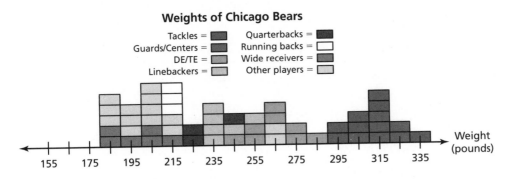

Weights of Chicago Bears

Tackles = ▓   Quarterbacks = ▓
Guards/Centers = ▓   Running backs = ☐
DE/TE = ▓   Wide receivers = ▓
Linebackers = ☐   Other players = ▓

Weight (pounds)

155   175   195   215   235   255   275   295   315   335

The weights are: 220, 200, 185, 240, 215, 222, 185, 180, 210, 196, 218, 190, 218, 185, 204, 180, 200, 219, 198, 196, 260, 211, 203, 239, 234, 258, 244, 230, 320, 310, 265, 309, 315, 295, 315, 275, 316, 333, 320, 308, 206, 200, 255, 267, 260, 287, 292, 300, 248, 310, 252, 238, 270.

a. Describe the data. How much are the weights dispersed from the mean weight? Explain your reasoning.

Definition of Dispersed: To disperse objects means to spread them over an area. For instance, the population of Texas is much more dispersed than the population of Rhode Island.

b. Does it appear that the weight of a football player is correlated to the position that he plays? Explain your reasoning.

Do you think your answer is valid for other types of professional sports, such as basketball, baseball, hockey, and soccer? Explain your reasoning.

12.2 Measures of Dispersion (continued)

2 ACTIVITY: Measuring the Dispersion of Data

Work with a partner. The diagram shows the weights of 40 players on the Los Angeles Angels baseball team in 2011.

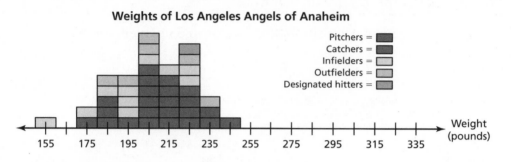

Weights of Los Angeles Angels of Anaheim

Pitchers =
Catchers =
Infielders =
Outfielders =
Designated hitters =

Weight (pounds)

155   175   195   215   235   255   275   295   315   335

The weights are: 200, 200, 185, 210, 215, 200, 221, 215, 220, 185, 175, 205, 235, 215, 240, 220, 200, 210, 150, 180, 227, 195, 175, 210, 200, 190, 220, 190, 185, 225, 195, 200, 230, 220, 190, 230, 200, 185, 200, 220.

a. Describe the data. How much are the weights dispersed from the mean weight? Explain your reasoning.

b. Compare the dispersions of the weights of players for a National Football League and Major League Baseball team.

c. Does it appear that the weight of a baseball player is correlated to the position that he plays? Explain your reasoning.

12.2 **Measures of Dispersion** (continued)

What Is Your Answer?

3. **IN YOUR OWN WORDS** How can you measure the dispersion of a data set? Illustrate your answer by using the positions and weights of the 15 players on the Boston Celtics basketball team in 2011.

   Forward: 235; power forwards: 253, 295, 245; small forwards: 235, 235; centers: 255, 240, 325; point guards: 205, 186, 200; shooting guards: 205, 210, 180

   Does it appear that the weight of a basketball player is correlated to the position that he plays? Explain your reasoning.

Name _____ Date _____

Find the mean and range of each data set. Then compare the data sets.

1. 800 meter dash times (in seconds)
Varsity: 137, 114, 125, 141, 132, 119
JV: 160, 151, 140, 147, 138, 176

2. Grades (out of 100) for a student
Tests: 81, 89, 75, 84, 89, 86
Quizzes: 98, 87, 71, 100, 57, 88

Find the mean and standard deviation of the data.

3. 2, 9, 4, 5, 8, 3, 10, 7

4. 11, 14, 8, 12, 16, 12, 6, 9

5.

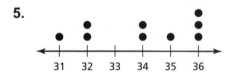

6.

Stem	Leaf
10	8
11	1 4 5
12	3 5
13	2 6 9
14	0 3

Key: 12 | 3 = 123

7. The weights (in pounds) of whitetail deer in two forests are shown.

Forest A	
140	159
155	137
146	149
143	151

Forest B	
148	171
157	152
163	173
156	160

a. Find the mean, range, and standard deviation of the weights in each forest. Compare your results.

b. Do you think a hunter would have greater success in Forest A or in Forest B? Explain.

12.3 Box-and-Whisker Plots
For use with Activity 12.3

Essential Question How can you use a box-and-whisker plot to describe a data set?

 ACTIVITY: Drawing a Box-and-Whisker Plot

Work with a partner.

The numbers of first cousins of the students in an eighth-grade class are shown.

A box-and-whisker plot uses a number line to represent the data visually.

Numbers of First Cousins			
3	10	18	8
9	3	0	32
23	19	13	8
6	3	3	10
12	45	1	5
13	24	16	14

a. Order the data set and write it on a strip of grid paper with 24 equally spaced boxes.

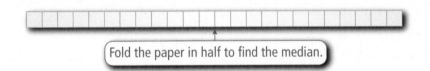

Fold the paper in half to find the median.

b. Fold the paper in half again to divide the data into four groups. Because there are 24 numbers in the data set, each group should have six numbers.

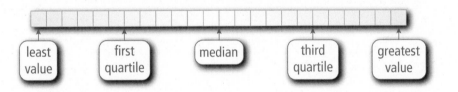

least value   first quartile   median   third quartile   greatest value

c. Use the number line. Graph the five numbers that you found in part (b).

```
  0   5  10  15  20  25  30  35  40  45  50
```

12.3 Box-and-Whisker Plots (continued)

d. Explain how the box-and-whisker plot shown below represents the data set.

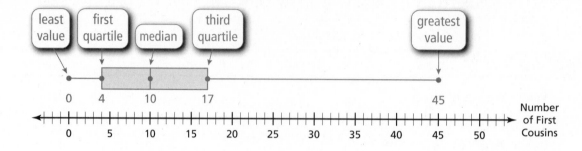

2 ACTIVITY: Conducting a Survey

Conduct a survey in your class. Ask each student to write the number of his or her first cousins on a piece of paper.

Two people are first cousins if they share at least one grandparent, but do not share a parent.

Collect the pieces of paper and write the data on the chalkboard.

Now, work with a partner to draw a box-and-whisker plot of the data.

12.3 **Box-and-Whisker Plots** (continued)

3 **ACTIVITY:** Reading a Box-and-Whisker Plot

Work with a partner. The box-and-whisker plots show the test score
distributions of two eighth-grade standardized tests. The tests were taken
by the same group of students. One test was taken in the fall and the other
was taken in the spring.

   a. Compare the test results.

   b. Decide which box-and-whisker plot represents the results of each. How
      did you make your decision?

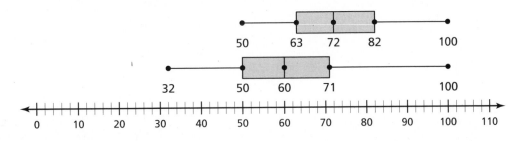

What Is Your Answer?

   4. **IN YOUR OWN WORDS** How can you use a box-and-whisker plot to
      describe a data set?

   5. Describe who might be interested in test score distributions like those
      shown in Activity 3. Explain why it is important for these people to
      analyze test score distributions.

Name_____ Date _____

Make a box-and-whisker plot for the data.

1. Hours of reading: 1, 6, 7, 5, 5, 8, 4, 8

2. Golf scores: −5, −12, 0, 2, −4, 3, −3, −7, −1, −3, −5, 0

3. The table shows quiz scores of 10 students. Make a box-and-whisker plot for the data. What does the box-and-whisker plot tell you about the data?

Quiz Scores (points)	
20	19
17	18
16	18
22	20
24	25

4. The box-and-whisker plot shows the number of pages in a stack of books. What is the range of the lower 25% of the data?

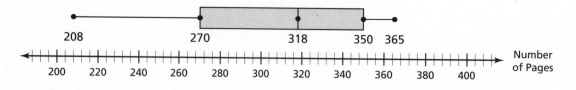

Name_____ Date _____

Essential Question How can you use a histogram to characterize the basic shape of a distribution?

1 ACTIVITY: Analyzing a Famous Symmetric Distribution

A famous data set was collected in Scotland in the mid-1800s. It contains the chest sizes, measured in inches, of 5738 men in the Scottish Militia.

Chest Size	Number of Men
33	3
34	18
35	81
36	185
37	420
38	749
39	1073
40	1079
41	934
42	658
43	370
44	92
45	50
46	21
47	4
48	1

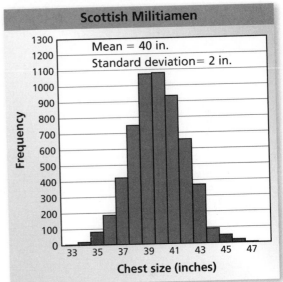

Work with a partner. What percent of the chest sizes lie within (a) 1 standard deviation, (b) 2 standard deviations, and (c) 3 standard deviations of the mean? Explain your reasoning.

12.4   **Shapes of Distributions** (continued)

2   **ACTIVITY:** Comparing Two Symmetric Distributions

Work with a partner. The graphs show the distributions of the heights of 250 adult American males and 250 adult American females.

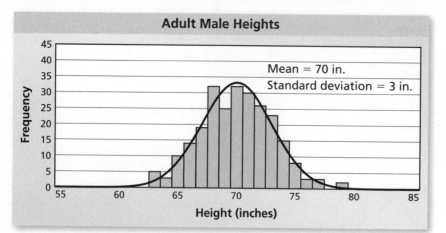

Adult Male Heights

Mean = 70 in.
Standard deviation = 3 in.

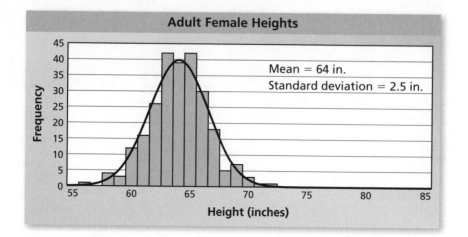

Adult Female Heights

Mean = 64 in.
Standard deviation = 2.5 in.

a. Which data set has a smaller standard deviation? Explain what this means in the real-life context.

b. Estimate the percent of male heights between 67 inches and 73 inches.

12.4 **Shapes of Distributions** (continued)

What Is Your Answer?

3. **IN YOUR OWN WORDS** How can you use a histogram to characterize the basic shape of a distribution?

4. All three distributions in Activities 1 and 2 are roughly symmetric distributions. The histograms are called "bell-shaped."

   a. What are the characteristics of a symmetric distribution?

   b. Why is a symmetric distribution called "bell-shaped"?

   c. Give two other real-life examples of symmetric distributions.

Name _____ Date _____

12.4 Practice
For use after Lesson 12.4

Display the data in a histogram. Describe the shape of the distribution.

1.

Shark Length (in feet)	Frequency
9	3
10	9
11	20
12	26
13	18
14	10
15	2

2.

Goals Scored in a Soccer Game	Frequency
0	4
1	8
2	5
3	3
4	1
5	1
6	0
7	1

Determine which measures of central tendency and dispersion best represent the data. Explain your reasoning.

3.
4.

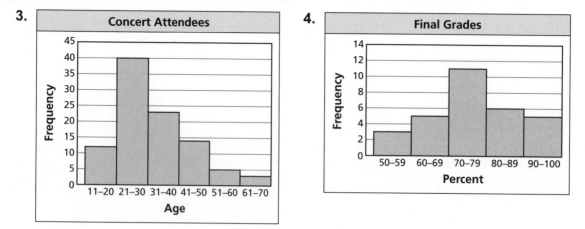

Name_____ Date _____

12.5 Scatter Plots and Lines of Fit
For use with Activity 12.5

Essential Question How can you use data to predict an event?

1 ACTIVITY: Representing Data by a Linear Equation

Work with a partner. You have been working on a science project for
8 months. Each month, you have measured the length of a baby alligator.

My Science Project

The table shows your measurements.

September

April

Month, x	0	1	2	3	4	5	6	7
Length (in.), y	22.0	22.5	23.5	25.0	26.0	27.5	28.5	29.5

Use the following steps to predict the baby alligator's length next September.

a. Graph the data in the table.

b. Draw the straight line that you think
best approximates the points.

c. Write an equation of the line you drew.

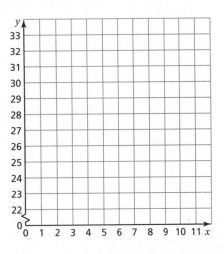

d. Use the equation to predict the baby
alligator's length next September.

12.5 Scatter Plots and Lines of Fit (continued)

2 ACTIVITY: Representing Data by a Linear Equation

Work with a partner. You are a biologist and are studying bat populations.

You are asked to predict the number of bats that will be living in an abandoned mine after 3 years.

To start, you find the number of bats that have been living in the mine during the past 8 years.

The table shows the results of your research.

7 years ago

this year

Year, x	0	1	2	3	4	5	6	7
Bats (thousands), y	327	306	299	270	254	232	215	197

Use the following steps to predict the number of bats that will be living in the mine after 3 years.

a. Graph the data in the table.

b. Draw the straight line that you think best approximates the points.

c. Write an equation of the line you drew.

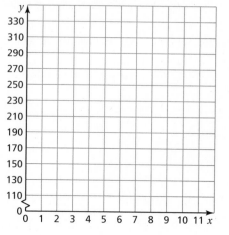

d. Use the equation to predict the number of bats after 3 years.

12.5 Scatter Plots and Line of Fit (continued)

What Is Your Answer?

3. **IN YOUR OWN WORDS** How can you use data to predict an event?

4. Use the Internet or some other reference to find data that appear to have a linear pattern. List the data in a table and graph the data. Use an equation that is based on the data to predict a future event.

Name_____ Date _____

Tell whether the data show a *positive*, a *negative*, or *no* relationship.

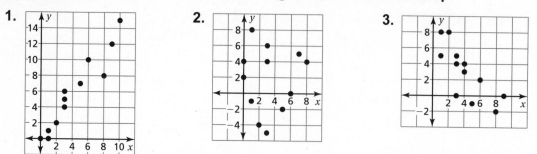

1.

2.

3.

4. The scatter plot shows the participation in a bowling league over eight years.

   a. About how many people were in the league in 2004?

   b. Describe the relationship shown by the data.

Bowling League

5. The table shows the money you owe to pay off a credit card bill over five months.

   a. Make a scatter plot of the data.

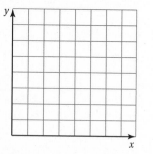

Months, x	Money owed (dollars), y
1	1200
2	1000
3	850
4	600
5	410

   b. Draw a line of fit.

   c. Write an equation for the line of fit.

   d. Predict the amount of money you will owe in six months.

12.6 Analyzing Lines of Fit

For use with Activity 12.6

Essential Question How can you find a line that best models a data set?

1 ACTIVITY: Comparing Lines of Fit

Work with a partner. You are researching the prices of liquid crystal display (LCD) televisions. The tables show the sizes and prices of several LCD televisions.

TV Size (in.), x	19	19	22	24	32
Price (dollars), y	170	180	170	250	320

TV Size (in.), x	32	37	40	40	46
Price (dollars), y	300	400	480	500	600

TV Size (in.), x	46	47	52	55	55
Price (dollars), y	850	800	950	1000	1150

a. Make a scatter plot of the data. Describe the pattern.

b. Draw a line of fit. Then have your partner draw a different line of fit.

c. Write an equation for each line of fit.

d. Compare your line of fit with your partner's line of fit. Are they similar? Which line of fit seems to model the data better? Why?

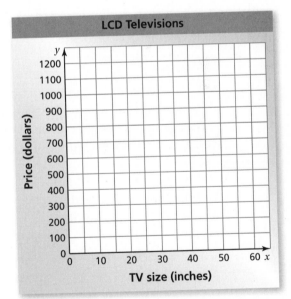

12.6 **Analyzing Lines of Fit** (continued)

2 **ACTIVITY:** Choosing a Line of Fit

Compare your line of fit with the lines of fit of the other students in your class. Which line of fit do you think best models the data? What criteria did you use when choosing the line of fit? Explain your reasoning.

3 **ACTIVITY:** Using a Graphing Calculator

The line of fit that models a data set most accurately is called the line of best fit. Graphing calculators use a method called linear regression to find a line of best fit. Use a graphing calculator to find an equation of the line of best fit for the data in Activity 1.

a. Enter the data from the tables into your calculator.

b. Use the *linear regression* feature of your calculator to find the equation of the line of best fit. The steps used to find the line of best fit depend on the calculator model that you have.

c. Compare the lines of fit from Activities 1 and 2 with the line of best fit. Are they similar? Explain.

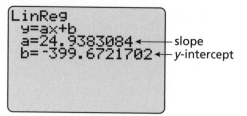

Name_____ Date _____

12.6 **Analyzing Lines of Fit** (continued)

4 ACTIVITY: Using a Line of Best Fit

Complete the table, which shows the sizes of four LCD televisions. Predict
the price of each television using the line of fit from Activity 2 and the line
of best fit from Activity 3. Then find the difference between the prices.

TV size (in.), x	Price using line of fit from Activity 2	Price using line of best fit: y = 24.9x − 400	Difference between the prices
26			
42			
50			
60			

How close are the predicted prices?

What Is Your Answer?

5. **IN YOUR OWN WORDS** How can you find a line that best models a
data set?

Name _____ Date _____

 Practice
For use after Lesson 12.6

Is the given model a good fit for the data in the table? Explain.

1. $y = -3x + 8$

x	0	1	2	3	4	5	6	7	8
y	9	3	2	0	−5	−5	−9	−15	−16

2. $y = 4x + 6$

x	−4	−3	−2	−1	0	1	2	3	4
y	−1	0	1	1	2	3	7	14	29

Use a graphing calculator to find an equation of the line of best fit for the data. Identify and interpret the correlation coefficient.

3.

x	−8	−6	−4	−2	0	2	4	6	8
y	10	7	1	0	−3	−5	−4	−14	−11

4.

x	1	2	3	4	5	6	7	8
y	8	6	4	2	0	2	4	6

Tell whether a correlation is likely in the situation. If so, tell whether there is a causal relationship. Explain your reasoning.

5. IQ (intelligence quotient) and income

6. grade in algebra and overall grade point average

Name_____ Date_____

12.7 Two-Way Tables
For use with Activity 12.7

Essential Question How can you read and make a two-way table?

Two categories of data can be displayed in a **two-way table.**

1 ACTIVITY: Reading a Two-Way Table

Work with a partner. You are the manager of a sports shop. The table shows the numbers of soccer T-shirts that your shop has left in stock at the end of the season.

		T-Shirt Size					Total
		S	M	L	XL	XXL	
Color	**Blue/White**	5	4	1	0	2	
	Blue/Gold	3	6	5	2	0	
	Red/White	4	2	4	1	3	
	Black/White	3	4	1	2	1	
	Black/Gold	5	2	3	0	2	
	Total						65

a. Complete the totals for the rows and columns.

b. Are there any black and gold XL T-shirts in stock? Justify your answer.

c. The number of T-shirts you ordered at the beginning of the season are shown below. Complete the two-way table.

		T-Shirt Size					Total
		S	M	L	XL	XXL	
Color	**Blue/White**	5	6	7	6	5	
	Blue/Gold	5	6	7	6	5	
	Red/White	5	6	7	6	5	
	Black/White	5	6	7	6	5	
	Black/Gold	5	6	7	6	5	
	Total						

12.7 Two-Way Tables (continued)

d. How would you alter the numbers of T-shirts you order for next season? Explain your reasoning.

2 **ACTIVITY:** Analyzing Data

Work with a partner. The three-dimensional two-way table shows information about the numbers of hours students at a high school work at part-time jobs during the school year.

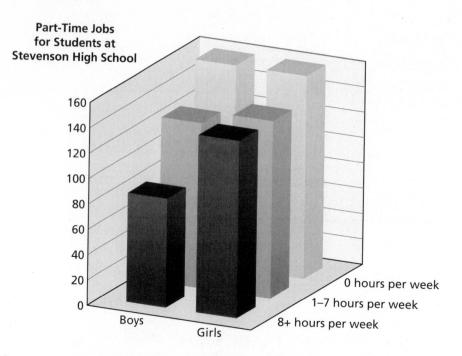

a. Make a two-way table showing the data. Use estimation to find the entries in your table.

12.7 Two-Way Tables (continued)

b. Write two observations you can make that summarize the data in your table.

c. A newspaper article claims that more boys than girls drop out of high school to work full-time. Do the data support this claim? Explain your reasoning.

What Is Your Answer?

3. IN YOUR OWN WORDS How can you read and make a two-way table?

4. Find a real-life data set that can be represented by a two-way table. Then make a two-way table for the data set.

12.7 Practice
For use after Lesson 12.7

1. You randomly survey students in a school about whether they got the flu after receiving a flu shot. The results of the survey are shown in the two-way table.

   a. How many of the students in the survey received a flu shot and still got the flu?

   b. Find and interpret the marginal frequencies for the survey.

		Flu Shot		
		Yes	No	Total
Flu	Yes	8	13	
	No	27	32	
	Total			

2. You randomly survey students in a school about whether they eat breakfast at home or at school.

   Grade 6 Students: 28 eat breakfast at home, 12 eat breakfast at school

   Grade 7 Students: 15 eat breakfast at home, 15 eat breakfast at school

   Grade 8 Students: 9 eat breakfast at home, 21 eat breakfast at school

   a. Make a two-way table that includes the marginal frequencies.

   b. For each grade level, what percent of the students in the survey eat breakfast at home? eat breakfast at school? Organize the results in a two-way table. Explain what one of the entries represents.

Name_____ Date_____

Essential Question How can you display data in a way that helps you make decisions?

 ACTIVITY: Displaying Data

Work with a partner. Analyze and display each data set in a way that best describes the data. Explain your choice of display.

a. **ROAD KILL** A group of schools in New England participated in a 2-month study and reported 3962 dead animals.

Birds 307
Mammals 2746
Amphibians 145
Reptiles 75
Unknown 689

b. **BLACK BEAR ROAD KILL** The data below show the numbers of black bears killed on a state's roads from 1993 to 2012.

1993	30	2003	74
1994	37	2004	88
1995	46	2005	82
1996	33	2006	109
1997	43	2007	99
1998	35	2008	129
1999	43	2009	111
2000	47	2010	127
2001	49	2011	141
2002	61	2012	135

12.8 Choosing a Data Display (continued)

c. **RACCOON ROAD KILL** A 1-week study along a 4-mile section of road found the following weights (in pounds) of raccoons that had been killed by vehicles.

13.4	14.8	17.0	12.9	21.3	21.5	16.8	14.8
15.2	18.7	18.6	17.2	18.5	9.4	19.4	15.7
14.5	9.5	25.4	21.5	17.3	19.1	11.0	12.4
20.4	13.6	17.5	18.5	21.5	14.0	13.9	19.0

d. What do you think can be done to minimize the number of animals killed by vehicles?

---

2 **ACTIVITY:** Statistics Project

ENDANGERED SPECIES PROJECT Use the Internet or some other reference to write a report about an animal species that is (or has been) endangered. Include graphical displays of the data you have gathered.

Sample: Florida Key Deer In 1939, Florida banned the hunting of Key deer. The numbers of Key deer fell to about 100 in the 1940s.

About half of Key deer deaths are due to vehicles.

12.8 **Choosing a Data Display** (continued)

In 1947, public sentiment was stirred by 11-year-old Glenn Allen from Miami. Allen organized Boy Scouts and others in a letter-writing campaign that led to the establishment of the National Key Deer Refuge in 1957. The approximately 8600-acre refuge includes 2280 acres of designated wilderness.

One of two Key deer wildlife underpasses on Big Pine Key.

The Key Deer Refuge has increased the population of Key deer. A recent study estimated the total Key deer population to be approximately 800.

What Is Your Answer?

3. **IN YOUR OWN WORDS** How can you display data in a way that helps you make decisions? Use the Internet or some other reference to find examples of the following types of data displays.

- Bar graph
- Circle graph
- Scatter plot

- Stem-and-leaf plot
- Box-and-whisker plot

12.8 Practice
For use after Lesson 12.8

Choose an appropriate data display for the situation. Explain your reasoning.

1. the number of people that donated blood over the last 5 years

2. percent of class participating in school clubs

Explain why the data display is misleading.

3.

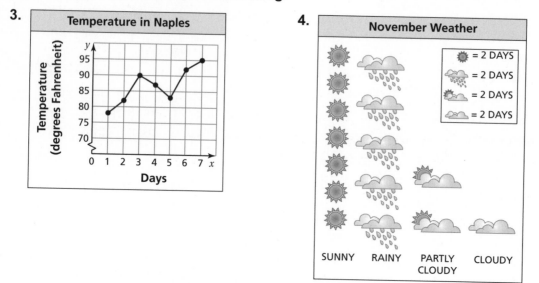

4.

5. A team statistician wants to use a data display to show the points scored per game during the season. Choose an appropriate data display for the situation. Explain your reasoning.

Glossary

This student friendly glossary is designed to be a reference for key vocabulary, properties, and mathematical terms. Several of the entries include a short example to aid your understanding of important concepts.

Also available at *BigIdeasMath.com*:

- multi-language glossary
- vocabulary flash cards

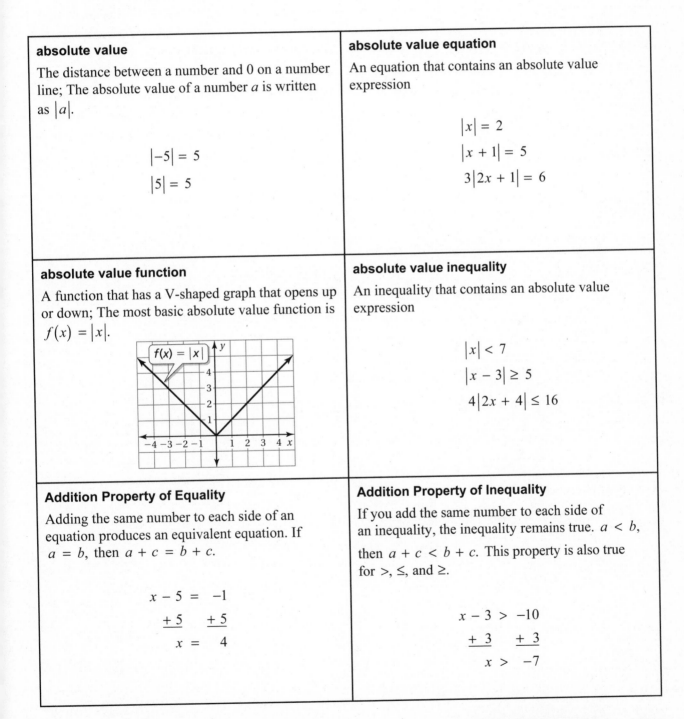

absolute value

The distance between a number and 0 on a number line; The absolute value of a number a is written as $|a|$.

$$|-5| = 5$$
$$|5| = 5$$

absolute value equation

An equation that contains an absolute value expression

$$|x| = 2$$
$$|x + 1| = 5$$
$$3|2x + 1| = 6$$

absolute value function

A function that has a V-shaped graph that opens up or down; The most basic absolute value function is $f(x) = |x|$.

$f(x) = |x|$

absolute value inequality

An inequality that contains an absolute value expression

$$|x| < 7$$
$$|x - 3| \geq 5$$
$$4|2x + 4| \leq 16$$

Addition Property of Equality

Adding the same number to each side of an equation produces an equivalent equation. If $a = b$, then $a + c = b + c$.

$$\begin{array}{r} x - 5 = -1 \\ +5 \quad +5 \\ \hline x = 4 \end{array}$$

Addition Property of Inequality

If you add the same number to each side of an inequality, the inequality remains true. $a < b$, then $a + c < b + c$. This property is also true for $>$, $\leq$, and $\geq$.

$$\begin{array}{r} x - 3 > -10 \\ +3 \quad +3 \\ \hline x > -7 \end{array}$$

Addition Property of Zero The sum of any number and 0 is that number. $$-5 + 0 = -5$$ $$a + 0 = a$$	**arithmetic sequence** A sequence in which the difference between consecutive terms is the same; This difference is called the common difference. 3, 5, 7, 9, ... Terms of an arithmetic sequence +2 +2 +2 Common difference
Associative Property of Addition Changing the grouping of addends does not change the sum. $$(-3 + 4) + 5 = -3 + (4 + 5)$$ $$(a + b) + c = a + (b + c)$$	**Associative Property of Multiplication** Changing the grouping of factors does not change the product. $$(-3 \bullet 4) \bullet 5 = -3 \bullet (4 \bullet 5)$$ $$(a \bullet b) \bullet c = a \bullet (b \bullet c)$$
asymptote A line that a graph approaches, but never intersects	**axis of symmetry** The vertical line that divides a parabola into two symmetric parts
base (of a power) The base of a power is the common factor. *See power.*	**binomial** A polynomial with two terms $$x^2 + 3x$$ $$2x - 1$$

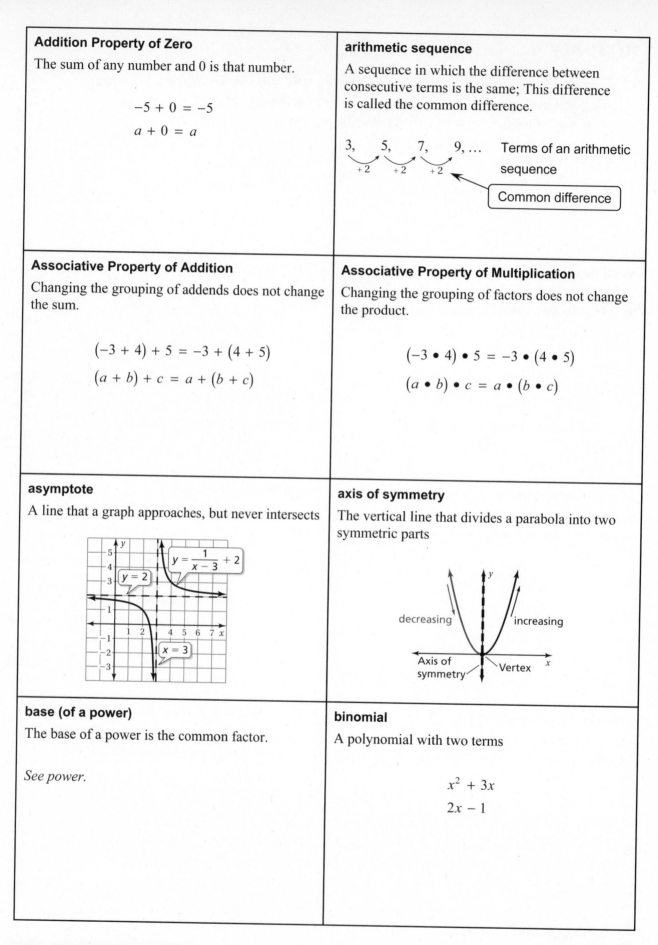

box-and-whisker plot

Displays a data set along a number line using medians; Quartiles divide the data set into four equal parts. The median (second quartile) divides the data set into two halves. The median of the lower half is the first quartile. The median of the upper half is the third quartile.

See five-number summary.

causation

When a change in one variable results in a change in another variable; This produces a strong correlation between the two variables.

time spent exercising and the number of calories burned

closed

A set of numbers is closed under an operation when the operation performed on any two numbers in the set results in a number that is also in the set.

The set of integers is closed under addition, subtraction, and multiplication; but not under division.

coefficient

The numerical factor of a term that contains a variable

In the algebraic expression $-5x + 1$, -5 is the coefficient of the term $-5x$.

common difference

The difference between consecutive terms of an arithmetic sequence

See arithmetic sequence.

common ratio

The ratio between consecutive terms of a geometric sequence

See geometric sequence.

Commutative Property of Addition

Changing the order of addends does not change the sum.

$$2 + 8 = 8 + 2$$
$$a + b = b + a$$

Commutative Property of Multiplication

Changing the order of factors does not change the product.

$$2 \bullet 8 = 8 \bullet 2$$
$$a \bullet b = b \bullet a$$

completing the square

A method for solving quadratic equations; In this method, a constant c is added to the expression $x^2 + bx$ so that $x^2 + bx + c$ is a perfect square trinomial.

$$x^2 + 6x + 9 = (x + 3)^2$$

$$x^2 + bx + \left(\frac{b}{2}\right)^2 = \left(x + \frac{b}{2}\right)^2$$

compound inequality

An inequality formed by joining two inequalities with the word "and" or the word "or."

$$x \geq 2 \text{ and } x < 5$$
$$y \leq -2 \text{ or } y > 1$$
$$4 < x - 1 < 7$$

compound interest

Interest earned on the principal and on previously earned interest

The balance y of an account earning compound interest is $y = P\left(1 + \dfrac{r}{n}\right)^{nt}$, where P is the principal (initial amount), r is the annual interest rate (in decimal form), t is the time (in years), and n is the number of times interest is compounded per year.

conjugates

Used to simplify radical expressions that involve a sum or difference of radicals in the denominator

$a\sqrt{b} + c\sqrt{d}$ and $a\sqrt{b} - c\sqrt{d}$ are conjugates.

constant term

A term without a variable

In the expression $2x + 8$, the term 8 is a constant term.

continuous domain

A set of input values that consists of all numbers in an interval

All numbers from 1 to 5

coordinate plane

A coordinate plane is formed by the intersection of a horizontal number line, usually called the x-axis, and a vertical number line, usually called the y-axis.

correlation

The relationship between paired data; The paired data have a positive correlation if y tends to increase as x increases, a negative correlation if y tends to decrease as x increases, and no correlation if x and y have no apparent relationship.

Positive relationship   Negative relationship   No relationship

correlation coefficient

When a calculator uses linear regression to find a line of best fit, it often gives a value r called the correlation coefficient. This value tells whether the correlation is positive or negative, and how closely the equation models the data. Values of r range from -1 to 1.

$r = -1$	$r = 0$	$r = 1$

Strong negative correlation   No correlation   Strong positive correlation

Cross Products Property

The cross products of a proportion are equal.

$$2 \bullet 6 = 3 \bullet 4$$

data

Information, often given in the form of numbers or facts

degree of a monomial

The sum of the exponents of the variables in a monomial; The degree of a nonzero constant term is 0.

The degree of 5 is 0.

The degree of x^2 is 2.

The degree of $2xy^3$ is $1 + 3 = 4$.

degree of a polynomial

The greatest degree of the terms of a polynomial

The degree of $6x^2 + x$ is 2.

The degree of $x^5 + x^2 - 8$ is 5.

denominator

The number below the fraction bar in a fraction

In the fraction $\frac{2}{5}$, the denominator is 5.

dependent variable

The variable that represents output values of a function

In the function $y = 2x - 3$, y is the dependent variable.

direct variation

Two quantities x and y show direct variation when $y = kx$, where k is a nonzero constant.

$y = kx, k > 0$ $y = kx, k < 0$

discrete domain

A set of input values that consists of only certain numbers in an interval

Integers from 1 to 5

discriminant

The expression $b^2 - 4ac$ of the associated equation $ax^2 + bx + c = 0$; The expression under the radical sign, $b^2 - 4ac$, in the quadratic formula; Used to determine the number of real solutions of a quadratic equation

The value of the discriminant of the equation $3x^2 - 2x - 7 = 0$ is

$$b^2 - 4ac = (-2)^2 - 4(3)(-7) = 88.$$

distance formula

The distance d between any two points (x_1, y_1) and (x_2, y_2) is given by the formula

$$d = \sqrt{(x_2 - x_1)^2 + (y_2 - y_1)^2}.$$

Distributive Property

To multiply a sum or difference by a number, multiply each number in the sum or difference by the number outside the parentheses. Then evaluate.

$$3(2 + 9) = 3(2) + 3(9)$$
$$a(b + c) = ab + ac$$
$$3(2 - 9) = 3(2) - 3(9)$$
$$a(b - c) = ab - ac$$

Division Property of Equality

Dividing each side of an equation by the same number produces an equivalent equation. If $a = b$, then $a \div c = b \div c, c \neq 0$.

$$4x = -40$$
$$\frac{4x}{4} = \frac{-40}{4}$$
$$x = -10$$

Division Property of Inequality (Case 1)

If you divide each side of an inequality by the same positive number, the inequality remains true.

$a < b$ and $c > 0$, then $\dfrac{a}{c} < \dfrac{b}{c}$. This property is also true for $>$, $\leq$, and $\geq$.

$$4x > -12$$
$$\frac{4x}{4} > \frac{-12}{4}$$
$$x > -3$$

Division Property of Inequality (Case 2)

If you divide each side of an inequality by the same negative number, the direction of the inequality symbol must be reversed for the inequality to remain true. If $a < b$ and $c < 0$, then $\dfrac{a}{c} > \dfrac{b}{c}$. This property is also true for $>$, $\leq$, and $\geq$.

$$-5x > 30$$
$$\frac{-5x}{-5} < \frac{30}{-5}$$
$$x < -6$$

domain

The set of all input values of a function

For the ordered pairs $(0, 6)$, $(1, 7)$, $(2, 8)$, and $(3, 9)$, the domain is 0, 1, 2, and 3.

equation A mathematical sentence that uses an equal sign to show that two expressions are equal $$4x = 16$$ $$a + 7 = 21$$	**equivalent equations** Equations that have the same solution(s) $$2x - 8 = 0 \text{ and } 2x = 8$$
excluded value A number that makes a rational function or a rational expression undefined. A number that makes the denominator equal to 0 The excluded value of $\dfrac{2}{x + 5}$ is -5.	**exponent** The number or variable that represents the number of times the base of a power is used as a factor *See power.*
exponential decay When a quantity decreases by the same factor over equal intervals of time *See exponential decay function.*	**exponential decay function** A function of the form $y = a(1 - r)^t$, where $a > 0$ and $0 < r < 1$ $$y = 20(0.15)^t$$ $$y = 500\left(\dfrac{7}{8}\right)^t$$ *See exponential decay.*
exponential function A function of the form $y = ab^x$, where $a \neq 0$, $b \neq 1$, and $b > 0$ $$y = -2(5)^x$$ $$y = 2(0.5)^x$$	**exponential growth** When a quantity increases by the same factor over equal intervals of time *See exponential growth function.*

exponential growth function	**expression**
A function of the form $y = a(1 + r)^t$, where $a > 0$ and $r > 0$ $$y = 20(1.15)^t$$ $$y = 500\left(\frac{7}{5}\right)^t$$ *See exponential growth.*	A mathematical phrase containing numbers, operations, and/or variables $$12 + 6, 18 + 3 \times 4,$$ $$8 + x, 6 \times a - b$$
extraneous solution	**factor**
A solution of a transformed equation that is not a solution of the original equation When you square each side of $x = \sqrt{x + 2}$, the resulting equation has two solutions, $x = -1$ and $x = 2$. However, $x = -1$ is an extraneous solution because it does not satisfy the original equation.	An integer or expression that divides an integer or expression without leaving a remainder -2, 3, and 4 are factors of 24. $(x - 4)$ and $(x + 3)$ are factors of $x^2 - x - 12$.
factored completely	**factored form**
A factorable polynomial with integer coefficients is said to be factored completely when no more factors can be found and it is written as the product of prime factors. $$3x^3 - 18x^2 + 24x = 3x(x^2 - 6x + 8)$$ $$= 3x(x - 2)(x - 4)$$	A polynomial is in factored form when it is written as a product of factors. $$x^2 + 2x = x(x + 2)$$ $$x^2 + 5x - 24 = (x - 3)(x + 8)$$
factoring by grouping	**five-number summary**
To factor polynomials with four terms, group the terms into pairs, factor the GCF out of each pair of terms, and look for a common binomial factor. $$x^3 + 3x^2 + 2x + 6 = (x^3 + 3x^2) + (2x + 6)$$ $$= x^2(x + 3) + 2(x + 3)$$ $$= (x + 3)(x^2 + 2)$$	The five numbers that make up a box-and-whisker plot (least value, first quartile, median, third quartile, and greatest value) *See box-and-whisker plot.*

focus

A fixed point on the interior of a parabola that lies on the axis of symmetry; A parabola "wraps" around the focus.

For functions of the form $y = ax^2$, the focus is $\left(0, \dfrac{1}{4a}\right)$.

FOIL Method

A shortcut for multiplying two binomials; To multiply two binomials using the FOIL Method, find the sum of the products of the **First** terms, **Outer** terms, **Inner** terms, and **Last** terms.

F $(x + 1)(x + 2)$ ➡ $x(x) = x^2$
O $(x + 1)(x + 2)$ ➡ $x(2) = 2x$
I $(x + 1)(x + 2)$ ➡ $1(x) = x$
L $(x + 1)(x + 2)$ ➡ $1(2) = 2$

function

A relationship that pairs each input with exactly one output

The ordered pairs $(0, 1)$, $(1, 2)$, $(2, 4)$, and $(3, 6)$ represent a function.

Ordered Pairs	Input	Output
$(0, 1)$	0	1
$(1, 2)$	1	2
$(2, 4)$	2	4
$(3, 6)$	3	6

function notation

A way to name a function using $f(x)$ instead of y; The notation $f(x)$ is read as "the value of f at x" or "f of x."

$y = 5x + 2$ can be written in function notation as $f(x) = 5x + 2$.

geometric sequence

A sequence in which the ratio between consecutive terms is the same; This ratio is called the common ratio.

1,   4,   16,   64, ...   Terms of a geometric sequence
  ×4   ×4   ×4   Common ratio

graph of an inequality

A graph that shows all of the solutions of an inequality on a number line

$x > -2$

graph of a linear inequality

A graph in two variables that shows all of the solutions of an inequality in a coordinate plane
The graph of $y = x - 3$ is the shaded half-plane.

graph of a system of linear inequalities

A graph of all the solutions of a system

$y < x + 2$

$y \geq 2x - 1$

greatest common factor (GCF)

The largest of the common factors of two or more nonzero integers or expressions

The common factors of 12 and 20 are 1, 2, and 4. So the GCF of 12 and 20 is 4.

The common factors of $3x^3$ and $6x^2$ are 1, 3, x, x^2, and $3x^2$. So the GCF of $3x^3$ and $6x^2$ is $3x^2$.

half-planes

In a coordinate plane, the regions on either side of a boundary line

See graph of a linear inequality.

hypotenuse

The side of a right triangle that is opposite the right angle

independent variable

The variable that represents input values of a function

In the function $y = 5x - 8$, x is the independent variable.

inequality

A mathematical sentence that compares expressions; It contains the symbols $<$, $>$, $\leq$, or $\geq$.

$$x - 4 < -14$$
$$x + 5 \geq -67$$

input

A number on which a function operates

See function.

integers

The set of whole numbers and their opposites

$$\dots -3, -2, -1, 0, 1, 2, 3, \dots$$

interest

Money paid or earned for the use of money

See compound interest and simple interest.

interquartile range

The difference of the third quartile of a data set and the first quartile of the data set; It represents the range of the middle half of the data.

The interquartile range of the data set is $42 - 18 = 24$.

first quartile   third quartile

15, **18**, 21, 28, 35, **42**, 55

inverse function

When a relation and its inverse are functions, they are called inverse functions. The inverse of a function f is written as $f^{-1}(x)$. To find the inverse of a function represented by an equation, switch x and y and then solve for y.

$f(x) = 2x - 5$ and $f^{-1}(x) = \dfrac{1}{2}x + \dfrac{5}{2}$ are inverse functions.

inverse relation

Switches the input and output values of a relation; If a relation contains (a, b), then the inverse relation contains (b, a).

$(-4, 7), (-2, 4), (0, 1), (2, -2), (4, -5)$

$(7, -4), (4, -2), (1, 0), (-2, 2), (-5, 4)$

inverse variation

Two quantities x and y show inverse variation when $y = \dfrac{k}{x}$, where k is a nonzero constant.

$y = \dfrac{k}{x}, k > 0$ $y = \dfrac{k}{x}, k < 0$

irrational number

A number that cannot be written as the ratio of two integers

$\pi, \sqrt{14}$

joint frequency

Each entry in a two-way table

		Student	
		Studied	Did Not Study
Grade	Passed	21	2
	Failed	1	6

joint frequency

least common denominator (LCD) of rational expressions

The least common multiple of the denominators of two or more rational expressions

The least common denominator of $\dfrac{3}{10x^2}$ and $\dfrac{5}{12x}$ is the least common multiple of $10x^2$ and $12x$, or $60x^2$.

legs

The two sides of a right triangle that form the right angle

See hypotenuse.

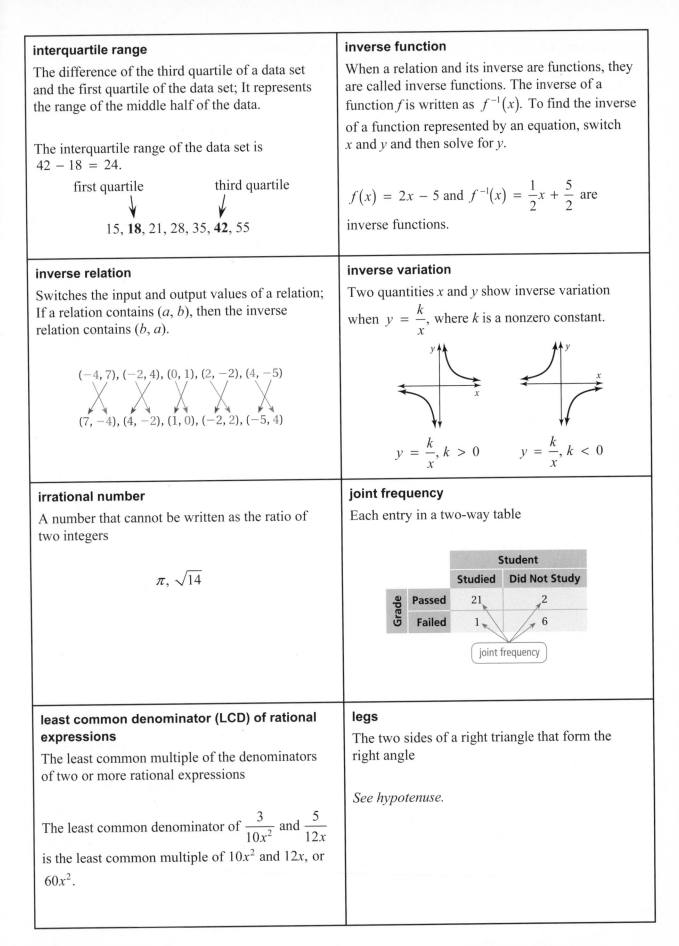

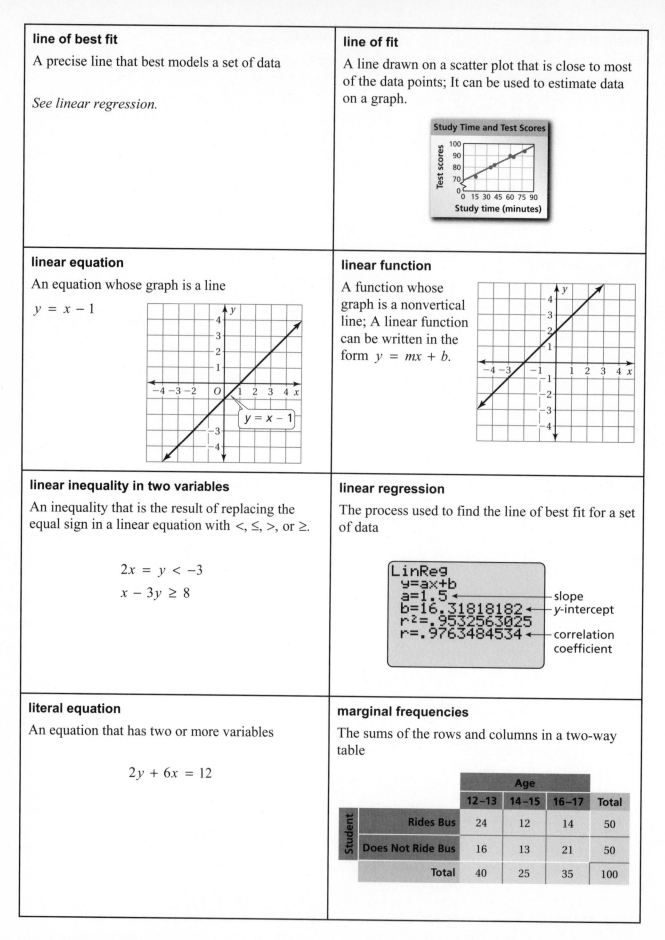

line of best fit

A precise line that best models a set of data

See linear regression.

line of fit

A line drawn on a scatter plot that is close to most of the data points; It can be used to estimate data on a graph.

linear equation

An equation whose graph is a line

$y = x - 1$

linear function

A function whose graph is a nonvertical line; A linear function can be written in the form $y = mx + b$.

linear inequality in two variables

An inequality that is the result of replacing the equal sign in a linear equation with $<$, $\leq$, $>$, or $\geq$.

$$2x = y < -3$$
$$x - 3y \geq 8$$

linear regression

The process used to find the line of best fit for a set of data

literal equation

An equation that has two or more variables

$$2y + 6x = 12$$

marginal frequencies

The sums of the rows and columns in a two-way table

		Age		
		12–13	14–15	16–17	Total
Student	Rides Bus	24	12	14	50
	Does Not Ride Bus	16	13	21	50
	Total	40	25	35	100

maximum value

The y-coordinate of the vertex of the graph of $y = ax^2 + bx + c$ when $a < 0$

mean

The sum of the values in a data set divided by the number of data values

The mean of the values 7, 4, 8, and 9 is

$$\frac{7 + 4 + 8 + 9}{4} = \frac{28}{4} = 7.$$

measure of central tendency

A measure that represents the center of a data set

The mean, median, and mode are all measures of central tendency.

measure of dispersion

A measure that describes the spread of a data set

The range and standard deviation are measures of dispersion.

median

For a data set with an odd number of ordered values, the median is the middle data value. For a data set with an even number of ordered values, the median is the mean of the two middle values.

The median of the data set 24, 25, 29, 33, 38 is 29 because 29 is the middle value.

minimum value

The y-coordinate of the vertex of the graph of $y = ax^2 + bx + c$ when $a > 0$

mode

The data value or values that occur most often; Data can have one mode, more than one mode, or no mode.

The modes of the data set 3, 4, 4, 7, 7, 9, 12 are 4 and 7 because they occur most often.

monomial

A number, a variable, or a product of a number and one or more variables with whole number exponents

$$-5$$
$$0.5y^2$$
$$4x^2y$$

Multiplication Properties of Zero and One

The product of any number and 0 is 0.

The product of any number and 1 is that number.

$$-5 \bullet 0 = 0$$
$$a \bullet 0 = 0$$
$$-6 \bullet 1 = -6$$
$$a \bullet 1 = a$$

Multiplication Property of Equality

Multiplying each side of an equation by the same number produces an equivalent equation. If $a = b$, then $a \bullet c = b \bullet c$.

$$-\frac{2}{3}x = 8$$
$$-\frac{3}{2} \bullet \left(-\frac{2}{3}x\right) = -\frac{3}{2} \bullet 8$$
$$x = -12$$

Multiplication Property of Inequality (Case 1)

If you multiply each side of an inequality by the same positive number, the inequality remains true. If $a < b$ and $c > 0$, then $a \bullet c < b \bullet c$. This property is also true for $>$, $\leq$, or $\geq$.

$$\frac{x}{2} < -9$$
$$2 \bullet \frac{x}{2} < 2 \bullet (-9)$$
$$x < -18$$

Multiplication Property of Inequality (Case 2)

If you multiply each side of an inequality by the same negative number, the direction of the inequality symbol must be reversed for the inequality to remain true. If $a < b$ and $c < 0$, then $a \bullet c > b \bullet c$. This property is also true for $>$, $\leq$, or $\geq$.

$$\frac{x}{-6} < 3$$
$$-6 \bullet \frac{x}{-6} > -6 \bullet 3$$
$$x > -18$$

negative exponent

For any integer n and any nonzero number a, a^{-n} is the reciprocal of a^n.

$$a^{-n} = \frac{1}{a^n}$$

negative number

A number less than 0

$$-0.25, -10, -500$$

nonlinear function

A function that does not have a constant rate of change; The graph of a nonlinear function is not a line.

nth root

When $b^n = a$ for an integer n greater than 1, b is an *n*th root of a.

$$\sqrt[3]{64} = \sqrt[3]{4 \bullet 4 \bullet 4} = 4$$
$$\sqrt[n]{a} = n\text{th root of } a$$

number line

A line whose points are associated with numbers that increase from left to right

numerator

The number above the fraction bar in a fraction

In the fraction $\dfrac{2}{5}$, the numerator is 2.

ordered pair

A pair of numbers (x, y) used to locate a point in a coordinate plane; The first number is the x-coordinate, and the second number is the y-coordinate.

The x-coordinate of the point $(-2, 1)$ is -2, and the y-coordinate is 1.

origin

The point, represented by the ordered pair $(0, 0,)$ where the x-axis and the y-axis meet in a coordinate plane

See coordinate plane.

output

A number produced by evaluating a function using a given input

See function.

parabola

The U-shaped graph of a quadratic function

perfect square

A number with integers as its square roots

16, 25, 81

perfect square trinomial

Trinomials of the form $a^2 + 2ab + b^2$ and $a^2 - 2ab + b^2$.

$$x^2 + 6x + 9 = x^2 + 2(3)x + 3^2$$
$$x^2 - 10x + 25 = x^2 - 2(5)x + 5^2$$

perpendicular lines Two lines in the same plane that intersect to form right angles; Two nonvertical lines are perpendicular if and only if the product of their slopes is -1.	**piecewise function** A function defined by two or more equations $$y = \begin{cases} x - 2, & \text{if } x \le 0 \\ 2x + 1, & \text{if } x > 0 \end{cases}$$

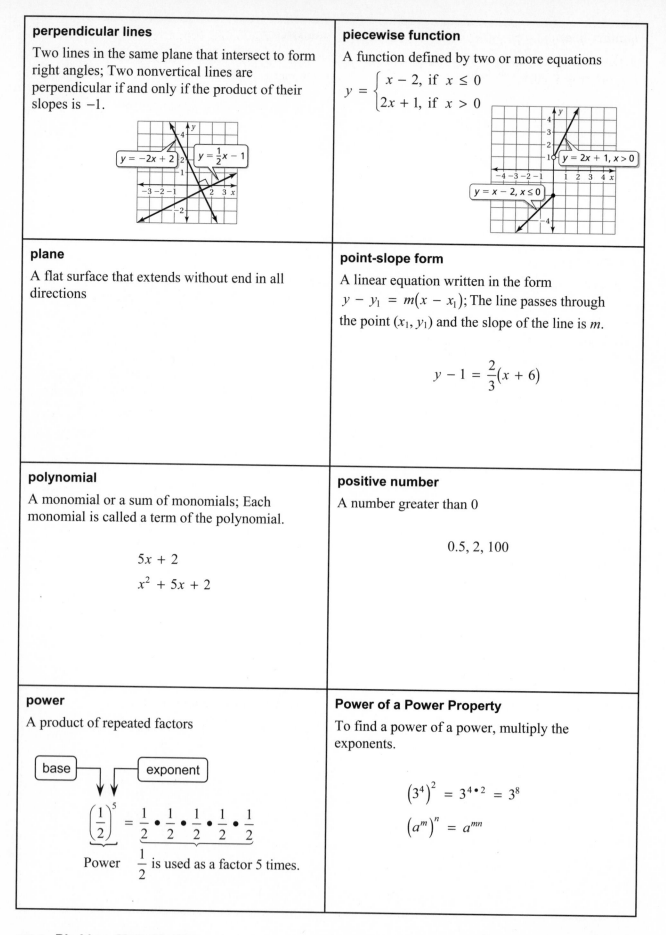

plane A flat surface that extends without end in all directions	**point-slope form** A linear equation written in the form $y - y_1 = m(x - x_1)$; The line passes through the point (x_1, y_1) and the slope of the line is m. $$y - 1 = \frac{2}{3}(x + 6)$$
polynomial A monomial or a sum of monomials; Each monomial is called a term of the polynomial. $$5x + 2$$ $$x^2 + 5x + 2$$	**positive number** A number greater than 0 $$0.5, 2, 100$$
power A product of repeated factors base exponent $$\left(\frac{1}{2}\right)^5 = \frac{1}{2} \cdot \frac{1}{2} \cdot \frac{1}{2} \cdot \frac{1}{2} \cdot \frac{1}{2}$$ Power $\frac{1}{2}$ is used as a factor 5 times.	**Power of a Power Property** To find a power of a power, multiply the exponents. $$\left(3^4\right)^2 = 3^{4 \cdot 2} = 3^8$$ $$\left(a^m\right)^n = a^{mn}$$

Power of a Product Property

To find a power of a product, find the power of each factor and multiply.

$$(5 \cdot 7)^4 = 5^4 \cdot 7^4$$

$$(ab)^m = a^m b^m$$

Power of a Quotient Property

To find a power of a quotient, find the power of the numerator and the power of the denominator and divide.

$$\left(\frac{3}{5}\right)^6 = \frac{3^6}{5^6}$$

$$\left(\frac{a}{b}\right)^m = \frac{a^m}{b^m}$$

prime number

A whole number greater than 1 whose only factors are 1 and itself

$2, 3, 5, 7, 11, 13, 17, 19, 23, 29, 31, \ldots$

prime polynomial

A polynomial that cannot be factored as a product of polynomials with integer coefficients

$$2x + 3$$
$$x^2 - x + 5$$
$$x^2 + 2x + 9$$

principal

An amount of money borrowed or deposited

You deposit $200 in an account that earns 4% compound interest per year. The principal is $200.

product

The result when two or more numbers or expressions are multiplied

The product of 4 and -3 is $4 \times (-3)$, or -12.

The product of $x + 2$ and $x - 5$ is
$(x + 2)(x - 5)$, or $x^2 - 3x - 10$.

Product of Powers Property

To multiply powers with the same base, add their exponents.

$$3^7 \times 3^{10} = 3^{7+10} = 3^{17}$$

$$a^m \cdot a^n = a^{m+n}$$

Product Property of Square Roots

The square root of a product equals the product of the square roots of the factors.

$$\sqrt{4 \cdot 3} = \sqrt{4} \cdot \sqrt{3} = 2\sqrt{3}$$

$$\sqrt{xy} = \sqrt{x} \cdot \sqrt{y}, \text{ where } x \geq 0 \text{ and } y \geq 0$$

Pythagorean Theorem

In any right triangle, the sum of the squares of the lengths of the legs is equal to the square of the length of the hypotenuse.

$a^2 + b^2 = c^2$

13 cm   5 cm
12 cm

$5^2 + 12^2 = 13^2$

quadratic equation

A nonlinear equation that can be written in the standard form $ax^2 + bx + c = 0$, where $a \neq 0$

$$x^2 + 4x = 12$$
$$-x^2 + 1 = 2x$$

quadratic formula

The formula below that can be used to find the real solutions of the quadratic equation $ax^2 + bx + c$, where $a \neq 0$ and $b^2 - 4ac \geq 0$:

$$x = \frac{-b \pm \sqrt{b^2 - 4ac}}{2a}$$

To solve $2x^2 + 13x - 7 = 0$, substitute 2 for a, 13 for b, and -7 for c in the quadratic formula.

$$x = \frac{-13 \pm \sqrt{13^2 - 4(2)(-7)}}{2(2)} \rightarrow x = \frac{1}{2} \text{ or } x = -7$$

quadratic function

A nonlinear function that can be written in the standard form $y = ax^2 + bx + c$, where $a \neq 0$

$$y = -16x^2 + 48x + 6$$

quartile

Divides a data set into four equal parts

See box-and-whisker plot.

quotient

The result of a division

The quotient of 10 and -5 is $10 \div (-5)$, or -2.

Quotient of Powers Property

To divide powers with the same base, subtract their exponents.

$$\frac{9^7}{9^3} = 9^{7-3} = 9^4$$

$$\frac{a^m}{a^n} = a^{m-n}, \text{ where } a \neq 0$$

Quotient Property of Square Roots

The square root of a quotient equals the quotient of the square roots of the numerator and denominator.

$$\sqrt{\frac{7}{9}} = \frac{\sqrt{7}}{\sqrt{9}} = \frac{\sqrt{7}}{3}$$

$$\sqrt{\frac{x}{y}} = \frac{\sqrt{x}}{\sqrt{y}}, \text{ where } x \geq 0 \text{ and } y > 0$$

radical sign	**radicand**
The symbol $\sqrt{}$ which is used to represent a square root $$\sqrt{25} = 5$$ $$-\sqrt{49} = -7$$ $$\pm\sqrt{100} = \pm 10$$	The number or expression under a radical sign The radicand of $\sqrt{25}$ is 25. The radicand of $\sqrt{x+1}$ is $x+1$.
range	**range (of a data set)**
The set of all output values of a function For the ordered pairs $(0, 6)$, $(1, 7)$, $(2, 8)$, and $(3, 9)$, the range is 6, 7, 8, and 9.	The difference between the greatest value and the least value of a data set; The range describes how spread out the data are. The range of the data set 12, 16, 18, 22, 27, 35 is $35 - 12 = 23$.
rate	**ratio**
A ratio of two quantities with different units You read 3 books every 2 weeks.	A comparison of two quantities using division; The ratio of a to b $\left(\text{where } b \neq 0\right)$ can be written as a to b, $a : b$, or $\dfrac{a}{b}$. 4 to 1, 4 : 1, or $\dfrac{4}{1}$
rational equation	**rational exponents**
An equation that contains one or more rational expressions $$\frac{5}{x+4} = \frac{4}{x-4}$$	The nth root of a positive number a can be written as a power with base a and an exponent of $1/n$. $$\sqrt[4]{81} = 81^{1/4}$$ $$\sqrt[n]{a} = a^{1/n}$$

rational expression

An expression that can be written as a fraction whose numerator and denominator are polynomials

$$\frac{3}{x + 1}$$

$$\frac{x - 2}{x^2 + 16}$$

rational function

A function of the form

$$y = \frac{\text{polynomial}}{\text{polynomial}}, \text{ where}$$

the denominator does not equal 0; The most basic rational function is

$$y = \frac{1}{x}.$$

rational number

A number that can be written as $\frac{a}{b}$, where a and b are integers and $b \neq 0$

$$3 = \frac{3}{1}, \qquad -\frac{2}{5} = \frac{-2}{5}$$

$$0.25 = \frac{1}{4}, \qquad 1\frac{1}{3} = \frac{4}{3}$$

rationalizing the denominator

The process of eliminating a radical from the denominator of an expression by multiplying the expression by an appropriate form of 1.

$$\frac{1}{\sqrt{10}} = \frac{1}{\sqrt{10}} \bullet \frac{\sqrt{10}}{\sqrt{10}} = \frac{\sqrt{10}}{\sqrt{100}} = \frac{\sqrt{10}}{10}$$

$$\sqrt{\frac{1}{3}} = \frac{\sqrt{1}}{\sqrt{3}} = \frac{1}{\sqrt{3}} \bullet \frac{\sqrt{3}}{\sqrt{3}} = \frac{\sqrt{3}}{\sqrt{9}} = \frac{\sqrt{3}}{3}$$

real numbers

The set of all rational and irrational numbers

$$4, -6.5, \pi, \sqrt{14}$$

recursive rule

Gives the beginning term(s) of a sequence and an equation that indicates how any term a_n in the sequence relates to the previous term

$$a_n = a_{n-1} + d, \text{ where } d \text{ is the common difference}$$

$$a_1 = 2, a_n = a_{n-1} + 3$$

$$a_n = r \bullet a_{n-1}, \text{ where } r \text{ is the common ratio}$$

$$a_1 = 1, a_n = 3a_{n-1}$$

relation

Pairs inputs with outputs; A relation that pairs each input with exactly one output is a function.

residual

The difference between the y-value of a data point and the corresponding y-value found using the line of fit; A residual can be positive, negative, or zero.

right angle An angle whose measure is 90°	**right triangle** A triangle that has one right angle
rise The change in y between two points on a line *See slope.*	**roots** The solutions of a polynomial equation The roots of the equation $(x + 9)(x - 4) = 0$ are $x = -9$ and $x = 4$.
run The change in x between two points on a line *See slope.*	**scatter plot** A graph that shows the relationship between two data sets using ordered pairs in a coordinate plane **Study Time and Test Scores**
sequence An ordered list of numbers $5, 10, 15, 20, \ldots, a_n, \ldots$ $2, 4, 8, 16, \ldots, a_n, \ldots$	**simple interest** Money paid or earned only on the principal Simple interest ⟶ ⟵ Annual interest rate (in decimal form) $I = Prt$ Principal ⟶ ⟵ Time (in years) You put $200 into an account. The account earns 5% simple interest per year. The interest earned after 3 years is $200 \times 0.05 \times 3$, or $30. The account balance is $200 + $30 = $230 after 3 years.

simplest form of a radical expression

A radical expression that has no perfect square factors other than 1 in the radicand, no fractions in the radicand, and no radicals appearing in the denominator of a fraction

$$\sqrt{27} = 3\sqrt{3}$$

$$\frac{2}{\sqrt{5}} = \frac{2\sqrt{5}}{5}$$

simplest form of a rational expression

A rational expression whose numerator and denominator have no common factors except 1

The simplest form of $\dfrac{4x}{2x(x + 7)}$ is $\dfrac{2}{x + 7}$.

slope

A ratio of the change in y (the rise) to the change in x (the run) between any two points, (x_1, y_1) and (x_2, y_2) on a line; It is a measure of the steepness of a line.

$$\text{slope} = \frac{\text{rise}}{\text{run}} = \frac{\text{change in } y}{\text{change in } x}$$

$$= \frac{y_2 - y_1}{x_2 - x_1}$$

slope-intercept form

A linear equation written in the form $y = mx + b$; The slope of the line is m and the y-intercept of the line is b.

The slope is 1 and the y-intercept is 2.

solution of an equation

A value that makes an equation true

6 is the solution of the equation $x - 4 = 2$.

solution of an inequality

A value that makes an inequality true

A solution of the inequality $x + 3 > -9$ is $x = 2$.

solution of a linear equation

An ordered pair (x, y) that makes a linear equation true; All of the points on the line are solutions.

$(2, -4)$ is a solution of $x + 2y = -6$

solution of a linear inequality

An ordered pair (x, y) that makes a linear inequality true; All of the points in the shaded half-plane are solutions.

$(2, 4)$ is a solution of $-x + 2y > 2$.

See graph of a linear inequality.

solution set	**solution of a system of linear equations**
The set of all solutions of an inequality	An ordered pair that is a solution of each equation in a system $(1, -3)$ is the solution of the following system of linear equations. $$4x - y = 7$$ $$2x + 3y = -7$$
solution of a system of linear inequalities	**square root**
An ordered pair that is a solution of each inequality in a system $(-2, 5)$ is a solution of the following system of linear inequalities. $$x - y < 4$$ $$2x - y \geq -9$$	If $b^2 = a$, then b is a square root of a. The radical sign, $\sqrt{}$, represents a nonnegative square root. The square roots of 25 are 5 and -5 because $5^2 = 25$ and $(-5)^2 = 25$. So, $\sqrt{25} = 5$ and $-\sqrt{25} = -5$.
square root equation	**square root function**
An equation that contains a square root with a variable in the radicand $$\sqrt{x} + 5 = 13$$ $$\sqrt{2x - 1} = \sqrt{x + 4}$$	A function that contains a square root with the independent variable in the radicand; The most basic square root function is $y = \sqrt{x}$. $$y = 3\sqrt{x - 5}$$ $$y = -\sqrt{x + 1} + 2$$
standard deviation	**standard form**
A measure of how much a typical value in a data set differs from the mean; It is given by standard deviation $$\sqrt{\frac{(x_1 - \bar{x})^2 + (x_2 - \bar{x})^2 + \cdots + (x_n - \bar{x})^2}{n}}$$ where n is the number of values in the data set. The symbol $\bar{x}$ represents the mean. It is read as "x-bar."	A linear equation written in the form $ax + by = c$, where a and b are not both zero $$-2x + 3y = -6$$

step function

A piecewise function defined by constant values over its domain

$$f(x) = \begin{cases} 50, & \text{if } 0 < x \le 1 \\ 75, & \text{if } 1 < x \le 2 \\ 100, & \text{if } 2 < x \le 3 \\ 125, & \text{if } 3 < x \le 4 \\ 150, & \text{if } 4 < x \le 5 \end{cases}$$

Subtraction Property of Equality

Subtracting the same number from each side of an equation produces an equivalent equation. If $a = b$, then $a - c = b - c$.

$$\begin{array}{r} x + 10 = -12 \\ \underline{-10 \quad -10} \\ x = -22 \end{array}$$

Subtraction Property of Inequality

If you subtract the same number from each side of an inequality, the inequality remains true. If $a < b$, then $a - c < b - c$. This property is also true for $>$, $\le$, and $\ge$.

$$\begin{array}{r} x + 7 > -20 \\ \underline{-7 \quad -7} \\ x > -27 \end{array}$$

system of linear equations

A set of two or more linear equations in the same variables; also called a linear system

$$y = x + 1 \qquad \text{Equation 1}$$
$$y = 2x - 7 \qquad \text{Equation 2}$$

system of linear inequalities

A set of two or more linear inequalities in the same variables

$$y < x + 2 \qquad \text{Inequality 1}$$
$$y \ge 2x - 1 \qquad \text{Inequality 2}$$

term (of a sequence)

Each number in a sequence; Each term a_n has a specific position n in the sequence.

$$5, \ 10, \ 15, \ 20, \ 25, \ ..., a_n, \ ...$$

| 1st position | 3rd position | nth position |

terms (of an expression)

The parts of an expression that are added together

The terms of $x^2 - 2x + 3$ are x^2, $-2x$, and 3.

theorem

A rule in mathematics

The Pythagorean Theorem

trinomial	**two-way table**
A polynomial with three terms $$x^2 + 5x + 2$$	Displays two categories of data collected from the same source
variable	**vertex (of a parabola)**
A symbol, usually a letter, that represents one or more numbers x is a variable in $2x + 1$.	The lowest or highest point on a parabola
vertex form	**Vertical Line Test**
A quadratic function of the $y = (x - h)^2 + k$, where $a \neq 0$; The vertex of the parabola is (h, k). $$y = (x - 2)^2$$ $$y = -2(x + 4)^2 + 3$$	A graph represents a function when no vertical line passes through more than one point on the graph. **Function**　　　**Not a function**
whole numbers	**x-axis**
The numbers $0, 1, 2, 3, 4, \ldots$	The horizontal number line in a coordinate plane *See coordinate plane.*

x-coordinate

The first coordinate in an ordered pair, which indicates how many units to move to the left or right from the origin

In the ordered pair $(3, 5)$, the *x*-coordinate is 3.

x-intercept

The *x*-coordinate of the point where a line crosses the *x*-axis

y-axis

The vertical number line in a coordinate plane

See coordinate plane.

y-coordinate

The second coordinate in an ordered pair, which indicates how many units to move up or down from the origin

In the ordered pair $(3, 5)$, the *y*-coordinate is 5.

y-intercept

The *y*-coordinate of the point where a line crosses the *y*-axis

See x-intercept.

zero (of a function)

An *x*-value for which $f(x) = 0$; A zero is located at the *x*-intercept of the graph of the function.

The zero of $f(x) = 2x - 6$ is 3 because $f(3) = 0$.

zero exponent

For any nonzero number a, $a^0 = 1$.

$$10^0 = 1$$
$$(-5)^0 = 1$$
$$x^0 = 1, \text{ where } x \neq 0$$

Zero-Product Property

If the product of two real numbers is 0, then at least one of the numbers is 0. If a and b are real numbers and $ab = 0$, then $a = 0$ or $b = 0$.

$$(x + 6)(x - 5) = 0$$
$$x + 6 = 0 \quad or \quad x - 5 = 0$$
$$x = -6 \quad or \quad x = 5$$

Algebra Tiles*

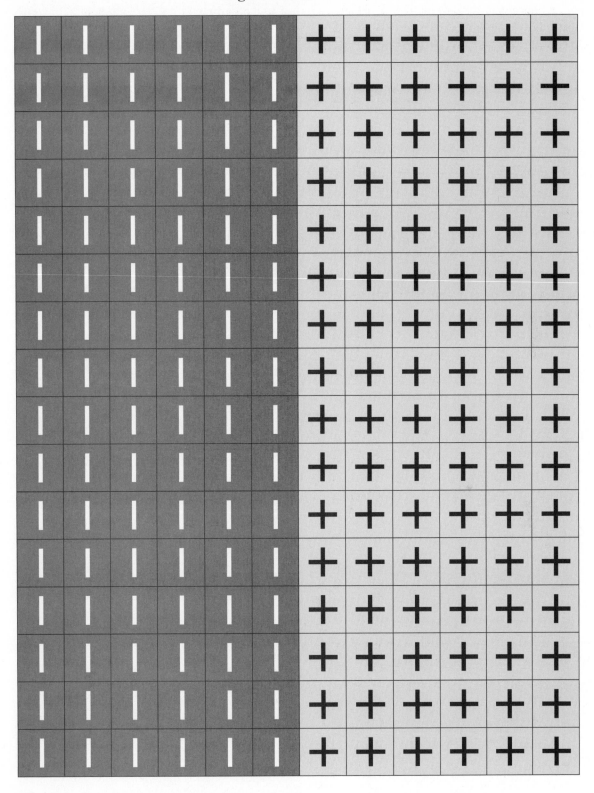

*Available at *BigIdeasMath.com*

Algebra Tiles*

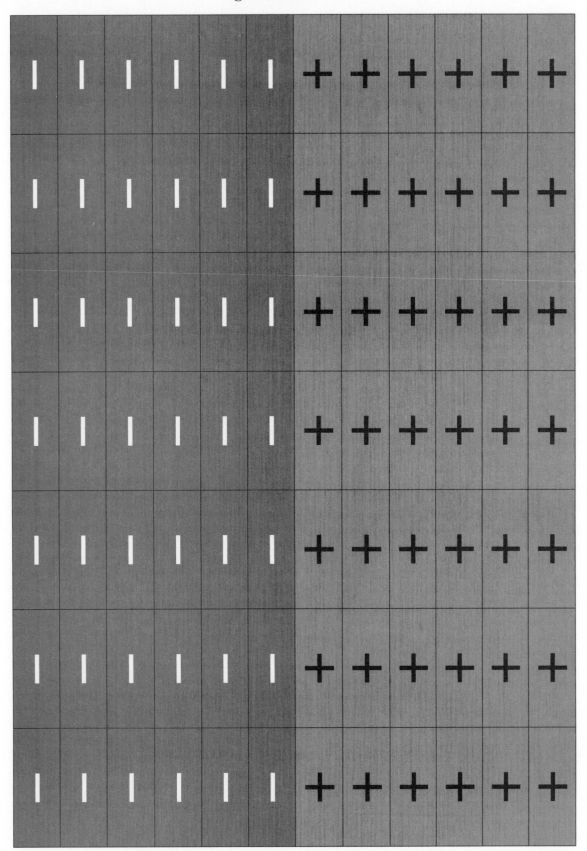

*Available at *BigIdeasMath.com*

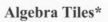
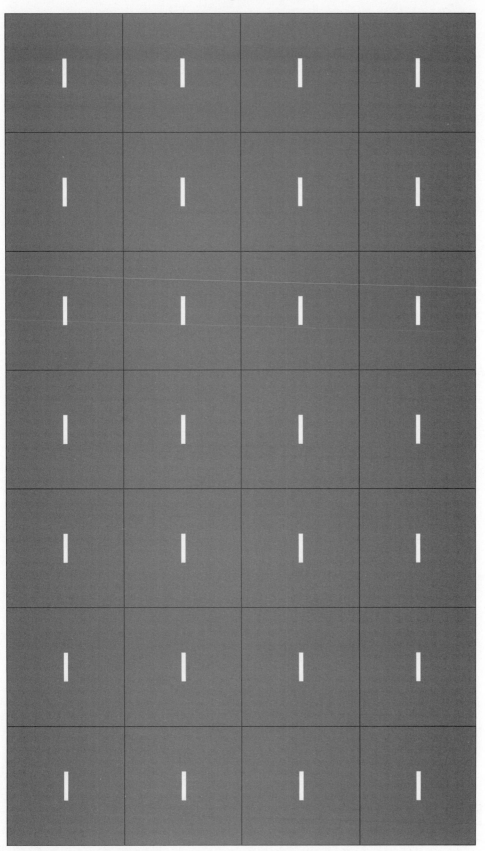

*Available at *BigIdeasMath.com*

Algebra Tiles*

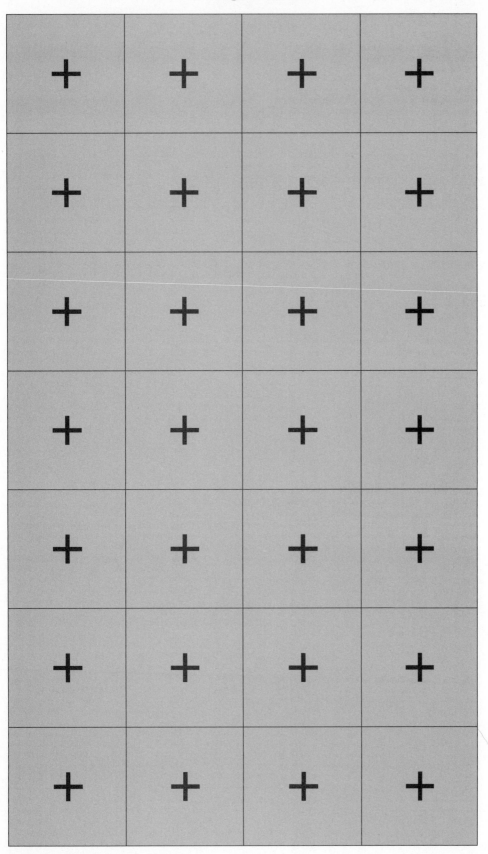

*Available at *BigIdeasMath.com*